Slaying the "Spirit" of Vatican II
With the Light of Truth

Slaying the "Spirit" of Vatican II With the Light of Truth

By Rev. Robert John Araujo, S.J.
and
The Bellarmine Forum

The Wanderer Forum Foundation, Inc./Bellarmine Forum
PO Box 542, Hudson, WI 54016-0542

ISBN: 978-0-9915883-9-8

Cover photo: *Roma, San Pablo, Vaticano*, by Luis Núñez.
Downloaded from www.pexels.com

Editor: Cindy Paslawski
Design: Rhonda Klein, Evergreen Press
White Bear Lake, Minnesota

Printed in the United States of America

TABLE OF CONTENTS

PREFACE

Mention the Second Vatican Council to many Catholics and the wound the radical changes created so many years ago is still painful. For some, the Second Vatican Council meant license to create a new modern church without sin, without so-called medieval trappings, without its hierarchical structure. The abandonment felt by the laity as the misinterpretations of Vatican II became widespread was intense. Priests, Sisters, schools, colleges were all on some tangent that seemed hell-bent on destroying the Catholic Church rather than strengthening it. And many of the flock, like those with itching ears for new things, followed right along.

Perceived chaos caused even faithful followers to feel there was no longer something to have faith in. But faith is like clutching the last straw in the raging waters and holding on. Like islands in an ocean of dissent, the few – laity, priests, and religious – determined to keep the faith: they read what they could, a difficult task when bookstores stocked more Hans Küng than papal encyclicals; spoke up for the truth when given the opportunity; and prayed for deliverance. These souls held on to keep the vigil light of faith lit, driving for miles for reverent Masses, maintaining prayer and devotions and the vision of Catholicism in spite of the disintegrating culture around them.

God's time is not our time. It has taken awhile for the "signs of the times" to change. It took two popes who kept the pressure on the dissidents, who held the true vision of what the Council meant. It took courageous young men who challenged the nonsense in the seminaries and Sisters who were bold enough to found new religious orders faithful to their consecration. And it took laity who held tightly to the promise of Christ that the gates of Hell would not prevail.

Perhaps there needed to be a rupture for the renewal to occur, to clean out the debris, the dead matter that the Council made visible. The Church could not move forward until those who would not serve finally revealed themselves and over time lost their power over the faithful. Through papal leadership, synods, encyclicals, and exhortations over many years, the true and empowering vision of the Council has begun to emerge. The liturgy has been re-translated, bringing back a wealth of meaning to the Sacrifice of the Mass; priestly formation is stressing holiness; the Church has called world attention to Christian family life, to mercy, and the poor.

It isn't over yet. The rest is up to us, the laity, to act. To do so we must set out armed with eternal standards, immersed in the Church's teachings, rich history, and culture. We must, as James Bemis writes, hold up a different image of mankind's place in the universe. "We should not endeavor to be 21st century Americans looking at the Church, but rather strive to be well-catechized Catholics critically examining 21st century America," and once again gear our Catholic evangelization toward saving souls. Positive action must be taken by all of us to live the faith with truth and holiness called for by the Second Vatican Council. The documents must be read and lived with the mind of the Church to truly renew our age.

What did the Council really say about liturgy, about freedom, about priests, religious life, married life? Is there hope? Can the Faith catch fire again and renew the face of the earth?

Open these pages and find out.

The Editor

INTRODUCTION

With the Light of Truth

Most Reverend Thomas John Paprocki
Bishop of Springfield in Illinois
Adjunct Professor of Law, Notre Dame Law School and Loyola University Chicago School of Law

On February 11, 1996, I preached a homily at St. John Cantius Church in Chicago entitled, "Reforming the Reform." The title was taken from the use of that phrase by then Joseph Cardinal Ratzinger, Prefect of the Congregation for the Doctrine of the Faith, who would some nine years later in 2005 become Pope Benedict XVI. My homily was warmly received with vigorous applause. What did I say that evoked such an enthusiastic response from a normally very reserved congregation?

I started by recalling that it was with a great sense of optimism and hope for bigger and better things that city planners in Chicago spent $17 million in 1979 to turn State Street into a downtown shopping mall. Four lanes were reduced to two on which cars were banned and traffic was restricted to buses only. Narrowing the street made it possible to widen the sidewalks from 22 feet to 40. Sidewalk planters, greenery and bubble-topped bus shelters were added to make the Great Street more enticing to shoppers. Instead, the exact opposite happened. With the arrival of the State Street Mall, the crowds disappeared. Major department stores folded up and left State Street within eight years of the renovation. Instead of attracting more customers to the Loop, the new mall apparently drove people away.

So it was not a total surprise when the Greater State Street Council and the City's Department of Transportation announced in January of 1996 that $24.5 million would be spent to renovate the renovation. A nine-block stretch of State Street between Wacker Drive and Congress Parkway would be restored to four lanes, traffic would be reopened to cars and taxis, and sidewalks would be narrowed to their original 22-foot width. The hope was that the pedestrians and shoppers would come back, that the stores would thrive again, and that State Street would once again be that Great Street. In making this announcement, the City was making a stunning admission: the 1979 renovation was a disastrous failure, and the City would spend $24.5 million to undo a $17 million mistake.

What was the point of saying all this in a homily? In many ways the State Street renovation of the renovation was analogous to the situation facing the Catholic Church, namely, that what is needed is a reform of the reform. In 1966, the Second Vatican Council was recently ended with its optimistic promise of reforming the liturgy and life of the Catholic Church in the modern world. There were vocations galore. Surely with the reforms and innovations of the Second Vatican Council the future could only get brighter.

What happened? Instead of building on what we had, the bottom fell out. Over the years and across North American and Western Europe, priests and nuns by the thousands abandoned their religious commitments; seminaries and convents emptied and closed; schools, hospitals and parishes closed and churches were torn down as regular Sunday Mass attendance plummeted.

Our late Holy Father, Pope John Paul II, whom I prefer to call St. John Paul the Great since his canonization as a saint, realized the challenges that were facing the Church as he repeatedly and courageously sought to keep the Church faithful to revealed truth, the deposit of faith, and moral integrity. His successor, Pope Benedict XVI, as mentioned earlier, when he was Prefect of the Congregation for the Doctrine of the Faith, called for a "reform of the reform."

Some might ask: how does a calling for a "reform of the reform" square today with the statement of Pope Francis in his address on the liturgical reform given on August 24, 2017, when he said that "we can affirm with certainty and magisterial authority that the liturgical reform is irreversible"? The answer is that there is a difference between saying something is "irreversible" and saying that it is "irreformable." I would posit that reform of the reform does not seek to reverse the reforms of the Second Vatican Council, particularly with regard to the liturgy, but rather to continue in an authentic way the reforms begun with the liturgical movement leading up to the Second Vatican Council, for example, by working toward an eventual consolidation of what we now call the Ordinary Form and the Extraordinary Form of the Mass into a singular form that integrates the best of both. Indeed, one cannot argue against the need for continued reform without contradicting the Second Vatican Council itself, which said in the *Decree on Ecumenism, Unitatis redintegratio* (n. 6), that the Church is called "to continual reformation" (*ad hanc perennem reformationem*) and is "always in need of this."

Such reformation must be done in an authentic manner in continuity with the intentions of Jesus Christ, Sacred Scripture, and the two-thousand-year tradition of the Church. Pope Benedict XVI reflected on this in an address to the Roman Curia in December, 2005:

> The question arises: Why has the implementation of the Council, in large parts of the Church, thus far been so difficult? Well, it all depends on the correct interpretation of the Council or – as we would say today – on its proper hermeneutics, the correct key to its interpretation and application. The problems in its implementation arose from the fact that two contrary hermeneutics came face to face and quarreled with each other. One caused confusion, the other, silently but more and more visibly, bore and is bearing fruit.
>
> On the one hand, there is an interpretation that I would call "a hermeneutic of discontinuity and rupture," it has frequently availed itself of the sympathies of the mass media, and also one trend of modern theology. On the other, there is the "hermeneutic of reform," of renewal in the continuity of the one subject – Church – which the Lord has given to us. She is a subject which increases in time and develops, yet always remaining the same, the one subject of the journeying People of God.

Pope Benedict XVI argued insistently that "the hermeneutic of discontinuity is countered by the hermeneutic of reform," as it was presented first by Pope John XXIII in his speech inaugurating the Council on October 11, 1962 and later by Pope Paul VI in his Discourse for the Council's Conclusion on December 7, 1965. He quoted Pope St. John XXIII's words which unequivocally expressed this hermeneutic of reform when he said that the Council wished "to transmit the doctrine, pure and integral, without any attenuation or distortion."

Thus, the Second Vatican Council must not be viewed as a rupture from the past that discards what came before it, but rather as a faithful development that respects the integrity of Sacred Tradition as handed down over the centuries from one generation to the next. Otherwise, it would make no sense to consider this newly created church as even being Christian except in some vaguely vestigial sense, for indeed, if the "hermeneutic of discontinuity and rupture" were to prevail, then there would be an entirely new religion distinct from the Catholic Church as it existed prior to 1962. Such an interpretation must be wholly rejected.

Some might also ask: was not the Second Vatican Council divinely inspired by the Holy Spirit, as we believe about an ecumenical council when the Pope gathers with the College of Bishops? What I said in my "Reforming the Reform" homily in 1996 remains true today: "Of course the Holy Spirit guided the work of Vatican II with tremendous benefit for the Church in many ways, but not everything that has been introduced into the Church in the past thirty [now fifty] years under the guise of the 'spirit of Vatican II' can authentically be attributed to that Council. Much has been mere human innovation and indeed experimentation, and it is this which is subject to human error. After all, Vatican II defined no infallible dogmas."

In suggesting that mistakes have been made, I do not mean to denigrate in any way the authentic Spirit-led movements of the Second Vatican Council which have so greatly benefited the Church and the world. Moreover, we cannot and we must not give up hope that we can overcome our challenges and difficulties. Already we can see seeds of hope bearing fruit in the founding of new religious communities and increased vocations to the priesthood in some places, the exponential growth of the Catholic Church in Africa, an increased awareness of the need for a new evangelization, and the call to intentional missionary discipleship and stewardship as a way of life.

The Second Vatican Council might seem like a distant memory to those who were alive then or simply as a historical footnote to those who were born in the years after the close of the Council, but even if one is not consciously aware of Vatican II in our current time, a review of what has transpired in the Catholic Church in the past fifty years should make it apparent that Vatican II has had a great impact on the life of the Church as we know it today. The positive developments we see – such as more and more parishes taking up Eucharistic adoration – should encourage us, while the negative aspects should not cause us to despair. After all, if a city can undo an urban planning debacle, then we should be confident that the Holy Spirit will guide the Church to correct her human mistakes. Thank God we have already begun to see some encouraging signs of hope for the future.

May God give us this grace.

PROLOGUE

The Origins of and Problems With
The "Spirit" of Vatican II
By David Paul Deavel

Introduction: An Uncomfortable Ride and a Basic Division

"You mean the primacy of Gregorian Chant in the Liturgy?" The response to my question was a silence less "sacred" and more "stony" or perhaps "angry."

I had hazarded this little question while riding in the back seat of a car coming back from a Fordham graduate student lunch with a Sister of Mercy ("Just call me Sharon!") and our driver, Bill, a chain-smoking Carmelite priest ("You can drop the 'Father'"), both of whom never wore any kind of religious garb. It was around the turn of the millennium, years after the close of the Second Vatican Council. The topic was the "difficulty" in the Church that stemmed from "conservatives" who wanted to hold religious, priests, professors, and catechists to a standard of Catholic teaching to which my companions clearly did not agree. The narrow-minded believers, they complained, had dared not only to question their authority but to make complaints to bishops and even "the Vatican." I had kept my mouth shut for most of the ride, not knowing how long traffic issues might make this trip, but finally piped up when Sharon (I have changed the names to protect the guilty) sighed, "I wonder if we'll ever see the promise of Vatican II fulfilled."

For me the promise of Vatican II involved things that had actually appeared in the Council documents. When I first dipped into them before I entered the Catholic Church, I found them to be the best written committee production ever. They were sensible, they were traditional, and they put traditional Catholic doctrine in a biblical and humanistic vein that gave them power. My own thought was that they put the romance back into Christian orthodoxy.

But I very soon encountered the somewhat more hazy notion of a Church that was more "progressive," "open," "ecumenical," "flexible," and backtracking on doctrines that were found difficult to swallow by non-Catholics and indeed many Catholics, particularly those doctrines that involved limits on sexuality, on ecumenical and interreligious activities, and on ideas that contrasted with elite and often left-wing opinions. For many, "Vatican II" meant that pretty much anything that had taken place before the Council was now off-limits, banned, or simply passé, even if those things were praised, called for, or commanded in the documents themselves. My garb-less religious fellow students' stony silence at my question came from the fact that when it came to the actual words of Vatican II, as for instance the *Constitution on the Sacred Liturgy*'s dictum (n.116) about Gregorian chant's "pride of place," such words could be put aside because though they were in the "letter," they really weren't in the so-called "spirit of Vatican II."

I. The Origins of the Spirit:
A Media Context for Seeing the Documents

The Second Vatican Council's proceedings were filled with drama that was heightened by the fact that this was the first Church Council to be held in the age of modern communications. People read about the Council in the newspapers from the reports of journalists and even priests. Many Americans gathered their understanding of what happened from the *New Yorker* reports made by Fr. Francis X. Murphy, a Redemptorist priest pseudonymously reporting as "Xavier Rynne."[1] The reports made by many like Murphy were easily digested because the narrative of the proceedings was often told through the lens of a "good guys and bad guys" narrative, what George Weigel has described in now politically incorrect terms as "cowboys versus Indians." Very simply put, there were the cowboys, a majority of bishops and many of the big name theologians from around the world who wanted *ressourcement* – a "return to the sources" of the Bible and Christian history to enrich the teaching, practice, and witness of the truth – and *aggiornamento* – an "updating" of the Church's message that would be more positive about the modern world, non-Catholic Christians, other religions, and the importance of the laity. And then there were the Indians, a minority group led by Cardinal Ottaviani, prefect of the Holy Office, a man whose cardinalatial motto was *semper idem*, "always the same." They wanted the Church, it was said, to retain a "fortress mentality" that was unyielding to all of the desires of the majority, to keep a "monopoly" on salvation, and to claim that the Church "had all the answers." This division was often painted in starkly political terms as between conservatives and liberals.

Like all generalizations, such a story had a degree of truth to it. But the reality was that the majority group was divided into two groups that agreed on some things but would ultimately part ways later (more on this division further on). At the time, however, there was a great desire on the part of many bishops and theologians of the world for changes in the Church's tone, many of its policies, and even the way of doing theology. There was also a great deal of worry on the part of a minority that the Church needed to be wary of being swept up in the spirit of the age and forget that her identity was trans-historical and was made up not only of practices and institutions that were revisable and even disposable, but also teachings and practices that were meant for all ages. They were also worried that a hasty or foolish revision of even changeable practices, with regard to the sacraments and the liturgy especially, would have a malign effect. The Council did sometimes seem like a pitched battle between two sides, especially if one were paying attention to the media, who loved events like the childish and uncharitable applause by the Council Fathers when Cardinal Ottaviani's microphone was turned off by the timekeeper.

The Rhine Flows into the Tiber, the 1967 history of Vatican II by the American Divine Word Missionary Ralph Wiltgen, showed that the ultimate result of the Council was that "the Rhine" which stood not just for German theology, but for the broader currents of biblical and liturgical study that had started well before the Council, was brought into and shaped its final results.[2] Wiltgen depicted the debates in a winsome fashion, with attention to the forming of alliances and factions within the Council, as well as the resulting compromises on the documents. There is a good bit of the cowboy and Indian in Wiltgen's narration, but it was sufficiently honest about the proceedings that it was republished by the distinctly non-progressive TAN Books.

Wiltgen and others have noted the very distinct changes in the Church that were decided or called for by the Council. There were important but controversial decisions from the first document on the liturgy onward, such as the allowance of certain parts of the Mass being performed in the vernacular at the discretion of the bishops, though it was maintained that "the use of the Latin language is to be preserved in the Latin rite, except where a particular law might indicate otherwise" (*Sacrosanctum concilium* n.36). There was also the call for a general revision of the rites of the Church. *Dei verbum*, the document on divine revelation, rethought the issue of Scripture and Tradition, considering them not as two separate streams but as one single channel of divine truth (*DV* n.9). *Lumen gentium*, the *Dogmatic Constitution on the Church*, placed the authority of the Pope within the context of the authority of the bishops of the world; it didn't limit his authority as teacher or legislator, as determined by Vatican I, to a situation in which he could not act without a majority of the world's bishops, but emphasized that he was both head and member of the college of bishops. It similarly emphasized that the bishops themselves had authority given by Christ to act – they were not simply assistants to the vicar of Christ, but exercised their office directly as bishops, though in union with the Roman Pontiff and under his jurisdiction.

Lumen gentium also broke ground by speaking of the relationship of other Christians and indeed other religious believers to the Catholic Church in more positive terms than had ever been done. *Dignitatis humanae*, perhaps the most controversial document, affirmed the rights of believers and indeed religious groups in all faiths to be free from state coercion as they followed their religious beliefs. The document certainly didn't say that one could do anything in the name of conscience, but that such uses of freedom still had to be "in conformity with the objective moral order" (*DH* n.7). And it certainly never equated Catholic faith with all faiths, but instead affirmed the Church as the "one true religion" with a divine mandate to spread the truth to all peoples (*DH* n.1).

A careful examination of the texts of Vatican II reveals that there was very little doctrinal discontinuity but a great deal more discontinuity in style of presentation and indeed practical recommendations for the Church. Indeed, as the late Cardinal Avery Dulles, S.J., wrote in an article that seeks to correct interpretations of the Council that contradict its letter, "the teaching of Vatican II" is "very solid, carefully nuanced and sufficiently flexible to meet the needs of our own time and place" and has an "artful blending of majority and minority perspectives" that should have forestalled the unilateral interpretations.[3]

But in the aftermath of the Council, close attention to long documents was never going to compete with media depictions of the vibrant personalities who had been shown all along as the good guys. And some of them were saying dramatic things.

II. Cowboy Theologians and Counter-Reaction

The reality that there were really more than two groups at the Council was quickly revealed afterward. The major problem for some of the cowboys at the Council's end was the very fact that the Council ended in documents with compromises. In their view the documents had not gone nearly far enough. Very quickly after the Council, direct statements such as the ones about Latin or Gregorian chant were seen as simply too conservative and pressure was exerted to rid the formal Latin rite of liturgy and fill the air with folk songs. Many said that the ecumenical possibilities offered by the documents didn't go far enough. The late 1960s and early 1970s were filled with events like joint-communion services with Protestants, lay people attempting to take priestly tasks on themselves, and all manner of other experimentation. The teaching of the Council on the possibility of salvation for those outside of the visible Catholic Church was expanded into a conviction that all religious traditions were paths to salvation in and of themselves and, further, that everyone was going to Heaven.

Many of the theologians who had been interpreters of the Council had formed a theological journal called *Concilium* in 1965 that began to push the boundaries on even basic doctrinal claims. As theologians such as Hans Küng, Edward Schillebeeckx, and Karl Rahner became more radical, a number of their colleagues such as Joseph Ratzinger and Henri de Lubac – who were no less in favor of *ressourcement* and *aggiornamento* – broke away by the early 1970s and founded *Communio*, which would instead seek to interpret the documents in the light of Tradition in a more serious way. Ratzinger recalled in his memoir that even during the Council itself, he had begun to sense that his fellow scholars "now understood themselves to be the truly knowledgeable experts in the faith and no longer subordinate to the shepherds." Concerning Rahner, perhaps the dominant figure in the immediate aftermath of the Council, Ratzinger wrote that though the two had similar convictions about many practical issues in the Council, the two were ultimately "on two different theological planets," agreeing on certain theological and practical matters "for entirely different reasons":

> Despite his early reading of the Fathers, his theology was totally conditioned by the tradition of Suarezian scholasticism and its new reception in the light of German idealism and of Heidegger. His was

a speculative and philosophical theology in which Scripture and the Fathers in the end did not play an important role and in which the historical dimension was really of little significance.[4]

Other faithful Catholics who had initially felt hopeful about the reforms of the Council – laymen like Jacques Maritain, Etienne Gilson, Christopher Dawson, and Dietrich von Hildebrand, and many priests who had taken part in the Council, like the Jesuits Henri de Lubac and Jean Danielou and the Oratorian Louis Bouyer – were now filled with anger and disgust. Maritain's *Peasant of the Garonne* (1968), in which the 85-year-old Thomist wrote about the Church's seeming "kneeling to the world" and Bouyer's *The Decomposition of Catholicism* (1970) were representative reactions to the trends in the Church.

But those who had been cowboys originally were still in the saddle in many dioceses around the world and subscribed to a number of intellectual theories that justified their seemingly endless revolution. The self-anointed experts/radicals had the ear of many good-hearted bishops and priests who often let them have their way.

III. Rupture

The first and most important theory was the "rupture" thesis presented by historians such as the University of Bologna's Giuseppe Alberigo.[5] Alberigo was the director of the University's Institute of Religious Studies, founded in 1953 by Fr. Gino Dossetti and continuing today as a major player in interpreting Vatican II. Alberigo and other historians and theologians were already interpreting Vatican II as an "event" in the midst of the Council. "Event" is a term of the historian. As theologian Joseph Komonchak has observed, "An event...means difference."[6] To be more concrete, "an 'event' represents novelty, discontinuity, a 'rupture,' a break from routine, causing surprise, disturbance, even trauma, and perhaps initiating a new routine, a new realm of the taken-for-granted."[7]

For many historians and theologians, Vatican II was a rupture with previous Catholic history. That this is so from the perspective of history is no doubt. The immediate history of the Church after the Council indeed represented all of the words in Fr. Komonchak's list. The question is what to do with all of the historical data about the Council and its consequences. Many theologians took the dramatic changes not only in the texts but in the Council and the years afterward and turned them into a theological theory of rupture in the Church.

Pope John XXIII, the convener of the Council, had himself said that what he wanted out of the Council was a "new Pentecost." The experiences of many of the people at the Council, especially the cowboys, was of a new beginning. Thus from the historians was fashioned a theological reasoning that rupture and newness were themselves the key to understanding the Council. As Cardinal Dulles described the theorists of this kind, "where there are ambiguities in the Council documents, these should always be resolved in favor of discontinuity."[8] We might add that for these theorists, even unambiguous statements should be resolved in favor of discontinuity.

In a 1987 article titled "Opposition to the Council (1966-1984)," Bologna theorist Daniele Menozzi, an Alberigo protégé who is now co-director of the influential journal *Rivista di Storia del Cristianesimo (Journal of the History of Christianity)* and professor of contemporary history at the Scuola Normale Superiore in Pisa, informs us that not only was Archbishop Lefebvre, founder of the Society of St. Pius X, "anticonciliar," but so were Maritain, de Lubac, Daniélou, Communion and Liberation, Opus Dei, and indeed, Pope Paul VI. Amusingly Menozzi says that the above groups "can indeed find in the final documents elements that support their vision of the direction enjoined by Vatican II, but they seem nonetheless to disregard its spirit."

How does Menozzi define the "spirit" by which we should understand the Council? In a section dedicated to showing how Paul VI was also in opposition to the Council, Menozzi explains that the pontiff's determination to apply the Council documents was because he believed that the closing of the Council was "an end to the effort to understand the limits and modalities of Church renewal." In other words, for Menozzi, Paul VI's attempt to apply the documents according to their letter meant that he was claiming that the Council was the end of renewal in the Church. For Menozzi and the Bologna theorists, everything had changed and would continue to change, even against the letter of the conciliar documents because "the Council, basing itself on what John XXIII had said in his opening discourse as he looked to the future, expressed in some passages of its documents [note that they are not cited], namely that there should be a continuous rereading of Christianity in the light of the signs of the times the Gospel was making visible in the contemporary world."[9]

IV. Reception

The theorists of "rupture" all take for granted that Vatican II was not only a good idea but was an event explicitly planned by the Spirit. This has been asserted strongly by Church historian and theologian Massimo Faggioli (b. 1970), perhaps the youngest and most visible of Alberigo's disciples. Faggioli has a full professorship at Villanova, regular columns with *La Croix* and the *Huffington Post*, and has won awards for several of his books. He acknowledges that the clash of narratives about Vatican II cannot be decided by the historian, but needs theological discernment. He calls for a "reception" of the Council by the whole Church, but like the rest of the Bologna school, he does not think that according the texts a final authority as to their meaning is a proper reception. He characterizes such an approach as rejecting the idea of the Council as a "beginning of renewal" and calls it "not only unfaithful to the intention and the history of Vatican II; it also shows scant confidence in the ability of the Church to manage change on the basis of the Spirit-assisted understanding of the 'signs of the times.'"[10]

For Faggioli, the proper reception of the documents is to understand them through a "hermeneutics" (theory of interpretation) of the Council. I would characterize four broad ways that theologians have used to interpret the Council and "receive" it. The first is through an interpretation of the overall themes. The Australian Jesuit Gerald O'Collins does this with some degree of success in his book, *The Second Vatican Council*.[11] O'Collins tends to stay very close to the text and is much more careful than many theorists of the Bologna school to attend to the specific words. Faggioli and other theorists of the Bologna School tend to read the text in the light of the primacy of one document or another (Faggioli reads it in the light of the *Constitution on the Sacred Liturgy*, while others read the Council through the lens of other documents). The third way of interpreting the Council by those in the rupture school is by looking at the "style" of writing of the Council. The Jesuit historian John O'Malley in his book *What Happened at Vatican II?* interprets the Council through this lens, noting that the classical expository style of Vatican II's documents, along with its tendency toward the positive, and its vocabulary all tell us something about the Council documents' meaning.[12] And the fourth is by looking at the history of how the documents themselves were formed, what was changed from the drafts, who suggested the changes, and seeing how the final product looked.

Of course, in the right context, such methods of interpretation can all be used with more or less benefit. We will of course find meaning by studying the themes of the documents, the ways in which one document interprets another, the style of the documents, and the history of its writing. But as Flannery O'Connor said, "the Theories are worse than the Furies." What becomes so damaging is when the theme, style, prioritization of texts by theologians, or supposed insights gained from the process of committee writing end up vitiating the doctrinal claims of the text itself. Because, for example, the texts of Vatican II speak about the possibility for salvation for those outside the Church in several places does not mean that this "theme" allows us to say that Vatican II teaches everyone will reach salvation.[13] The claims made by many theologians for "developments in doctrine" are often reversals not merely of practices or revisable doctrine, but even of infallibly declared teachings of previous councils and popes. Many theologians said that because *Lumen gentium* (n.8) claimed that the Church of Christ "subsists in," rather than "is," the Catholic Church, that the Council taught the Catholic Church is just one of many "subsisting" Churches that are all equal.

There is something deeply troubling about the Bologna school and its intellectual heirs' use of "hermeneutics" to allow themselves to skate by doctrinal and practical decisions of the Council and then condemn others who think differently. Massimo Faggioli has no sorrow that Latin and Gregorian chant have been banished despite the call for their prominence at the Council, but sees any calls for a reception of the Council that might include a liturgy more in continuity with the period before the Council as opposition to the Council. For him, a Vatican II ecclesiology cannot include traditional liturgy – even one that follows the 1970 *Missal*.[14]

But there is a further problem with the "Spirit of Vatican II" proponents. Many of them rightly complain that the focus on the Pope as a kind of inspired oracle whose ideas and directions must always be the best does not reflect the teaching of the Church that the Pope can teach infallibly under certain very limited conditions. (This means not that we must accept as infallible either his themes or his style or even his practical decisions – even though we are usually obligated to obey the last – but that we must accept his teaching on faith and morals in an absolute way when he teaches infallibly but also with a submissive spirit even when he is teaching non-infallibly.) We even acknowledge that not all popes are good popes. But the kind of exaggerated claims they reject with regard to Popes they then apply to Vatican II, making it – or rather their interpretation of it – into what some have called a "superdogma" that necessitates a retraction of everything the so-called reformers don't like.

The "rupture school" asks us not just to accept that Vatican II is a valid Council or that it teaches doctrine infallibly, but accept that it is "inspired" and that we must approve absolutely the way it stated things, its emphases, its practical decisions, and even the post-conciliar decisions that were said to be based on it – as long as the "Spirit of Vatican II" school agrees with those decisions. Though the Bologna school and other theologians have criticized popes and previous councils of the Church for their policies and decisions, they do not allow others to criticize the policies and decisions of Vatican II unless the criticisms comport with the progressive viewpoint. When that is the case, then defenders of the Council's decisions are labeled "anti-conciliar."

This simply isn't required of Catholics. One can think the Council's practical decisions and the way that it expressed things were done well or badly. A Council whose practical decisions or modes of expression – especially when not defining any doctrines – were ill-done is no more a slight to the Holy Spirit than the fact of a bad pope. Both are realities through which God's providence will work.

Conclusion: To Know Christ in the Tradition

I still think as I did when I first encountered the texts of Vatican II that there is gold there. But for that gold to be found, the reception of Vatican II will have to involve not just looking at Vatican II's documents, decisions, and the decisions made in the time after it, but also to the whole history of the Church's teaching and life. As Joseph Ratzinger said when Prefect of CDF:

> Many interpretations give the impression that, from Vatican II onward, everything has been changed, and that what preceded it has no value or, at best, has value only in the light of Vatican II. The Second Vatican Council is not treated as part of the entire living Tradition of the Church, but as an end of Tradition, a new start from zero.[15]

On the contrary, Vatican II is part of the long history of the Church. Its dogmatic teaching must be accepted and its practical decisions – and particularly the ways those were implemented by popes, bishops, priests, and laypeople – need to be evaluated in the light of the whole history of Tradition and by how well they help others know Christ.

ENDNOTES

1. Those interested in reading or re-reading Rynne/Murphy's reports, along with a new afterword by the author, can see them in *Vatican Council II* (New York: Orbis, 1999).

2. Ralph Wiltgen, SVD, *The Rhine Flows into the Tiber: A History of Vatican II* (Rockford, IL: TAN Books, 1978 [1967]).

3. Avery Dulles, "Vatican II: The Myth and the Reality," *America*, February 24, 2003 issue, online at http://www.americamagazine.org/issue/423/article/vatican-ii-myth-and-reality.

4. Joseph Ratzinger, *Milestones* (San Francisco: Ignatius, 1998), 133, 128.

5. Alberigo (1926-2007), taught at the University of Bologna for thirty years. After World War II the former law student and historian-in-training met Gino Dossetti, the former vice-secretary of the Italian Christian Democratic Party. Dossetti wished to begin a community of study of Church reform and located it in Bologna. It was there that Alberigo and his wife helped found the Institute, a community of religious and historians (the religious community later split off) that put together a history of the Ecumenical Councils and then, under Alberigo's direction, the five-volume history of the Second Vatican Council that advanced the ideas not only of a rupture with the pre-conciliar period but also a post-conciliar period in which renewal meant going beyond the texts of the Council.

6. Joseph Komonchak, "Interpreting the Council and Its Consequences," in *After Vatican II: Trajectories and Hermeneutics*, James L. Heft and John O'Malley, eds. (Grand Rapids, Mich.: Eerdmans, 2012): 164-72, at 166.

7. Joseph Komonchak, "Vatican II as an 'Event,'" in *Vatican II: Did Anything Happen?* David Schultenover, ed. (New York: Continuum, 2007): 24-51, at 27.

8. Dulles, "Vatican II: The Myth and the Reality."

9. Danele Menozzi, "Opposition to the Council (1966-84)," in *The Reception of Vatican II*, Giuseppe Alberigo, Jean-Pierre Jossua, and Joseph Komonchak, eds. Translated by Matthew J. O'Connell (Washington, DC: Catholic University of America Press, 1987): 325-48, at 328 and 332.

10. Massimo Faggioli, *Vatican II: The Battle for Meaning* (New York: Paulist Press, 2012), 124.

11. Gerald O'Collins, *The Second Vatican Council* (Collegeville, MN: Michael Glazier/Liturgical Press, 2014).

12. John W. O'Malley, *What Happened at Vatican II* (Cambridge, Mass.: Belknap Press of Harvard University Press, 2008).

13. See Ralph Martin, *Will many be saved?: what Vatican II actually teaches and its implications for the new evangelization* (Grand Rapids, Mich.: Eerdmans, 2012), for some pertinent examples of this view.

14. See Massimo Faggioli, "Quaestio Disputata: *Sacrosanctum concilium* and the Meaning of Vatican II," *Theological Studies* 71 (2010) 438-452 and his book *True Reform: Liturgical Reform and Ecclesiology* (Collegeville, Minn.: Liturgical Press, 2012).

15. 1988 address of Cardinal Ratzinger to the Bishops of Chile on the Lefebvre schism, at http://www.catholicculture.org/culture/library/viewcfm?id=3032&repos=1&subrepos=&searchid=292734

DAVID PAUL DEAVEL is editor of *Logos: A Journal of Catholic Thought and Culture* and visiting assistant professor of Catholic Studies at the University of St. Thomas (Minnesota). He has a Ph.D. in theology from Fordham University. He is the vice president of the Newman Association of America and a contributing editor for *Gilbert*, the magazine of the American Chesterton Society. He has published over 250 articles, essays, and reviews in a number of books as well as a wide variety of popular and scholarly journals including *America, Books & Culture, Catholic World Report, Chesterton Review, Christian Century, Commonweal, First Things, National Review, Journal of Markets and Morality, New Blackfriars, Nova et Vetera,* and *Touchstone*. In 2013, the Acton Institute presented him with the Novak Award for promising scholarship on the connections between religion and economic liberty. He lives in St. Paul, Minnesota, with his wife Catherine, an associate professor of philosophy at the University of St. Thomas, and their seven children.

The Second Vatican Council:
The Reality and the Myth About the Nature of the Church

By Rev. Robert John Araujo, S.J.

*I am the vine; you are the branches. If a man remains in me and I in him,
he will bear much fruit; apart from me you can do nothing.* John 15:5

Introduction

Since the Second Vatican Council (hereinafter, the Council), the Church's faithful and others have encountered diverse, sometimes conflicting explanations about the Council's work. In some instances, these accounts are well-founded because they are based on the texts representing and memorializing the Council's labors. However, other descriptions of the Council's work are problematic as they reinvent or revise the history of the Council and the fruits of its labor; moreover, the accompanying interpretations produced by this second category of descriptions of the Conciliar documents are flawed because the interpretation fails to take stock of all the documents that concern related issues.

As one trained in the law, I have come to understand the importance of texts and their meaning which are essential to an objective comprehension of what they signify and what they do not. The significance of texts is important to both theology, philosophy, literature, history, *and* the law. Following the importance of the texts themselves is the relevance of how they are interpreted. In this regard, the intent and objectives of the authors of the texts are critical to the reader's understanding and to the import generally.[1] While speaking of objectives, mine is to develop an uncomplicated method of interpretation that will be useful to reading the texts of the Council dealing with the nature of the Church and how her members are to interact with and to relate to one another. Here I submit that what is essential to understanding the meaning of individual texts is the further need to read *together* the several documents issued by the Council that address the same subject matter.

The Council heralded the dignity of the human person and the societies to which the individual person belongs in several of its documents – texts which reveal the intent, objectives, and contexts of the Council's work. In the *Pastoral Constitution on the Church in the Modern World, Gaudium et spes (GS)*, the Council Fathers offered an important expression relevant to this paper, i.e., it is the dignity of the human person that establishes the foundation for relationship – relationship with others, with the world, and with the Church.[2]

The opening quotation from St. John's Gospel provides our Lord's perspective on the nature of the Church – we as the members of the Church are in communion with Him, but He is the vine on which we, the branches, are grafted. While asserting that the Church is a "mystery," the *Pastoral Constitution* also acknowledges that the Church was founded by Christ to fulfill eschatological and salvific purposes which begin in the temporal world but are only fully achieved in the world of eternity.[3] Regarding the Church's nature, the Council Fathers agreed that the Church is a family constituted by Christ to be a society that is established on relationships and is directed to the purposes just mentioned in the temporal and eternal spheres.[4] Once again, the image of the vine and its branches comes to mind. As a leaven for the "soul for human society," the Church relies on the "talents and industry" of her individual members.[5] But the question that will be pursued here is how she does this. The Council supplied answers to this question in the texts it issued which address the Church's nature.

Many questions about what the Conciliar documents mean must be addressed by objectively reading the texts individually, and then, together as I have argued. This seems to be an obvious and promising approach, but all too often texts, and the common or related themes that they address, are read and, therefore, understood in a fragmented fashion. Consequently, their more authentic meanings can be lost as a result of this fragmentation. In the final analysis, all relevant documents of the Council are critical to the task in seeking the best possible understanding of what the Council said and what it did not say. When this approach consisting of a careful reading and consideration of the relevant documents has been neglected, understanding of the Council's work product are flawed. This becomes acutely patent when the nature of the Church is the question under investigation.

One important illustration of the misunderstanding of the Council's work in this context can be found in the 1968 Statement of several theologians (published in *The New York Times*) who publicly opposed Pope Paul VI's encyclical, *Humanae vitae*.[6] The Pope's encyclical reaffirmed the Church's opposition to artificial birth control and her positions on other matters related to marriage, family life, and human nature. While the Statement against the encyclical appeared to address artificial birth control and individual conscience, it was, in effect, a challenge to papal authority and the *Magisterium*; moreover, it was an unambiguous attempt to redefine the Church's nature. The Statement was, by its own admission, purportedly based on the work of the Council. To justify the Statement's objectives, the authors asserted that:

> We take exception to the ecclesiology implied and the methodology used by Paul VI in the writing and promulgation of the document: *They are incompatible with the church's authentic self-awareness as expressed in and suggested by the acts of the Second Vatican Council itself.*[7]

This was a remarkable set of claims not only because they challenge papal authority but also because they present an erroneous understanding of how the Council defined the nature of the Church. My task will be an intentional effort to remedy this misunderstanding.

A strategy was subsequently developed to implement the Statement.[8] The tactic would be applied to any moral issue because "the Pope can only recommend a stance on a particular moral issue and not bind the consciences of Catholics."[9] In essence, the stratagem was designed to create an explanation of the Church's nature which ignores the essential hierarchical relationship of the Church's members as specifically and unambiguously defined by the Council.[10] Notwithstanding the clarity of the texts, the plan underpinning the Statement asserted that the autonomy of each member of the Church is based on an individual conscience that is subjectively formed. Thus, each person would be purportedly authorized to reach an individual position on crucial matters. But this tactic fails to comprehend the nature of the Church because it, in fact, is not substantiated by the documents of the Council which address the issues discussed in the Statement.[11]

Paul VI's actions surrounding the drafting and promulgation of *Humanae vitae* were in accord with the acts of the Second Vatican Council. In stark contrast, the astonishing and bold challenge from dissenting theologians expressed in their Statement is inconsistent with the Council's accomplishments and the import of the documents which they drafted and adopted. The dissenters who crafted the Statement, while praising the Pope and the *Magisterium* on the one hand, had the objective of critiquing – perhaps even ridiculing – them on the other hand.[12] The tactic underpinning their strategy was to portray the Pope's view as merely one of several or many views to which respect was due regarding an acceptable (tolerable) understanding of the Church, her nature, and ecclesiastical authority. Interestingly, the ploy offered praise to the Pope in order to demonstrate that he is "an example of how each Catholic must prayerfully come to his own moral decision on birth control."[13] But to borrow from an old advertising line about variations in gasoline mileage, the actual outcome of the applications of conscience may vary. Would this tactic apply only to the issue of birth control? Apparently not, because the strategy for opposition would apply to any moral issue because, as the authors of the Statement asserted, "the Pope can only recommend a stance on a particular moral issue and not bind the consciences of Catholics."[14] But this explanation is inconsistent with the conclusions of the Council as recorded in the documents it produced.

The challenges to papal authority, the *Magisterium*, and the authentic meaning of the documents of the Council continue to the present day. As some contemporary literature demonstrates, there is a misapprehension that the Council welcomed a democratization of what the Church teaches and why the Church teaches what she teaches.[15]

The thesis that I intend to advance is a counterpoint to this. As I shall demonstrate through an objective and careful reading of the relevant Conciliar documents, the "church's authentic self-awareness" or nature is discernible by reading a number of the crucial texts authored by the Council. When these texts are carefully read, it becomes clear that Paul VI possessed and exercised a clear and accurate understanding of the nature of the Church supported by the conclusions of the Council on the relevant issues. The objective of my essay is to present dispassionately the reality of the Council so that anyone will be better equipped to understand accurately the work of the Council, particularly in how it defined the nature of the Church as a hierarchical structure in which the categories of members have specific tasks to perform; however, notwithstanding the different tasks, a strong and essential bond of relationship – as reflected in the analogy of Christ's "I am the vine, you are the branches[16] – is imperative to a proper understanding of the Church's organic and unified nature.

It has been over a half century since the Council concluded its work on December 8, 1965. Since then, Catholics have encountered explanations of the meaning of the Council by fellow Catholics and others which are based less on the texts of the Council and more on the ambiguous *spirit* of Vatican II. The documents which the Council Fathers produced are, in fact, the authentic source of the spirit of the Council because they are the product of the Council that was presented to Pope Paul VI for his approval. Still, there are occasions when some opinions argue that the spirit of the Council is elsewhere. It might be in the notes of certain bishops or the journals of *periti* and other documentation that are extrinsic to the Constitutions, Declarations, and Decrees issued by the Council and approved by the Pope. These arguments are problematic when the "spirit" they project constitute a revision of the fruits of the Council as recorded in the official texts.[17]

This project and its objectives are geared to assist those who wish to know what the Council did and what it did not do, particularly in the context of explaining ecclesiology, that is, the nature of the Church. I will organize the structure of this paper in a thematic way that examines the texts and relates them to one another. Then, by considering the intent and purpose of each document, it should become clear how each element of the Church relates to one another in a coherent fashion and organic relationship. The documents in my survey begin with the most crucial text that is the nucleus of the Council's fruit, i.e., the *Dogmatic Constitution on the Church, Lumen gentium (LG)*. The *Dogmatic Constitution* addresses each of the Church's constituencies which encompass: the bishops; the clergy; persons in consecrated and religious life; and the laity. Following each constituency discussion in the *Dogmatic Constitution*, I shall then turn to the particular document or documents dealing with this particular category. So, in addition to *Lumen gentium*, I consider the other texts dealing with: bishops *Christus Dominus, (CD)*; priests *Presbyterorum ordinis (PO)* and priestly formation *Optatam totius (OT)*; religious life *Perfectae caritatis (PC)*; and, the laity *Apostolicam actuositatem (AA)*. The roadmap of my presentation follows: section I offers an overview of the *Dogmatic Constitution*; section II addresses the role of bishops and their relationship to the Pope; section III investigates the presbyterate; section IV considers those in consecrated and religious life; section V examines the laity; and section VI offers some concluding observations.

This discussion should present, in an objective fashion, the reality of the Church's nature as defined by the Council. What follows is a guide to the documents and, therefore, the meaning of Vatican II that is founded on the wisdom of St. Augustine of Hippo: *tolle lege*, take up and read! And with this reading, an explanation and a consequent understanding of the reality of what the Council did and did not do will follow, and the myth which surrounds the Council in explaining the nature of the Church should dissolve.

I. Overview of *Lumen Gentium* – Light of Nations
the *Dogmatic Constitution on the Church*

Lumen gentium, without doubt, is the foundational text of the Council. Among all the documents issued, it establishes the framework for explaining the Church and who she is. The *Dogmatic Constitution* addresses relevant issues dealing with the Church's nature that include: 1. the people of God; 2. the hierarchical structure of the Church, with special reference to the bishops and priests as their collaborators; 3. the laity; and 4. persons in religious life.

The *Dogmatic Constitution* begins with a discussion of the Church as the People of God. God, throughout human history and across all races, expresses love for those who fear Him and do what is right and avoid what is wrong. His salvation is directed both to individuals and to the body of them as one people – a body that acknowledges God's truth and serves Him in holiness. The covenant with God, ratified in Christ, brings together Jew (old) and gentile (new) in one Spirit. This unification by covenant is the People of God.[18]

One area that has been a source of confusion for many is the concept of priesthood that intersects the People of God. The Council's explanation of priesthood states that, "Though they differ from one another in essence and not only in degree, the common priesthood of the faithful and the ministerial or hierarchical priesthood are nonetheless interrelated: each of them in its own special way is a participation in the one priesthood of Christ."[19] The ministerial priest, i.e., a member of the presbyteral order, by operation of his "sacred power," has a specific role to teach and rule the priestly people as he acts in the person of Christ.[20] The priesthood of faithful laity, on the other hand, exists in their joining in the offering of the Eucharist and by their participation in the Church's sacramental life and prayer.[21]

Nevertheless, the lay faithful have active responsibilities which rely on their particular gifts, particularly in the temporal order of the world. They have a responsibility, as branches engrafted on the vine of Christ, to spread and defend the faith by word and deed as "true witnesses of Christ" to the temporal world.[22] While there are these differences, there is also a unity in the different roles attributed to the nature of those in the presbyterate and those in the laity through Holy Communion in the Body of Christ. The Council explained that the laity have special responsibility for the family, which is "the domestic church" where parents become the first instructors of the faith of the Church's newest members.[23] It is in this "domestic church" where her members must learn and live the "universal agreement in matters of faith and morals" that is initiated and sustained by the Spirit of God's truth.[24]

The universal dimension of the People of God must never be forgotten. Ironically, in the present age where globalization is the buzz word often used to describe many matters addressing a kind of secular universality, some Catholics, especially in the United States, like to consider themselves different from their co-religionists elsewhere; however, the rationale for the purported differences is typically thin. Regardless of the nation of which one is a member, the universality "which adorns the people of God" exists to bring all members of the human family back to its source and head who is Christ.[25] This fact demonstrates the "catholicity" (the universality) of the Church. This universality exists around the world and permeates the local churches represented in the individual dioceses. An important point about the "particular Churches" is that while they may have their own traditions that reflect certain elements of a local culture, they must not stand in opposition to the primacy of the Chair of Peter, i.e., the Pope.[26] Consequently, the Pope, as Christ's Vicar and as the successor of St. Peter, has a crucial role that must be exercised in the Church's true nature.

The unity of the Church is also expressed through all of her members, for the Church has been given the responsibility to go out to the world and preach the Good News to everyone.[27] A portion of this duty is to assist those who may otherwise be prone to falling into doctrinal error which compromises the integrity of the faith which the Church holds, advances, and protects. These are the obligations of every disciple who follows Christ.[28] Here the Council Fathers saw need to explicate the specific duties of the various members of the Church taking stock of her "hierarchical structure." In light of this fact, I now turn to the components which constitute this structure and begin with the bishops.

II. Bishops

Chapter III of the *Dogmatic Constitution* discusses the hierarchical structure of the Church and the special emphasis on the bishops. Indeed, there has been much discussion and debate about the Church's hierarchical nature, the Petrine Office, the collegiality of the bishops, and the primacy of Peter (the Pope).[29] An in-depth examination of these issues goes beyond the scope of this paper. What is relevant to this paper, however, is not what scholars researching records and diaries have concluded about these matters but what the Council concluded and said about them as recorded by the Council's documents. The hierarchical nature of the Church as explained by the Council is a point often overlooked by those who might criticize the Church as a hierarchical institution. It is useful to understand why the Council acknowledged this fundamental point. It did so in the context of its conclusion that the Church's bishops are the successors of the Apostles and, therefore, are the shepherds of the Church.[30] But they are not shepherds alone, for their vital unifying force is the Roman Pontiff, the successor of Peter, the permanent and visible source and foundation of the unity of faith and communion. The Pope is fortified in his office by the teachings of the Church, the perpetuity of the institution, the meaning and reasoning of the primacy of his office, and the *Magisterium*.[31] As the Council Fathers stated, "this Council is resolved to declare and proclaim before all people the doctrine concerning bishops, the successors of the apostles, who together with the successor of Peter, the Vicar of Christ, the visible Head of the whole Church, govern the house of the living God."[32] There is little doubt that this conviction of the Council suggests anything other than a hierarchical nature of the Church and her structure.

The Apostles and their successors, the bishops, have been entrusted by Christ with the principal responsibility of preaching the Good News.[33] To ensure the continuity of their work, the Apostles were also authorized to choose and commission their successors. By this means, the apostolic succession and tradition of the Church is manifested and preserved.[34] While the bishops preside in "place of God over the flock," they have been given the assistance of priests and deacons.[35] Led by Peter and his successors, the bishops are to continue as the Church's shepherds and whoever "hears them, hears Christ, and he who rejects them, rejects Christ and Him who sent Christ."[36] The leadership of Peter, the Pope, is not an inconsequential matter.

Bishops, who are fortified by the Holy Spirit, must be always mindful of the fact that they have been given great responsibilities. Through their Episcopal consecration, they possess and exercise the fullness of the sacrament of Holy Orders – the "supreme power of the sacred ministry."[37] The fact of supremacy once again more than suggests something about the hierarchical nature of the Church. In order to complete the tasks of this ministry, the bishops have the distinct authority and office of teaching within and governance of the Church that "can be exercised only in hierarchical communion with the head [i.e., the Pope] and the members of the college."[38] Thus, if there is no communion with the Pope, the authority of teaching and governance of any bishop is deficient. This says something about the unique authority of the Pope and how the bishops are subject to his office. As the Council acknowledged:

> "The college or body of bishops has no authority unless it is understood together with the Roman Pontiff, the successor of Peter as its head. The Pope's power of primacy over all, both pastors and faithful, remains whole and intact. In virtue of his office, i.e., as Vicar of Christ and pastor of the whole Church, the Roman Pontiff has full, supreme and universal power over the Church. And he is always free to exercise this power."[39]

Implicit in this authority of the Pope is the supreme power of the Church being situated in Christ's Vicar and in no one else. Consequently, the bishops who exercise the principal authority in their local churches must nevertheless remain subject to the supreme power of the Pope who is entrusted with the authority of Peter over the universal Church. Although the bishops are leaders of the local flocks, the Pope is shepherd of the entire flock – for he, Peter, expresses the unity of the flock in and of Christ.[40]

Even though the individual bishops are the visible principle and foundation of the local churches, the Pope is at the head of the universal Church of which the local churches are constitutive elements. Thus, when exercising responsibilities affecting his particular church, each bishop must be mindful of the welfare of the universal Church. This is true because every bishop's actions (or inactions) must promote and safeguard the unity of faith and the welfare of the universal Church and its catholicity.[41]

The fact that the Church is hierarchical does not mean or necessitate entitlement to perks to the Apostles' successors, for the office of bishop is not a conferral of privilege or prerogative but is a commission for service with the authority of an Apostle – that is *diakonia* or ministry.[42] Since the Pope is the servant of the servants of God, the bishops are then the servants of the servant of the servants of God. They thus have an office to fulfill and responsibilities that must be met. Inherent in these responsibilities is the critical duty to address errors that may or do threaten the souls entrusted to the care of the bishops. In the twenty-first century we witness on several fronts – clerical, religious, and laity – sources of error which become the responsibility of bishops to address with charity, wisdom, *and* authority. In this regard, a critical passage of *Lumen gentium* needs to be recalled:

> In matters of faith and morals, the bishops speak in the name of Christ and the faithful are to accept their teaching and adhere to it with a religious assent. This religious submission of mind and will must be shown in a special way to the authentic *Magisterium* of the Roman Pontiff, even when he is not speaking *ex cathedra*; that is, it must be shown in such a way that his supreme *Magisterium* is acknowledged with reverence, the judgments made by him are sincerely adhered to, according to his manifest mind and will. His mind and will in the matter may be known either from the character of the documents, from his frequent repetition of the same doctrine, or from his manner of speaking.[43]

While infallibility is the sole prerogative of the Pope, bishops must proclaim the Church's teaching so that the integrity of her doctrine is not compromised in any way; furthermore, they must agree on the positions to be definitively held.[44] This principle is patent when the bishops gather with the Pope in an ecumenical council as they did from 1962-65.

As the Eucharist is central to the liturgy of the Church, every celebration of the Eucharist, to be legitimate, must be under the tutelage of the local bishop.[45] The bishops are also the original and principal ministers of Confirmation, and they remain the dispensers of Holy Orders. They must also remain a positive influence for the good of the souls entrusted to them by way of personal example. While the authority of bishops is extensive and relates to the office of the Roman Pontiff, their exercise of authority is not in their name but in that of Christ.[46]

The bishops must never be viewed as a challenge to power which is proper and universal to the Pope; however, the authority of the bishops is complementary to that of Peter and reinforced by the Holy Spirit.[47] To properly execute the duties of their office, bishops must never lose sight of the example of the Good Shepherd: they must be prepared to offer themselves for the lives of their flock; they must be compassionate; and, they must be attentive to the concerns of those whom they lead.[48]

These important elements of the *Dogmatic Constitution* are complemented by the *Decree Concerning the Pastoral Office of Bishops in the Church (Christus Dominus)*. The *Decree* is subdivided into three chapters. The first addresses the relationship between the bishops and the universal Church and considers the subject within two areas: 1. the role of bishop in the universal Church, and 2. the relation between the bishops and the Apostolic See and the Pope. The second chapter takes account of the bishops and their particular churches or dioceses by looking at three major issues: 1. the bishops' duties; 2. the boundaries of dioceses; and 3. those who assist bishops execute their pastoral office (coadjutor and auxiliary bishops; diocesan curia and commissions; the diocesan clergy; and men and women religious). The third and final chapter investigates the issue of how bishops cooperate for the common good of the many churches by examining three issues: 1. synods, councils, and episcopal conferences (such as the United States Conference of Catholic Bishops); 2. the boundaries of ecclesiastical provinces and the erection of ecclesiastical regions; and 3. bishops who hold inter-diocesan offices and responsibilities.

This paper will focus on the first chapter of the *Decree* which speaks most directly to the issues dealing with the nature of the Church. The Council begins the *Decree* by recalling how Jesus sent the apostles into the world to glorify God and to build up the Body of Christ, the Church.[49] As St. Peter's successor, the Pope is charged with the overarching duty of protecting the faithful who are Christ's people. With this commission comes "supreme, full, immediate, and universal authority over the care of souls by divine institution."[50] The Pope, as the first bishop, is also charged with the care of the common good of the universal Church and all the churches within it.

In essence, the primacy of Peter is the primacy of the Pope.[51] The bishops, appointed by the Holy Spirit and in accordance with the apostolic succession, succeed in the work of the Apostles and collaborate with the Pope, *under his authority*, to continue the work of Christ with the commission of teaching all nations and consecrating them in truth and sustenance. All bishops are therefore "true and authentic teachers of the faith."[52] Their exercise of authority comes through episcopal consecration in communion with and under the authority of the Pope.[53] While they exercise the authority of their dioceses individually, each bishop is united with all others in a college.[54]

The Council reiterated that each bishop is in a "hierarchical communion" with all other bishops and the Pope, and they fall within the uninterrupted apostolic succession of the first Apostles.[55] This college of bishops with the Pope as its head constitutes the "supreme, plenary power over the Universal Church."[56] The Council Fathers were quite clear that this authority, an ecumenical council, cannot be exercised without the agreement of the Pope. It is within the competence of the Pope to devise and implement the ways and manners of appointing bishops.[57] Although bishops are chosen by the Pope to be the shepherd of a particular diocese, each bishop is bound with his brother bishops in a "concern for all the churches" as they all share in the responsibility for the Universal Church.[58] The universality of this work requires each bishop to be prepared to send his own priests into the Lord's vineyard where "the harvest is great but the laborers are few."[59] Regardless of where they are situated in the world, bishops must assist other local churches where the need for the corporal works of mercy are great but not answered completely.

At the outset of this part of the *Decree*, the Council Fathers wasted no time in acknowledging that while a bishop, as a successor to the Apostles, has "all the ordinary, proper, and immediate authority" needed to exercise his pastoral office, the Pope has authority that no bishop can infringe.[60] The Council noted that there was some need for the Roman curia to undergo study, but the Fathers also suggested that it would be desirable for some diocesan bishops to be appointed to these Roman offices so that "the thinking, the desires, and the needs of all the churches" would be known to the Pope; moreover, they saw an opportunity for making the views of the laity "who are outstanding for their virtue, knowledge, and experience" evident within the working of the Roman curia.[61]

As every bishop has the important role of being a "witness of Christ for all men," he has the primary responsibility for the faithful in his dioceses as well as those who have "fallen away" or are "ignorant of the Gospel."[62] Another principal duty of each bishop, then, is to be a teacher of the Gospel to all within his territorial jurisdiction.[63] The responsibilities of this teaching office cannot be taken lightly. Good teaching is an acquired skill necessitating patience and perseverance. Every bishop is primarily responsible for ensuring that the faithful and all others understand the doctrine of the Church – especially those matters dealing with "the human person with his freedom and bodily life, the family and its unity and stability, the procreation and education of children, civil society with its laws and professions, labor and leisure, the arts and technical inventions, poverty and affluence."[64] As the Council Fathers stated:

> The bishops should present Christian doctrine in a manner adapted to the needs of the times, that is to say, in a manner that will respond to the difficulties and questions by which people are especially burdened and troubled. They should also guard that doctrine, teaching the faithful to defend and propagate it. In propounding this doctrine they should manifest the maternal solicitude of the Church toward all men whether they be believers or not. With a special affection they should attend upon the poor and the lower classes to whom the Lord sent them to preach the Gospel.[65]

The bishops have the additional duty of engaging the all members of society in constructive dialogue relying on clarity of speech, humility, charity, and prudence.[66] Nonetheless, their teaching must be clear and be based on Sacred Scripture, the Church's tradition and liturgy and history, and the *Magisterium*.[67] Anyone who assists bishops must have the necessary training that furthers rather than frustrates these duties. While the bishop must work with many people in exercising the responsibilities of his office, he must regard his priests as "sons and friends" and listen to them.[68] But, "with active mercy bishops should pursue priests who are involved in any danger or who have failed in certain respects."[69] The bishops and their collaborators have a network of apostolates to further the Gospel: catechetical, missionary, charitable, social, familial, educational, or anything else pursuing a pastoral aim.[70] A special charge for bishops was that of encouraging "Catholic Action"[71] amongst the laity. While this lay organization has and continues to exist in Europe, it is not an entity identifiable with the United States. Perhaps it should be.

The Council Fathers realized that a bishop needs certain things to be an effective successor to the Apostles. A major prerequisite is independence from all civil authorities.[72] This is a matter of great and grave concern for the Church today around the world and including the United States. The manifestations of this independence or *libertas ecclesiae* include the capacity to communicate with the Apostolic See, other ecclesiastical authorities, and the faithful entrusted to his care. Nonetheless, a bishop must also set a good example of dual citizenship by collaborating with public authorities and advocating respect for just laws and the legitimately constituted civil authorities when matters dealing with the common good and (public) morality are at stake.[73] In the context of the Church's freedom, the Council concluded that the right of appointing bishops exclusively belongs to the "competent ecclesiastical authority" and that, in order to protect the freedom of the Church, any rights or privileges formerly held by civil authorities to elect, nominate, present, or designate candidates for episcopal office must be terminated.[74] This remains a difficult and delicate problem in some parts of the world, particularly the People's Republic of China.[75]

The Council further acknowledged the need for and role of those who assist diocesan bishops in the work of each diocese. The first category of assistants is coadjutor and auxiliary bishops who are to assist the bishop for "the good of the Lord's flock" which is the bishop's "supreme consideration."[76] This is where auxiliary bishops can assist where circumstances do not permit the bishop to fulfill properly all his episcopal duties.[77] Coadjutor bishops are relied upon to meet some special need of the diocese. Both auxiliary and coadjutor bishops must exercise their responsibilities with "single-minded agreement" with the bishop.[78] A coadjutor bishop may or may not have the right of succession when the bishop departs from his episcopal care of the diocese.[79] I now turn to the other categories of persons who are essential to the consideration of the nature of the Church: priests; men and women religious; and the laity.

III. Priests

The diocesan and religious clergy are special assistants of the bishop in view of their presbyteral office. This work most evidently surfaces in parishes; however, the clergy may be assigned to other duties involving various charitable institutions such as schools or other institutions affiliated with the works of the Church. While not possessing the highest degree of priesthood, the members of the presbyterate, nonetheless, are united with their bishops in the exercise of preaching the Gospel, leading the faithful *in personam Christi* in divine worship.[80] In their ministry to the faithful, all clergy exercise a vital role in bringing the sacraments to the faithful. In this regard there is special emphasis on their unique role in the celebration of the Eucharist which necessitates their admittance to Holy Orders. Another primary duty of the clergy is the indispensable role they have in the sacrament of Penance, which reconciles the faithful with God and neighbor.[81]

It goes without further emphasis that members of the presbyterate are the principal collaborators with the bishops to ensure that the responsibilities of the latter are generously and respectfully met. The relationship between bishop and priest is characterized this way: following the example of Christ, bishops are to look upon their priests not as servants but as friends and sons.[82] Because of their common sacred ordination and mission to serve God's people, all members of the presbyterate must view themselves as brothers ready to come to the spiritual or material aid of their brothers in ministry.

The Council Fathers issued two documents on priests: the *Decree on the Ministry and Life of Priests* (*Presybyterorum ordinis*) and the *Decree on Priestly Formation* (*Optatam totius*). These decrees will be considered in the order listed. The *Decree on the Ministry and Life of Priests* is divided into three chapters addressing: 1. priesthood in the mission of the Church; 2. the ministry of priests, focusing on their functions; the relationship between priests and the other faithful; and, the distribution of priests and priestly vocations; and, 3. the life of priests which considers their call to perfection; the particular spiritual needs of priestly life; and, the means of support for priestly life. The *Decree on Priestly Formation* is much shorter than the *Decree on the Ministry and Life of Priests* but nonetheless addresses important matters dealing with: 1. the programs of priestly formation to be undertaken in individual countries; 2. the intensified encouragement of priestly vocations; 3. the programming of major seminaries; 4. the deepening of spiritual formation; 5. the revision of ecclesiastical studies; 6. the promotion of strictly pastoral training; and 7. the refinement of training after the course of studies.

At the outset, the *Decree on the Ministry and Life of Priests* is clear that it applies to all priests, diocesan and religious – especially religious who are "devoted to the care of souls."[83] All priests receive a mission, through their ordination, in "the service of Christ the Teacher, Priest, and King"; consequently, their ministry is vital to "the Church here on earth [that] is unceasingly built up into the People of God, the Body of Christ and the Temple of the Holy Spirit."[84]

The Council Fathers acknowledged that all the faithful are members of "a holy and royal priesthood" as previously mentioned; however, those in presbyteral orders (i.e., the ordained clergy – be they religious or diocesan) have a particular and unique function by sharing in the ministry of the bishops regarding matters dealing with sanctification and ruling of the Body of Christ especially in the realm of sacramental life.[85] There is a substantive difference, then, between their priesthood and that of the faithful who are not in orders. While all Christians are called into discipleship through baptism, priests have a particular and distinctive discipleship requiring a focused dedication of their lives "in the things that belong to God in order to offer gifts and sacrifices for sins."[86] But their service to God and the Church occurs in this world. What is needed for them to advance the particular discipleship to which they are called through ordination are certain virtues, which include "goodness of heart, sincerity, strength and constancy of mind, zealous pursuit of justice, affability, and others."[87] Sadly, not all priests have demonstrated this appropriation of virtue into their lives and have thus committed great crimes against their neighbors and sins against God.

Like any other vocation within the Church, particular functions are associated with the priesthood – all deal with salvation. As previously noted, priests have been conferred with the special obligation of making the sacraments and the grace they offer – instruments of salvation – to the faithful because priests have the obligation of proclaiming "the lasting truth of the Gospel to the particular circumstances of life."[88] In essence, the clergy have the principal duty of being God's ministers of sacred functions. As the Council asserted, "They must coax their people on to an ever more perfect and constant spirit of prayer for every grace and need."[89] A solemn element of priestly work is to demonstrate the need not to adopt the ways of the world but the ways of God in Christian life: "They should act toward men, not as seeking to please them, but in accord with the demands of Christian doctrine and life."[90]

Leading ceremony and nothing else is not enough in the life of priestly service to the Church. Priests must help all they minister to perfect

Christian maturity and to lead good Christian lives –especially in and through the family. Pastors in parishes have the additional responsibility of the formation of "a genuine Christian community" characterized by their exercise of missionary zeal directed toward the dissemination of the Gospel and the salvation of souls.[91] Most importantly in all contexts of priestly ministry, "priests are never to put themselves at the service of some human faction of ideology, but, as heralds of the Gospel and shepherds of the Church, they are to spend themselves for the spiritual growth of the Body of Christ."[92]

For priests to remain faithful to their vocation, they must persist in the hierarchical communion with the bishops; however, bishops are to listen to the priests and the counsel they can provide.[93] Their relationship must be a healthy and respectful one considering the challenges which the apostolic undertakings of the present age must confront especially for bishops and priests.[94] All priests are called to work with the lay faithful in a manner so that they are "not to be ministered unto, but to minister" to others for the salvation of the souls.[95] However, this directive does not preclude entrusting duties to the laity that serve the Church and rely on the initiatives of the laity, for the labor of all is directed to perfecting the common good.[96] We see today much good evidence of the healthy collaboration of all the members of the Church – be they ordained or not – in advancing the Kingdom of God. Hence, all Catholics must be mindful that the Church's teachings have the critical role of asserting the truth of God so that the faithful will not "be carried about by every wind of doctrine."[97] This is where the authentic formation of priests has a critical role which cannot be dismissed.

In the *Decree on Priestly Formation (Optatam totius)*, the Council provides instructions for the formation of all priests in the universal Church. As the promotion of vocations clearly can begin at an early stage, the moral, spiritual, and intellectual instruction of young men cannot be ignored at any stage of the person's formation.[98] This instruction begins in the home, but then it continues throughout the education and formation a man who is called to priestly life must receive. The emphasis must be on formation that will develop throughout the life of priestly ministry concerning proper intention; freedom to serve; sound spiritual, moral, and intellectual qualifications and development; and an appropriate physical and psychological health.[99] In this regard, a healthy understanding of clerical celibacy and the temptations that can lure a man away from this gift are essential.[100] Today we see too much evidence where this is not the case; moreover, this evidence is not restricted to those cases of notoriety which come to public attention. Still many men who are called to orders have displayed and exercised the virtues that are essential to priestly service of God's people.

Another crucial element of priestly formation is to work effectively and harmoniously with their fellow priests and the laity in many capacities.[101] A priest's intellectual formation must never lose sight of the question: *quid est homo* – what is the human person and what is his or her destiny.[102] While a sound foundation in scripture and dogmatic theology are essential to the intellectual training, the Council emphasized the need for solid moral theological formation in order to assist the faithful with the issues they encounter in human existence.[103] This is a matter of crucial importance in the present age where we see many people drift from the Gospel values that need to intersect all aspects of human existence. All this implies that those teaching these important subjects are themselves competent to do so in service to God's holy Church.[104]

IV. Consecrated and Religious Life

Some clergy are members of religious institutes, but not all members of religious institutes are priests. Some are brothers or women in religious or consecrated life. To these individuals and the contributions to the nature of the Church I now turn. Chapter VI of *Lumen gentium* begins by concentrating on the evangelical counsels of poverty, chastity, and obedience that have long been the cornerstone of religious life in the Church. After all, the faithful are reminded that the counsels are not a burden but a gift from God and afford the stable foundation for religious life in men's and women's communities.[105] The counsels are instruments which make the men and women religious effective collaborators of those to whom hierarchical office has been entrusted. The counsels also provide the structure for vigorous apostolic or contemplative life that serves the welfare of the entire Body of Christ, the Church. Through the fraternal association that is inherent in the counsels, the "militia of Christ" is reinforced.

The Council Fathers expressed with clarity that religious life is not some middle ground or hybrid entity between lay and clerical life;

rather, it draws from both of these groups to serve as witness of the gift of the evangelical counsels in the prayer and work of the Church and by a special bond to God through the exercise of the gifts of apostolic or contemplative life.[106] In short, the life of the evangelical counsels consecrates the person fully in service to and for the welfare of the Church and God's people in diverse but rich ways.[107] Moreover, the counsels are a means to ensure that men and women religious maintain their dedication to their vocations and to those individuals who are competent ecclesiastical authorities.

Today there is much evidence that some members of religious institutes by word and deed distance themselves and their activities from these competent ecclesiastical authorities. This is not restricted to any particular person, group, congregation, or institute. However, the Council Fathers emphasized that it is the proper duty of the ecclesiastical hierarchy to regulate the practice of the evangelical counsels and those who profess vows or in some other fashion follow the evangelical counsels.[108] While the rules of the religious institutes are presented by the institute to the hierarchy, the latter have the responsibility and authority to approve and adjust them.[109] In this way, the competent ecclesiastical authorities have the further obligation to ensure that the religious institutes remain faithful to the plan of the orders' founders and the deposit of faith.

Any institute or any member of an institute can be removed from the jurisdiction of local ordinaries by the Pope and be "subjected to himself alone."[110] Members of the religious institutes are nonetheless obliged to "show reverence and obedience to bishops" because of the latter's pastoral authority in the local churches where the religious institutes work and pray for the "need for unity and harmony in the apostolate."[111] This is crucial especially on those occasions where some are inclined to take a position in opposition to the Church's teachings. To borrow again from Fr. Murray, this is a perilous theory and course that hinders the work to which men and women religious are called to perform in fulfillment of their individual and corporate ministry.[112]

It is pertinent to note here that the Council saw religious institutes not as a parallel ecclesiastical structure but as an organic element of the one universal Church, for the members of these institutes are called to a life to assist in the "increased holiness of the Church, for the greater glory of the one and undivided Trinity, which in and through Christ is the fount and the source of all holiness."[113] Complementing these fundamental principles found in the *Dogmatic Constitution* is the *Decree on Religious Life*.

The *Decree* acknowledges how the Church profits from the diversity of experiences, charisms, and talents which each of the consecrated and religious communities presents to the People of God.[114] For these gifts to flourish, it is essential that the wide variety of communities of men and women religious remain uniformly faithful to the original spirit of their institutes as appropriately adapted to the "changed conditions" of the modern world.[115] Otherwise the justification for their existence becomes ambiguous.

While the Council urged renewal of religious institutes that would include abandoning out-dated laws and customs,[116] it was further noted that the approval of the Holy See for this process is essential.[117] This principle is consistent with both the hierarchical structure of the Church and the Church's need for universality. Renewal does not mean reinventing or compromising the faith and the moral life that must accompany the faith. By living, working, and praying in fidelity to the Church and the charism of the founder/foundress, men and women religious are able to serve the Church with their entire self-less beings by a vigorous practice of virtue: including obedience, humility, fortitude, and chastity.[118] Daily prayer *and* the Eucharist are essential to the vitality of religious life as they cultivate a stronger bond with the universal Church's mission.[119] As with priestly formation, religious formation must be accomplished by selecting directors, spiritual fathers, and instructors who "are carefully chosen and thoroughly trained."[120] I now turn last, but not least, to the vital roles exercised by the laity that are essential to understanding the nature of the Church.

V. The Laity

Since the conclusion of the Council, the role of the laity in the Church has been a frequent topic of discussion.[121] Many, but not all, the contributors to these discussions have been well-informed regarding the important roles that the laity have in the life and work of the Church which the Council fathers addressed in *Lumen gentium* in Chapter VI and other texts, especially the *Decree on the Laity, Apostolicam actuositatem*. However, some voices are ill-informed or confused regarding the laity and their specific tasks; consequently, it will be necessary to consider carefully the role of the laity as explained by the Council in these important documents.

In the *Dogmatic Constitution*, the Council noted that the laity are, because of the nature of their vocation and their state of life, well-suited to be the Church's principal voice and God's conscious instruments in the temporal world. As the Council Fathers recognized, "there are certain things which pertain in a special way to the laity, both men and women, by reason of their condition and mission."[122] Their work as disciples of Jesus Christ in temporal affairs is simultaneously a great challenge and grace of the apostolate of the laity. After all, this is the venue in which they expend much of their energy day after day. This is a point, moreover, that cannot be over-emphasized. At the same time, it is important to recognize that this apostolate necessitates a strong bond with the universal Church and its hierarchical order. Fidelity to this union is needed if their great role in executing their functions which contribute to the Church's welfare across the world is to be successful. If the clergy, especially the bishops, are the principal teachers, the laity are the implementers of the Church's teachings especially in the realm of temporal affairs.

But, precisely, who are the laity? The Council identifies them as those persons not in clerical orders or in professed religious life. While the laity are "sharers in the priestly, prophetical, and kingly functions of Christ," their core mission in the world emerges from their lay nature to engage and influence in a positive fashion the realm of temporal affairs for the furtherance of the common good.[123] While those in orders and religious life are not excluded from the material affairs of the world, the laity have been endowed with their particular gifts to engage the temporal affairs of the world and order these affairs "according to the plan of God."[124] As members of the secular professions, trades, and other occupations, the laity have the daily contact with the family and social life that places them at the heart of the material issues that absorb the energies of the world. Because they are at the center of temporal affairs, the laity have much to offer in the way of sanctification of the world for they are God's leaven propelled by the Holy Spirit. This point cannot be overemphasized.

The laity, moreover, are best suited to make Christ known to others who inhabit the realm of the temporal by their display of faith, hope, and charity in the affairs of the secular order.[125] This is a great task and responsibility, but if the world can be transformed and more attuned to Christ's mission and message, the laity are the transformers as long as they remain in union with the rest of Christ's Church. The laity, their pastors, and their fellow disciples who are in religious life are bound to one another by a mutual need that leads all the members of the Church to their own conversion and, then, that of the world where the laity expend most of their energy. Each group comprises a set of branches on the vine of Christ – an image that well describes the nature of the Church to which the laity are crucial members. The lay apostolate is a remarkable calling to discipleship that is often overlooked, especially by some critics of the Church's teachings.[126] But this is one reason why the Council Fathers recalled St. Augustine who said: "What I am for you terrifies me; what I am with you consoles me. For you I am a bishop; but with you I am a Christian. The former is a duty; the latter a grace. The former is a danger; the latter, salvation."[127]

Nevertheless, while there are many people with many gifts who are constitutive members of the Church, they contribute to the one Body of Christ under one head.[128] Those who are called to the apostolate of the laity participate with others in the salvific mission of Christ and His Church. As Pope Pius XI acknowledged in his encyclical letter *Quadragesimo anno*, the laity make the Church present and operative in those places and circumstances where they are best suited to introduce the Church – for they combine "harmoniously the diligent practice of their occupation with the salutary precepts of religion, protect effectively and resolutely their own temporal interests and rights, keeping a due respect for justice and a genuine desire to work together with other classes of society for the Christian renewal of all social life."[129]

The laity also serve as crucial collaborators with the hierarchy.[130] For it is the laity and their "noble duty" which extend the divine plan of salvation to all people in all corners of the world because their labors encompass temporal activities, prayers, and other apostolic endeavors that are synonymous with the Church's activity in the secular world.[131] In whatever they do, from family life to the noble and humble deeds of the human person, their every activity can serve as a witness to the One who came to save all, for it is the laity who can "consecrate the world itself to God."[132] The laity, by exercising their proper functions while conscious of their noble calling, are the light shining brightly in a world that can be easily overcome by darkness.[133] They evangelize by remaining living witnesses who offer testimony of the Gospel in the temporal sphere where the overwhelming majority of the human race subsists.

One particular and major source of their testimony of the Gospel can be found in married and family life.[134] As one considers the sad state of the moral status of the world today, the extraordinary treasure in Christian family life cannot be overemphasized or understated. This is a critical function that properly belongs to the Christian lay faithful. It is within the truly Christian home and the environment that it produces where faith, hope, and charity prevail. Moreover, it is the place of education where these Christian virtues are passed on to succeeding generations. Again, the value of this apostolate must not be forgotten because the moral foundation of the good citizen and Christian begins with family life soon after birth.

In order to be their best and to execute their responsibilities well, the laity must be taught well by good teachers who teach not only by word but by the example of their own deeds. This is where the unity of the Church and its hierarchical order have key functions to exercise. Knowing that the temporal sphere is governed by its own principles and infused with its own ways, the laity who exercise their apostolate in the temporal sphere must also be guided by the ways of God. Thus, the laity, to exercise properly their role in the temporal order, must be aware of those ominous doctrines which do not serve God and His people well – especially those doctrines which have "no regard whatever for religion" and which attack and destroy the religious liberty of its citizens.[135] It is the faithful laity who must courageously demonstrate that such doctrines are to be rejected.[136]

But if the laity are to understand the difference between sound and treacherous doctrines, they must be attuned to the Church's teachings and this requires fidelity to the instruction provided by their spiritual shepherds.[137] The bishops, then, have the humbling responsibility to ensure that what they teach and what they permit others to teach is sound and faithful because this will have a direct effect on the formation of the laity and an indirect effect on the formation of the cultures which the laity can and do shape because of their direct insertion in the temporal affairs of human existence. Consequently, the Council Fathers realized that a "great many wonderful things are to be hoped for from this familiar dialogue between the laity and their spiritual leaders: in the laity a strengthened sense of personal responsibility; a renewed enthusiasm; a more ready application of their talents to the projects of their spiritual leaders."[138]

The *Decree on the Laity* complements the norms of the *Dogmatic Constitution*. The *Decree* also acknowledges the crucial role and responsibility that the laity have to exercise with zeal in a world that requires their Christian service for attaining the common good.[139] As Catholics, the laity have been called by baptism to engage in God's plan of redemption that includes participation in the vocation of an apostolic life.[140] Considering the diversity of persons who inhabit the world, there are many ministries and apostolates in the Church but only one mission.[141] As a result of these related principles essential to the Church's essence, the apostolate of the laity relies on the rich differences of missionary zeal and Christian activity, but the organic nature of the Church requires that a discipline exists which channels the energy of Christians into a coherent mission of following Christ. For the laity, the direction of their apostolic zeal is geared to "penetrating and perfecting of the temporal order."[142] The objective of the lay apostolate is like any other apostolic activity exercised within the Church: the salvation of the members of the human family in preparation for meeting God.[143] Acknowledging the presence of temptation and sin, the Council recognized that the laity have a particular duty to rectify "the distortion of the temporal order and direct it to God through Christ."[144] This is a great challenge, but to borrow from the spiritual quality of their work in the Church's name, the benefits transcend anything the secular culture that is devoid of God can offer.

Of special significance to the Church is the work of its lay members who are involved with the administration of public affairs. These members of the faithful have an important access to form the civil authority through law and public policy that furthers the common good based on the Gospel.[145] This is of critical concern today as many public officials who profess to be Catholic and claim to rely on their Catholicism act in fashions which contradict the teachings of the Church and the essential principles of the Gospel. Unfortunately, not all public servants who consider themselves Catholic and administer, legislate, or adjudicate on behalf of the state follow the norms established for the faithful disciple.[146] The faithful exercise of the lay apostolate in public affairs requires a combination of prayer, humility, and skill seasoned with knowledge of the ways of the world that is not open to Christ and that denigrates His Church.

For all who follow Christ, the exhortation must be this: *be not afraid, for I am with you always.*[147] In most cases, the apostolate of the laity is a kind of "Catholic Action" where the laity collaborate in the "apostolate of the hierarchy."[148] Although the Church relies on the creative talents of her lay members, it should be recalled that no project may use the name "Catholic" in its title or works without the consent of lawful Church authority.[149] In those institutions directed by laity which are engaged in some form of education or formation of others, it is imperative that these lay institutions conform to moral principles that are consistent with and reflect Church teachings. If they do not, the proper ecclesiastical authorities have both the right and the duty to intervene for the benefit of all.[150] Essential to ensure the integrity of the service of the lay apostolate to the Church is a mechanism of ongoing spiritual and doctrinal formation.[151] Once more, the image of Christ that He is the vine and the members of the Church are His branches demonstrates the need for this.

VI. Conclusion

The Council concluded that the Church and Her people are unfailingly holy when in communion with Christ.[152] Consequently, all members of the Church are called to holiness which must be reflected in the fruits of their diverse works and activities. Because human beings can be sinful as well as holy, depending on how they exercise consciously the gift of free will, the need to strive to greater Christian perfection remains: "Be therefore perfect, even as your heavenly Father is perfect."[153] In this regard, a wise and holy counsel that applies to all members of the Church is contained in the prayer Jesus taught us: forgive us our trespasses as we forgive those who trespass against us. All the faithful must be reminded that they follow in the footsteps of Christ and must, therefore, conform to Him.[154] The diversity of the Church's members does not deny the unity of holiness.[155] To set the proper example in their lives and in their teaching, the Church's shepherds have a special duty to demonstrate the need for and unity of holiness. The call to holiness requires that all disciples – clerical, religious, or lay – must seek the virtue of love and perfect it.[156] Living a well-grounded life based on the sacraments is an important step in responding to the call to holiness, in being faithful to one's discipleship, and in nurturing and defending the nature of the Church.

The Church and her members also need a requisite measure of freedom to accept and exercise these rights and duties. Here we must turn to the *Declaration on Religious Liberty, Dignitatis humane personae (DH)*, to understand as best we can the role of freedom in the nature of the Church which is the means by which her members exercise their prudent judgment to seek the truth and justice by which the Church exists in the temporal world.[157] Significantly, it is this text which asserts that "the one true religion subsists in the Catholic and Apostolic Church" by which God spreads this religion among all people.[158] But the freedom of which the Council Fathers spoke is not simply individual, it must also be a freedom of the Community – the Church, the People of God, the Body of Christ.[159] The freedom, then, that properly belongs to the Church is not private, rather, it is one that must be exercised in public for the individual believer and for the community of believers, i.e., the Church.[160] It would be contrary to the nature of the Church if one or some of her members take and defend a position, internally or externally to the community of believers, that brings harm to the rest of the community or any of its members. This would not be an exercise of freedom or conscience, but it would be a threat that undermines the Body of Christ and antithetical to the nature of the Church.[161]

ENDNOTES

1. My essay on method in interpretation...

2. *Gaudium et spes*, n. 40. Hereafter referred to as *GS*.

3. *Id.*

4. *Id.*

5. *Id.*

6. The text of the Statement was published in *The New York Times*, July 31, 1968, p. 16.

7. *Ibid.* (Italics added)

8. "Strategy for Opposition," John Leo, *The New York Times*, July 31, 1968, p. 16.

9. *Ibid.*

10. John O'Malley makes several observations about the contention between the hierarchical nature of the Church and the collegiality of bishops with the Pope in *What Happened at Vatican II*. Whether there were contentious discussions about the relationship between these two subjects is essentially resolved by the texts, however. While texts are subject to careful study and interpretation, they do speak. Surely the documents of Vatican II have a voice. They do not address all matters, but those they do are readily identifiable, especially when it comes to the nature, the makeup of the Church. It will be good to point out the pages where John discusses this - usually in the context of *Lumen gentium* (hereafter referred to as *LG*), "papal primacy," and "collegiality." We are in debt to John, and to Matthew Levering and Matthew Lamb for their project *Vatican II: Renewal within Tradition* - especially

Avery Dulles's chapter on *Lumen gentium*. For Dulles, see pages 31-4. For Marchetto, see pages 437-9.

11. In addition, Fr. John Courtney Murray, S.J., who was a major contributor to the formulation of the *Declaration on Religious Liberty, Dignitatis humanae personae*, offered a crucial insight demonstrating the extent of the weakness of the Statement and its strategy when he concluded: "It is worth noting that the Declaration [*Dignitatis humanae personae*] does not base the right to the free exercise of religion on 'freedom of conscience.' Nowhere does this phrase occur. And the Declaration nowhere lends its authority to the theory for which the phrase frequently stands, namely, that I have the right to do what my conscience tells me to do, simply because my conscience tells me to do it. This is a perilous theory. Its particular peril is subjectivism - the notion that, in the end, it is my conscience, and not the objective truth, which determines what is right or wrong, true or false." *The Documents of Vatican II: with Notes and Comments by Catholic, Protestant, and Orthodox Authorities*, editors Abbott and Gallagher, (America Press: New York, 1966), p. 679, n. 5.

12. "Strategy for Opposition," John Leo, *op. cit.*, p. 16.

13. *Ibid.*

14. *Ibid.*

15. See, e.g., James F. Keenan, S.J., *A History of Catholic Moral Theology in the Twentieth Century: From Confessing Sins to Liberating Consciences*, (Continuum: New York, 2010).

16. 1 *John* 15:5.

17. Recently John W. O'Malley, S.J., the distinguished Church historian and keynote speaker at this gathering noted the "spirit of the Council" does not imply something at odds with the "letter" or as I prefer to say, the texts of the Council. He correctly asserts that different people driven by the "spirit of the Council" may not agree on important points because they have different "spirits." As O'Malley argues, "if careful attention is paid to the 'letter' of the Council's documents - that is, to certain basic orientation found in them - it is possible to uncover that 'something further' denoted by 'spirit.'" John W. O'Malley, S.J., "The Council's Spirit - Vatican II: The Time for Reconciliation," *Conversations on Jesuit Higher Education*, 42 Fall 2012, p.3. O'Malley makes another crucial point regarding coherence and interpretation. I think he and I are in agreement regarding the need to interrelate the texts of the Council for as he says, "the documents of Vatican II are not a grab bag of discreet units but, taken together, they constitute a single, though complex, testament." *Id.*

18. *LG*, n. 9; cf., 1 *Peter* 2:9-10.

19. *Id.*, n. 10; cf Pius XII, Alloc. *Magnificate Dominum*, 2 Nov. 1954: *AAS* 46 (1954) p. 669. Encyclical Letter, *Mediator Dei*, 20 Nov. 1947: *AAS* 39 (1947) p. 555.

20. *LG*, n. 10

21. *Id.*, n. 10

22. *Id.*, n. 11.

23. *Id.*

24. *Id.*, n. 12.

25. *Id.*, n. 13.

26. *Id.*

27. *Id.*, n. 17.

28. *Id.*

29. In the context of the debates and discussions of the Council regarding these issues, the five volume *The History of Vatican II*, Alberigo and Komonchak, editors, (Orbis Maryknoll: Maryknoll, 2006) is a useful source from which insights into the positions of Fathers of the Council and their *periti* can be obtained. Regarding the final texts, volume V of the same series, may be consulted. In addition, the five-volume *Commentary on the Documents of Vatican II*, Vorgrimler, general editor, (Crossroads: New York, 1989), should be consulted. In addition, the *Acta et documenta Concilio Oecumenico Vaticano II apparando / cura et studio Secretariae Pontificiae Commissionis Centralis Praeparatoriae Concilii Vaticani II*, (Typis Polyglottis: Vaticanis, 1960-69) is another important resource.

30. *Id.*, n. 18.

31. *Id.*

32. *Id.*

33. *Id.*, n. 19-20.

34. *Id.*, n. 20

35. *Id.*

36. *Id.*

37. *Id.*, n. 21.

38. *Id.*

39. *Id.*, n. 22

40. *Id.*, n. 21.

41. *Id.*, n. 23; cf. Pius XII, *Encyclical Letter Fidei donum*, 21 Apr. 1957: *AAS* 49 (1957) p. 237.

42. *LG*, n. 24.

43. *LG*, n. 25.

44. *Id.*

45. *Id.*, n. 26.

46. *Id.*, n. 27.

47. *Id.*

48. *Id.*

49. *Christus Dominus*, n. 1. Hereafter referred to as *CD*.

50. *Id.*, n. 2.

51. *Id.*

52. *Id.*

53. *Id.*, n. 3

54. *Id.*

55. *Id.*, n. 4.

56. *Id.*

57. *Id.*, n. 5.

58. *Id.*, n. 6.

59. *Matthew* 9:37; *Luke* 10:2.

60. *CD*, n. 8.

61. *Id.*, n. 9-10.

62. *Id.*, n. 11.

63. *Id.*, n. 12.

64. *Id.*

65. *Id.*, n. 13.

66. *Id.*

67. *Id.*, n. 14.

68. *Id.*, n. 16.

69. *Id.*

70. *Id.*, n. 17.

71. Fr. John Hardon, S.J., *Modern Catholic Dictionary*. Doubleday. New York. 1980. See also John DeJak, "Catholic Action: The Essence of the Lay Apostolate," *Catholic Social Teaching and the Common Good, Bellarmine Forum* magazine (vol II, n.1), 2012. p.30.

72. *CD*, n. 19. *The Declaration on Religious Freedom*, discussed elsewhere in this paper, establishes the framework of the *libertas ecclesiae*.

73. *Id.*

74. *Id.*, n. 20.

75. In this regard, see Pope Benedict XVI's *Letter to the Catholic Church in the People's Republic of China*, May 27, 2007, http://www.vatican.va/holy_father/benedict_xvi/letters/2007/documents/hf_ben-xvi_let_20070527_china_ en.html.

76. *CD*, n. 25.

77. *Id.*

78. *Id.*

79. *Id.*, n. 26.

80. *LG*, n. 28.

81. *Id.*

82. *Id.*

83. *Presbyterorum ordinis*, n. 1.

84. *Id.*

85. *Id.*, n. 2.

86. *Id.*, n. 3.

87. *Id.*

88. *Id.*, n. 4.

89. *Id.*, n. 5.

90. *Id.*, n. 6.

91. *Id.*

92. *Id.*

93. *Id.*, n. 7.

94. *Id.*

95. *Id.*, n. 9.

96. *Id.*

97. *Id.*

98. *Optatam totius*, n. 2.

99. *Id.*, n. 6.

100. *Id.*, n. 10.

101. *Id.*, n. 11.

102. *Id.*, n. 15.

103. *Id.*, n. 16.

104. While having specific duties within the hierarchy, deacons also have a vital role in the Church's ministry of service to Her members. (*LG*, n. 29) They are competent to administer baptism, to serve as a Eucharistic minister, to assist at or to bless sacramental marriages in the Church's name, to bring Viaticum to the dying, to proclaim Sacred Scripture and preach, to instruct the faithful, and to officiate at funerals and burials of the deceased. (*LG*, n. 29) The Council noted that the diaconate can be conferred upon men of more mature age or those who are married. It may also be conferred upon younger men, for whom the law of celibacy must remain intact if they are not of the married state prior to their ordination. (*LG*, n. 29)

105. *LG*, n. 43.

106. *Id.*

107. *Id.*, n. 44.

108. *Id.*, n. 45.

109. *Id.*

110. *Id.*; cfr. Leo XIII, *Const. Romanos pontifices*, 8 maii 1881: *AAS* 13 (1880-81) p. 483. Pius XII, *Allocution Annus sacer*, 8 dec. 1950: *AAS* 43(1951) p. 288.

111. *LG*, n. 45.

112. See, *supra*, note 11.

113. *LG*, n. 47.

114. *Perfectae caritatis*, n. 1.

115. *Id.*, n. 2.

116. *Id.*, n. 3.

117. *Id.*, n. 4.

118. *Id.*, n. 5.

119. *Id.*, n. 6.

120. *Id.*, n. 18.

121. Illustrations here: Russell Shaw, Paul Lakeland, Stephen Pope, von Balthasar, etc.

122. *LG*, n. 30.

123. *Id.*, n. 31.

124. *Id.*

125. *Id.*

126. *Id.*, n. 32.

127. *S. Augustinus, Serm.* 340, 1: PL 38, 1483.

128. *LG*, n. 33.

129. *Quadragesimo anno*, n. 33.

130. *LG*, n. 33.

131. *Id.*, n. 34.

132. *Id.*

133. *Id.*, n. 35.

134. *Id.*

135. *Id.*, n. 36.

136. Illustrations here: F4F; Catholic Action in Europe; faithful NGOs

137. *Id.*, n. 37.

138. *Id.*

139. *AA*, n. 1

140. *Id.*, n. 2.

141. *Id.*

142. *Id.*

143. *Id.*, n. 5.

144. *Id.*, n. 7.

145. *Id.*, n. 14.

146. See, e.g., the *Doctrinal Note on Some Questions Regarding the Participation of Catholics in Public Life* issued by the Congregation for the Doctrine of the Faith on November 24, 2002 and approved by Pope John Paul II on November 21, 2002.

147. Cf. *Matthew* 14: 27; 28:20

148. *Apostolicum actuositatem*, n. 20. Hereafter referred to as *AA*.

149. *Id.*, n. 24. Here, illustrate by the example of CFFC in 2000-1.

150. *AA*, n. 24.

151. *Id.*, n. 28.

152. *LG*, n. 39.

153. *Id.*, n. 40.

154. *Id.*, n. 40.

155. *Id.*, n. 41.

156. *Id.*, n. 42.

157. *Dignitatis humanae*, n. 1.

158. *Id.*

159. *Id.*, n. 3.

160. *Id.*, n. 4.

161. *Id.*, n. 14. See also, 11, note.g

FR. ROBERT JOHN ARAUJO, S.J. completed law school, entered military service, and had a successful business career prior to entering the Society of Jesus in 1986. After his discharge from the United States Army, he was an attorney advisor and supervisory trial attorney with the Office of the Solicitor of the U. S. Department of the Interior from 1974 to 1979. In 1979, he left government service to join the Law Department of the Standard Oil Company [Ohio] (now BP-Amoco). After his corporate experience, he joined the law firm of Tillinghast, Licht & Semonoff, in Providence, RI. As a member of the Jesuits, he taught law at Boston College Law School, 1988-1993; Chamberlain Fellow, Columbia Law School, New York, 1989-1990; Adjunct Professor of Law, Georgetown University Law Center, Washington, D.C, 1993; Robert Bellarmine Professor in American and Public International Law, Gonzaga University, Spokane, Washington, 1994-2005. From 2005 to 2008 he taught at the Pontifical Gregorian University in Rome. He was also the John Courtney Murray S.J., University Professor at Loyola University Law School in Chicago. Fr. Araujo held eight academic degrees; in addition to his teaching duties, he advised the Vatican on Public and International Law as Senior Legal Advisor to the Holy See and frequently assisted the Holy See's Permanent Observer to the United Nations. He was active in pastoral ministry in Spokane and in New York; during his graduate law studies in England, he assisted at Corpus Christi Church, Oxford. Father gave many talks around the country, including a Wanderer Forum Foundation Focus on Faith retreat in Portland, Oregon. He has also written for the *Forum Focus* magazine and its successor, the *Bellarmine Forum* magazine. He passed to eternity on October 21, 2015.

The Popes Of Conciliar Renewal

By Laurene K. Conner

(Editor's Note: This article was published in the *Forum Focus* magazine in 2002. It was the last Mrs. Conner wrote due to failing health.)

His Holiness Pope John Paul II on October 17, 1978, the day after his election to the See of Blessed Peter, celebrated Mass in the Sistine Chapel with the College of Cardinals. Following Mass in his address to the cardinals and "all who listen to us," he mentioned "the unceasing importance of the Second Vatican Council." He described it as "a milestone...an event of the utmost importance in the almost two-thousand-year history of the Church and...in the religious and cultural history of the world."

"There is one section," he said, "to which greater attention will have to be given – that is to the ecclesiological section. Venerable brethren and sons of the Catholic world, it is necessary for us once again to take into our hands the 'Magna Charta' of the Council – the *Dogmatic Constitution [on the Church] Lumen gentium*...so that with renewed and invigorating zeal we may meditate on the nature and function of the Church, its way of being and acting. This should be done...in order to contribute to bringing about a fuller closer unity of the whole human family."

Quoting John XXIII, he added, "The Church of Christ is the light of the nations." Pope John Paul II noted that these words were repeated by the Council "for the Church is the universal sacrament of salvation and unity for the human race" (*Lumen gentium* n.1, 48; *Decree ad gentes* n.1).

Hence, the Pope continued, "The assent to be given to this document of the Council seen in the light of Tradition and embodying the dogmatic formulae issued over a century ago by the First Vatican Council, will be to us pastors and to the faithful a decisive indication and a rousing stimulus so that...we may walk in the paths of life and of history" (*Talks of John Paul II, 1978-1979*, Daughters of St. Paul, p. 50-64).

With these words, Pope John Paul II clearly established a century-long link between the two Vatican Councils. The Councils were not to be seen as individual events but rather as a continuation of the teaching role of the Church in the modern world.

In fact, the idea of convening a second Vatican Council was not initiated by Pope John XXIII. In the decades after Vatican I, those governing the See of Peter had made many comments regarding the continuation of the work of Vatican I and the need for such a wide-scale gathering. The words of these pontiffs provide a clear indication of the mind of the Church over the years leading up to Vatican II. Pope John XXIII was merely acting on the prompting of the Holy Spirit in regard to the timing of the event.

Historical Backdrop

The 32-year reign of Pius IX, 1846-1878, was the longest in the history of the Church. He lived in the age that followed the skepticism of Voltaire, Diderot, Rousseau, among others; the age that witnessed the French Revolution and the rationalism, pantheism, naturalism of the Enlightenment. It was an age in which traditional values were discarded for a liberalism based on a denial of liberty itself. He was also the Pope during the time of some of the greatest saints of the Church, including the Cure of Ars, Bernadette, Catherine Laboure, and Peter Julian Eymard.

Pius IX had an abiding devotion to the Blessed Virgin and in 1854 he proclaimed the dogma of the Immaculate Conception, a feast that is celebrated each year on December 8. Pius chose this date for the major acts of his pontificate.

At least since the French Revolution, liberalism had become more or less identified with a philosophy that stressed human freedom to the neglect and even denial of the rights of God in religion, the rights of society in civil law, and the rights of the Church in her relation to the state. It was in this sense that liberalism was condemned by Pope Pius IX in his encyclical, *Quanta cura*, published December 8, 1864, with its Syllabus of Errors condemning liberalism, secularism, and religious indifferentism. It listed the prevailing errors that aimed at the undermining of society, morality, and religion (*Modern Catholic Dictionary*, Fr. John Hardon, p. 317).

The Spanish statesman and philosopher, Juan Donoso Cortes, in his critique of liberalism and socialism, had a direct influence on the teaching of his friend, Pius IX. Donoso held liberalism to be a "way-station" to socialism and socialism was the logical culmination of liberal principles.Catholicism is the truth; liberalism an error, and socialism a more extreme case of that same error. The history of liberalism over the past century and a half attests to the clarity of Donoso's vision. The Church and society face much the same ferment today and this is what makes Pius IX "more than a prophet."

The First Vatican Council

On December 8, 1869, Pius IX formally opened the First Vatican Council. Over 700 bishops had assembled in Rome to consider two principal drafts on faith and church. The one on faith was unanimously adopted on April 24, 1870 and duly confirmed by Pius IX in the formal constitution, *Dei Filius*. The Constitution on the Church, *De ecclesia*, prompted a great variety of opinions and discussions that lasted for months. Finally in July, 1870, the constitution, *Pastor aeternus*, which defined the pope's primacy and infallibility was adopted.[1]

During this same period, political unrest was sweeping European nations, spurred by liberalism, freemasonry, and the rising evil of communism. The movement for a united Italy began in 1861. Through political agitation, the Papal States came to be viewed as an obstacle to Italian unification and on September 20, 1870, King Victor Emmanuel's troops seized Rome and the Papal States.[2] Rome subsequently became the capital of Italy. These events led to the prorogration of the Council, which had only resolved the first part – the power of the papacy of its intended examination of the Church in the world. The work initiated with the First Vatican Council was understood by Pius IX and his successors to need completion. Pius IX died on February 7, 1878. He was beatified on September 3, 2000.

Leo XIII succeeded Pius IX to the throne of Peter in 1878. He was the Pope leading the Church at the turn of the century and he solidified a new role of leadership for the Church against the ills of modern society. He believed the Church was not to be confined to addressing only the spiritual realm, but that the spiritual authority vested in the Church by Christ demanded a role of authority and papal leadership in the secular world as well.

A Light To Safely Follow

In the encyclical letter, *Immortale Dei*, "On the Christian Constitution of State," promulgated in 1885 Pope Leo XIII wrote: "Pius IX brand(ed) publicly many false opinions [in *Quanta cura*] which were gaining ground and afterwards ordered them to be condensed in summary form in order that in this sea of error Catholics might have a light which they may safely follow." This "light" extended to many areas. To name just a few of the errors:

- "The Church is not a true, perfect, and wholly independent society...but it is for the civil power to determine what are the rights of the Church."

- "The State as the origin and source of all rights enjoys a right that is unlimited."

- "The Church must be separated from the State and the State from the Church."

- "It is untrue that the civil liberty of every form of worship and the full power given to all...leads to the ready corruption of the mind and morals...and to the spread of the plague of religious indifference."

Leo foresaw that education in the principles of the Faith must underlie any visible challenge to the world. His efforts concentrated on expanding the Church's teaching in philosophy, study of the Bible (*Providentissimus Deus*), and science (*Humanum genus*) as well as solidifying Catholic social thought in *Rerum novarum*.

Pope Leo XIII died in 1903. His successor, Pope St. Pius X, continued the impetus of Vatican I by the strengthening of the role of the papacy in the Church and the world. He promoted scholastic philosophy, established the Pontifical Biblical Institute and started work on the Code of Canon Law. He boldly spoke out against the Modernist heresy.

But Pius X also knew the Church needed to have a greater impact beyond the doors of its buildings: The state needed Christianization. Pius X knew people needed to be educated in their faith before they could be a positive force in society and formed the Confraternity of Christian Doctrine for instructing children. He promoted Catholic Action, an organization of Catholics devoting themselves to serving the Church by apostolic works in the world. And perhaps overlooked in Pius X's influence in the Church and State were his efforts in liturgical renewal. He reinstated congregational singing of plainchant in the Mass. This work is now viewed as a precursor to Vatican II's *Constitution on the Liturgy* (*St. Joseph Church History*, Fr. Lawrence Lovasik, S.V.D., p.163). Pius X died in 1914 and was canonized in 1954.

His successor, Benedict XV, who began discussions with Mussolini to resolve the Roman Question, ruled until 1922. Benedict was pope during World War I, an event which he called the suicide of civilized Europe. His efforts on behalf of prisoners and the wounded, and in providing food for the needy were unparalleled. He drew up a peace plan, parts of which were incorporated in Woodrow Wilson's Fourteen Points. A tribute engraved upon a statue erected of him in the courtyard of St. Esprit Cathedral in Istanbul captures best his life's work: "The great Pope of the world tragedy...the benefactor of all people, irrespective of nationality or religion." Benedict XV issued the Code of Canon Law, a work begun under Pius X; called for dedication to preaching the Word in *Humani generis redemptionem*; and expanded Marian theology to include Mary as Mediatrix of grace and Co-Redemptrix–teachings accepted by later popes and incorporated into Vatican II's *Lumen gentium*.

Pius XI: A Man of Prophetic Vision

Pope Pius XI's reign forged a link between Pius IX and John XXIII, between Vatican I and Vatican II. Pius XI ruled the Church through the terribly difficult years between the two World Wars, (1922-1939). The book, *Pius XI, A Close-up* written in 1957 by his secretary, Carlo Cardinal Confalonieri, records the accomplishments of his pontificate. Many salient points are found in its pages.

In his encyclical, *Ubi arcano Dei*, December 23, 1922, Cardinal Confaloniere wrote that "Pius XI mentioned his desire to seek from God 'some manifest sign regarding the expressed will and intent to continue the ecumenical council to which Pius IX had prepared a wide field of labor, but had been able to achieve only partially....' In future discourses and encyclicals Pius XI laid out...the general program for a possible future council."

He "was a man of prophetic vision" and much of what was accomplished after his death can be attributed to the foundation he laid, "including the Second Vatican Council" though "it was not until the pontificate of John XXIII...that the Council was convened" (pp. xii, xiii, xiv).

"He foretold the history of decades to come; he sought the restoration of the social order, the interior renewal of all Christians, and a basis for continuity of Vatican policy in the world....He was not interested," however, "in coming to terms with the evils of the modern world. He saw Communism and Marxism as but one more phase in the struggle with the principalities and powers of darkness" (xiv, xv).

The motivating principle of Pius XI's pontificate was embodied in the motto, *Pax Christi in Regno Christi* – the Peace of Christ in the Reign of Christ. Pius XI, in his encyclical letter *Quas primas* instituted the Feast of the Kingship of Christ. This solemnity is now observed throughout the whole world on the last Sunday of the liturgical calendar. He also authored encyclical letters that are part of the social doctrine of the Church: *Divini illius magistri*, "On the Christian Education of Youth" – 1927; *Casti connubii*, "On Christian Marriage" – 1930; *Quadragesimo anno*, "On the Social Order" – 1931, the fortieth anniversary of Leo XIII's *Rerum novarum*; and *Divini redemptoris*, "On Atheistic Communism" – 1937. Here Pius XI drew explicit reference to Pius IX's "solemn condemnation" in 1864 of "that infamous doctrine of so-called communism which is absolutely contrary to the Natural Law itself" and Leo XIII had defined it as "the fatal plague" (n.4).

With reference to his own pontificate Pius XI stated: "We too have with urgent insistence denounced the current trend to Atheism which is alarmingly on the increase....We raised a solemn protest against the persecutions unleashed in Russia, in Mexico, and now in Spain" (n. 5). He noted that "the lamentable ruin into which *amoral liberalism* has plunged us...can only be rectified by an infusion of social justice" (n. 32) and he wrote of "materialistic and atheistic propaganda" (n. 39).

The scholarly Pope Pius XII, who reigned from 1939 to 1958, continued setting the stage for a future council, particularly in the area of liturgy. In *Mediator Dei*, written in 1947, Pius XII referenced the Councils of Trent and Vatican I, as well as the work of his predecessors Pius X and XI. In that encyclical, Pius XII addressed many of the concepts which found their way into the *Constitution on the Sacred Liturgy* and the two constitutions on the Church in the world.

It remained for John XXIII, whose reign was less than five years, to heed the whisperings of the Spirit and convene the Second Vatican Council, October 11, 1962, undertaking a renewal effort in the face of a changing world.

In 2000, at the beatification of John XXIII on September 3, Pope John Paul II firmly established the bond between Vatican I and II. He declared

Vatican II a "prophetic intuition" of John XXIII, opening a new page in Church history and a "season of hope" for the world. He stressed that John XXIII was more like Pius IX than commonly thought, especially on a spiritual and human level. He went on, "The renewal Pope John had set in motion with Vatican II did not affect the Church's doctrine, but the way of expressing it" (*Inside the Vatican* October, 2000).

The Completion of Vatican I

Pope John XXIII in his opening address to Vatican II stated, "At the present time, what is needed is that the entire Christian teaching...be accepted by all in our time with fresh zeal, with serene and tranquil minds, as it still shines forth in the acts of the Council of Trent and First Vatican Council. It is necessary that the same doctrine be more fully and deeply understood, that consciences be more deeply imbued and formed by it. It is necessary that such certain and immutable doctrine, to which we owe the obedience of faith, be expounded with the method that our times require" (*L'Osservatore Romano*, June 6, 2001).

John XXIII died June 3, 1963, and was succeeded to the Chair of Peter by Pope Paul VI whose primary consideration was to bring Vatican II to a successful conclusion. His many accomplishments included renewals in liturgy and revamping the Roman Curia by internationalizing it with non-Italians. The Holy Office was renamed the Congregation for the Doctrine of the Faith. It was the first congregation to be reformed by Paul VI through a *motu proprio* on December 7, 1965, the last day of the Council. This congregation is the custodian of Catholic orthodoxy. When Paul VI gave it precedence in the post-conciliar reform, he wrote: "It is the congregation which deals with questions of greatest importance" (*The Ratzinger Report*, 1985).

Paul VI internationalized the influence of the papacy by pastoral journeys to the Holy Land and India (1964); the United Nations and New York City (1965), Fatima (1967), Colombia (1968), Uganda (1969), Asia, Australia, and the Pacific Islands (1970). In various encyclicals, he reaffirmed the Church's teachings on artificial birth control and abortion, and priestly celibacy; he wrote on Mary and the Holy Eucharist, and issued *The Credo of the People of God*, a listing of Catholic teachings.

Pope Paul VI died August 6, 1978. The time since the end of the Council saw unprecedented turmoil in the Church, a veritable crisis of authority. That is what faced the next pope.

After the short reign (3 weeks) of John Paul I in 1978, Karol Wojtyla was elected as the 264th successor to St. Peter. He had attended all the sessions of Vatican II. He was an author of *Gaudium et spes, the Pastoral Constitution on the Church in the Modern World* and he contributed to other Vatican II documents on religious freedom and social communication. Wojtyla, who took the name John Paul II for his pontificate, was well aware of the link between the Vatican Councils and his mission to implement their goals.

The Extraordinary Synod

John Paul II's papacy was worldwide and visible as he traveled to the ends of the earth calling all to follow Christ. He did not hesitate to speak with the moral authority to the issues of the day in his role as leader of souls. Like his predecessors, he saw to education in the faith, and like Pius IX and John XXIII, he wanted the renewal and teachings of the Councils made a part of daily life. He initiated a meeting of prelates to accomplish this goal.

In 1985 at a Mass commemorating the 20th Anniversary of Vatican Council II, Pope John Paul II announced he was calling an Extraordinary Synod of Bishops to discuss "the fundamental event in the life of the contemporary Church." He made this announcement in the Basilica of St. Paul-Outside-The-Walls, where Pope John XXIII had announced January 25, 1959, that he was calling a council of the entire Church.

Pope John Paul II said, "The aim is not only to commemorate the Vatican Council," but also "to favor further deepening and constant engrafting of Vatican Council II into the Church's life" as the third millennium of history approached.

The Final Report of the 1985 Extraordinary Synod made note of the lack of zeal for the Second Vatican Council in the first world countries (n.3), the growth of consumerism (n.3), and the problem of "partial and selective reading of the Council, as well as a superficial interpretation of its doctrines" (n.4).

In particular, the bishops stated:

"...the Council must be understood in continuity with the great Tradition of the Church....The Church is one and the same through all the Councils....The Church makes herself credible if She speaks less of Herself and ever more preaches Christ crucified....The message of the Church as described in the Second Vatican Council is Trinitarian and Christocentric" (n.5).

According to George Weigel, the Extraordinary Synod was "a call for affirmation." "The issues at the synod," he wrote, "were in large part those discussed by Cardinals Wojtyla and Ratzinger prior to the conclaves of 1978. The Church's engagement with the modern world would have to be distinctively ecclesial or it would betray Christ's great commission 'to go and make disciples of all nations' and nothing less than that was what the Church was *for*. Christ's commission made the Church a servant of human dignity...the 'Church in the modern world' had to be the *Church engaging modernity*" (*Witness to Hope*, p. 503). (emphasis in original)

To assist this engagement of the modern work, Bernard Cardinal Law of Boston, proposed that a "compendium" of all Catholic doctrine regarding both faith and morals be prepared (*Ibid*, p.504-505), a proposal endorsed by Pope John Paul II who "saw the Synod as he had seen Vatican II as a preparation for the Church's entrance into the third millennium of Christian history" (*ibid*, p.505).

Atheism - A Serious Problem

Germane to this documentation is our conciliar Popes' awareness of the inherent dangers of atheism.

Pope John XXIII in his apostolic constitution *Humanae salutis* (December 25, 1961) stated:

We have to reckon with a *completely new* and *disconcerting phenomenon*, namely, the *existence* of a *militant Atheism which has invaded entire peoples*." (emphasis in original)

The Second Vatican Council document, *Gaudium et spes*, promulgated by Pope Paul VI, December 7, 1965, stated: "Atheism must be accounted among the most serious problems of this age and is deserving of closer examination" (n. 19).

Karol Wojtyla, who came to the Council as administrator of the Archdiocese of Krakow, Poland, and by its conclusion had been made its Archbishop, was a major contributor to this document. During the third session of the Vatican Council, he maintained that the Church in dialogue with the world, always looked at history through the prism of the redeeming Cross of Christ. That God had entered the created world to redeem it and has "fixed once and for all the Christian meaning of 'the world'....The story of creation and redemption *is* the world's story, properly understood. Telling the world's story as that kind of story and thus bringing the world to conversion was the greatest service the Church could do" for it.

It was in this memorable speech to the assembled bishops that Archbishop Wojtyla then took up the question of Atheism as part of the Church's "dialogue with everyone." "The Church's dialogue with Atheism should begin not with arguments or proofs about the existence of God, but with a conversation about the human person's 'interior liberty.' In that kind of conversation, the Church might be able to show the Atheist a path beyond the radical loneliness and radical alienation that came from rejecting God in the name of liberation from alienation....Christian faith is not alienating; Christian faith is liberating in the most profound sense of human freedom. *That* was what the Church should propose to 'the modern world'" *(Witness To Hope*, p.166-169). (emphasis in original)

Fr. John A. Hardon, S.J., in *The Modern Catholic Dictionary*, notes that the Second Vatican Council, in *Gaudium et spes*, (Chapter 1, n. 19) "identified no less than eight forms of disbelief under the single term, Atheism." *The Catechism of the Catholic Church*, deals with the subject of atheism in paragraphs 2123-2126. It refers to the definite teaching in *Gaudium et spes* specifically in n.2123: "Many...of our contemporaries either do not at all perceive or explicitly reject this intimate and vital bond of man to God. Atheism must, therefore, be regarded as one of the most serious problems of our time" *(Gaudium et spes*, n. 19).

A Legacy To Claim and Cherish

On Sunday, November 26, 2000, the Solemnity of Christ the King, Pope John Paul II celebrated Mass in St. Peter's Square for the Jubilee of the Apostolate of the Laity. On that occasion with "thousands of people from around the world participating, the Holy Father gave a copy of the Documents of Vatican II to ten representatives of the lay Christian faithful." In his homily the Pope said:

> "*We must return to the Council. We must once again take the Documents of the Second Vatican Council in hand to rediscover the great wealth of its doctrinal and pastoral motives.*"

"Dear lay faithful, as witnesses to Christ, you are especially called *to bring the light of the Gospel to the vital nerve centers of society... Holiness continues to be the greatest challenge* for believers. We must be grateful to the Second Vatican Council which recalled *how all Christians are called to the fullness of Christian life*, and the perfection of charity" (*L'Osservatore Romano*, November 29, 2000). (emphasis in original)

On January 6, 2001, the Solemnity of the Epiphany, His Holiness Pope John Paul II penned another message to all the particular Churches:

"With the passage of the years *the Council documents have lost nothing of their value or brilliance*. They need to be read correctly, to be widely known and taken to heart as important and normative texts of the Magisterium, within the Church's Tradition....I feel more than ever in duty bound to point to the Council as *the great grace bestowed on the Church in the 20th Century*: There we find a sure compass by which to take our bearings in the century now beginning" (Apostolic Letter, *Novo millennio ineunte*, "At the Beginning of the Third Millennium," n. 57, text from *L'Osservatore Romano,* January 10, 2001).

Benedict Continues the Catholic Restoration

Until his death April 5, 2005, Pope John Paul II worked on Catholic restoration. He clarified some basic philosophical and theological principles in his writing, particularly in *Fides et ratio, Veritatis splendor, Evangelium vitae,* the *Catechism*. He tied them to the impetus given to their expression by the Council.

Joseph Cardinal Ratzinger was elected Pope on April 19, 2005, taking the name Benedict XVI. In his general audience in St. Peter's Square on April 27, 2005, Pope Benedict explained, "Filled with sentiments of awe and thanksgiving, I wish to speak of why I chose the name Benedict. Firstly, I remember Pope Benedict XV, that courageous prophet of peace, who guided the Church through turbulent times of war. In his footsteps I place my ministry in the service of reconciliation and harmony between peoples."

Pope Benedict XVI continued the work of John Paul II – especially the fight against atheism. Benedict XVI also advocated a life connected to God through prayer and a return to fundamental Christian values to counter secularization in the world. He asked that the Tridentine Mass be available more widely, and stressed the use of Latin during the Mass. He continued the explication of the relationship between faith and reason (e.g., Regensburg Address), the tightening up of the liturgy and prayer life of the Church (*Summorum pontificum*), and he insisted on the Second Vatican Council being seen through the lens of Tradition.

In his opening address launching the Year of Faith (Oct. 11, 2012), Pope Benedict XVI said:

"The Year of Faith which we launch today is linked harmoniously with the Church's whole path over the last fifty years: from the Council, through the *Magisterium* of the Servant of God Paul VI, who proclaimed a Year of Faith in 1967, up to the Great Jubilee of the year 2000, with which Blessed John Paul II re-proposed to all humanity Jesus Christ as the one Saviour, yesterday, today and forever. Between these two Popes, Paul VI and John Paul II, there was a deep and complete convergence, precisely upon Christ as the centre of the cosmos and of history, and upon the apostolic eagerness to announce Him to the world....

"I believe that the most important thing, especially on such a significant occasion as this, is to revive in the whole Church that positive tension, that yearning to announce Christ again to contemporary man. But, so that this interior thrust towards the new evangelization neither remain just an idea nor be lost in confusion, it needs to be built on a concrete and precise basis, and this basis is the documents of the Second Vatican Council, the place where it found expression....

"The Council Fathers wished to present the faith in a meaningful way; and if they opened themselves trustingly to dialogue with the modern world it is because they were certain of their faith, of the solid rock on which they stood....If today the Church proposes a new Year of Faith and a new evangelization, it is not to honour an anniversary, but because there is more need of it, even more than there was fifty years ago!

"In the Council's time it was already possible from a few tragic pages of history to know what a life or a world without God looked like, but now we see it every day around us. This void has spread. But it is in starting from the experience of this desert, from this void, that we can again discover the joy of believing, its vital importance for us, men and women. In the desert we rediscover the value of what is essential for living; thus in today's world there are innumerable signs, often expressed implicitly or negatively, of the thirst for God, for the ultimate meaning of life....This, then, is how we can picture the Year of Faith, a pilgrimage in the deserts of today's world, taking with us only what is necessary: neither staff, nor bag, nor bread, nor money, nor two tunics – as the Lord said to those He was sending out on mission (cf. *Lk* 9:3), but the Gospel and the faith of the Church, of which the Council documents are a luminous expression, as is the *Catechism of the Catholic Church*, published twenty years ago" (zenit.org).

Continuity

As Benedict XVI said, the new evangelization is needed, even more so now than 50 years ago at the opening of the Second Vatican Council. The void has spread, but in her Councils, the Church holds out the illumination that can fill the darkness. Whether from Peter to Benedict XVI or from Christ to 2013, from Council to Council, the Church holds out Christ as our hope, the light to all nations.

ENDNOTES

1. *Pastor aeternus* is the title of the *Dogmatic Constitution on the Church of Christ*, issued by the First Vatican Council on July 18, 1870, in which four doctrines of the Faith were defined:

• the apostolic primacy conferred on Peter;

• the perpetuity of the Petrine Primacy in the Roman Pontiffs;

• the meaning and power of the papal primacy; and

• the infallible teaching authority (Magisterium) of the Roman Pontiff.

(*Modern Catholic Dictionary*, p. 407)

2. The Papal States came into existence in 756 when Pepin the Short (the father of Charlemagne) gave Italian territory, including Rome, Ravenna, Bologna, and Ferrara, to the Pope Stephen III. In 1859, the land included about 16,000 square miles, twice the size of New Jersey. Throughout the centuries, the Papal States were governed by the Pope and became involved in European disputes just as any other country at the time. After the First Vatican Council ended, the Papal States were dismantled in 1870, with only the Vatican, St. John Lateran, and Castel Gandolfo remaining in papal hands. In protest, Pius IX withdrew into the Vatican as a voluntary prisoner because as he made clear, he could not move about Rome as a subject while insisting he was her sovereign. It was a policy followed until the reign of Pius XI with the Lateran Agreement of 1929. Negotiations for the solution of this issue covered two and one-half years with about two hundred meetings held in the presence of the Holy Father. The Lateran Treaty was signed February 11, 1929, and "established Vatican City as a sovereign state under the authority of the Pope. The Holy See, in turn, recognized the Italian State with Rome as its political capital. The Italian State recognized the Catholic, Apostolic, and Roman religion as the sole religion of the State. It declared the sovereign independence of the Holy See in the international field, and the Holy See's sovereign jurisdiction in Vatican City. At the same time a concordat was signed providing for the teaching of the Catholic religion in the public schools, the civil recognition of marriages performed according to Canon Law, and the freedom of Catholic Action provided it is nonpolitical" (*Modern Catholic Dictionary*, p. 309-310).

LAURENE CONNER was one of the co-founders of the Wanderer Forum Foundation with her husband, the late Stillwell J. Conner and Alphonse J. Matt Sr., in 1965. She served as Secretary/Treasurer of the Foundation, managing the annual National Forums, selecting topics and speakers to fit the yearly themes for the event. She also managed the correspondence which led to the realization that there was a need for published documentation for Catholics about some of the experimentation in the wake of the Second Vatican Council. She served as co-editor and research director for *Forum Focus* magazine since its origin in 1985, until her retirement in 2003. Some of the topics covered included the original Campaign for Human Development, the left-leaning bent of the bureaucracy of the U.S. Catholic Conference at the time, secularism, liturgical innovation, and a variety of lay movements. One issue of the magazine, "Unholy Alliance", concerned liberation theology, Jesuits, Communists, and subversive activities in Latin America. Mrs. Conner and Frank Morriss collaborated on this extensive study which included translated news articles by a Latin journalist about the reality of what was going on behind the scenes of the open turmoil. This issue is still available from the Foundation and in recent years had been sent to young Jesuits in El Salvador by a priest who had helped in the research. He reported the piece had a profound and positive influence on their thinking. Mrs. Conner wrote many articles and reported on many Church conferences for *The Wanderer* newspaper. Mrs. Conner passed from this life July 2, 2007.

The Four Constitutions of Vatican II: An Overview
By Michael Adkins

Introduction

Pope Benedict XVI, prior to his resignation from the papal office, convoked a Year of Faith whereby he encouraged Catholics to take the opportunity to learn more about their faith, particularly through an engagement with the teachings of the Second Vatican Council. The concerns and pastoral approach of the Council, now fifty years old, still present an interpretive challenge to Catholics on how to implement the Council in the twenty-first century. Even the Holy Father, in his final address to the clergy of Rome, spoke of great confusion about the Council and how the media has managed to usurp the "Council of the Fathers" and promote a "Council of the Media."[1]

The purpose of this article is to summarize the four major constitutions of the Second Vatican Council in order to assist the faithful in understanding what the Council actually said as well as its impact on the Church in the modern world: what was maintained in continuity and what was legitimately developed or reformed.

Sacrosanctum Concilium
The Constitution on the Sacred Liturgy
Promulgated by Pope Paul VI On December 4, 1963

According to the Council Fathers, the liturgy reminds the faithful and others of "the real nature of the true Church she is both human and divine, visible and yet invisibly equipped, eager to act and yet intent on contemplation, present in this world and yet not at home in it."[2] Holy Mother Church, according to the Council Fathers, "desires to undertake with great care a general restoration of the liturgy itself. For the liturgy is made up of immutable elements divinely instituted, and of elements subject to change."[3] With this in mind, a revision of the Roman rite should be undertaken so as "to express more clearly the holy things which they signify, [for Christians] should be enabled to understand them with ease and take part in them fully, actively, and as befits a community."[4] The document makes clear that the proposed principles of reform mainly concern the Roman rite of the Catholic Church.[5] The principles of reform are to be carefully undertaken "in the light of sound tradition" in order to renew a deepened engagement and participation in the sacred liturgy.[6] At the same time, the document expresses haste: "The liturgical books are to be revised as soon as possible."[7]

Unlike the other three constitutions, *Sacrosanctum concilium* is largely composed of lists of proposals toward the reform of the liturgy; it is technical and, at times, tedious. The document centers itself upon a reform of the Roman Missal (chapters 1-2), but it also proposes comprehensive reforms of the rites of sacramentals (ch. 3), all six rites of the sacraments (ch. 3), the Divine Office (ch. 4), the liturgical calendar (ch. 5), sacred music (ch. 6) and sacred art (ch. 7). In order to briefly and adequately summarize the proposed reforms, I have identified what I believe to be the three-fold approach of the Council Fathers:

• To retain, restore and develop tradition;

• To promote active participation, community and the didactic nature of the liturgy;

• To adapt the liturgy appropriately to the cultures and peoples of mission territory.

To Retain, Restore and Develop Tradition

Early in the document, the Council Fathers state that "sound tradition may be retained, and yet remain open to legitimate progress" and any "new forms adopted should in some way grow organically from forms already existing."[8] As a key example of restoration, the sacred Council announced the restoration of the catechumenate for adults, today called RCIA or Rite of Christian Initiation of Adults.[9] Also restored is the traditional sequence of hours in the Divine Office in order that "they [once again] be related to the time of day when they are prayed."[10] With regard to preservation, of great interest are the sacred Council's remarks on Latin: "particular law remaining in force, the use of the Latin language is to be preserved in the Latin rites,"[11] and "a suitable place may be allotted to the mother tongue... nevertheless steps should be taken so that the faithful may also be able to say or sing together in Latin those parts of the Ordinary of the Mass which pertain to them."[12] Without a doubt, the Council Fathers did not intend to suppress use of Latin in the liturgy, and yet they open up the possibility of development by the incorporation of vernacular tongues.[13] With regard to sacred music, the

Council Fathers make clear that Gregorian chant is "specially suited to the Roman liturgy; therefore, other things being equal, it should be given pride of place in liturgical services,"[14] and the pipe organ "is to be held in high esteem, for it is the traditional musical instrument."[15] That said, the document states that "other instruments also may be admitted for use in divine worship" as well as "other forms of music, especially polyphony,"[16] allowing for "legitimate" and "organic" development of the liturgical tradition. Speaking of sacred art and architecture, the Council Fathers note that the Church has never exclusively adopted one particular style of art, but rather has permitted and encouraged various styles from every period "according to the natural talents and circumstances of peoples, and the needs of the various rites."[17] With this in mind, the document states: "The art of our own days...shall also be given free scope in the Church, provided that it adorns the sacred buildings and holy rites with due reverence and honor."[18]

To Promote Active Participation, Community and the Didactic Nature of the Liturgy

Throughout *Sacrosanctum concilum*, the Council Fathers emphatically promote the laity's engagement and active participation in the liturgy in order that they may not be "strangers or silent spectators," but rather "conscious of what they are doing."[19] In order to engage the laity, the Council Fathers wish to remove anything that might distract or hinder the faithful from the central act and message of the liturgy; hence, for example, the proposals to remove of any unnecessary accumulation of sacramental elements which "crept into the rites" over the centuries.[20] They propose that the liturgy be streamlined to express "noble simplicity"[21] and that the immutable parts of the Mass (e.g. the Liturgy of the Word and the Liturgy of the Eucharist), be more clearly delineated.[22] Likewise, the rites of all the sacraments, by recommendation of the sacred Council, are to be revised along the same principles as the Roman rite of the Mass.[23] A key element of the reform is the revision of the liturgical calendar. Many reforms are proposed with regard to the calendar, but most notable are the desires to adapt and simplify the calendar "for modern circumstances"[24] and to emphasize the liturgical season over various feasts of saints and other local traditions.[25] The goal of these reforms is to focus the cycle of the calendar on the paschal mystery which culminates in Lent and Easter. Likewise, the Sunday Mass is to be of great importance and regarded as "the foundation and kernel of the whole liturgical year."[26]

With regard to "active participation," the vernacular will also be of great assistance, as the people will be more apt to vocally participate in the ritual as well as understand the readings from Scripture. The Tridentine rite is largely silent, and it is clear that the Council Fathers wish to engage *physically* the laity *so as to hone their focus*: "the people should be encouraged to take part by means of acclamations, responses, psalmody, antiphons, and songs, as well as by actions, gestures, and bodily attitudes. And at the proper times all should observe a reverent silence."[27] It is clear that the sacred Council did not intend "active participation" to mean that the laity *do more acts*, but rather *be actively engaged* in worship; provisions for the laity to undertake any new ministerial roles or tasks in the liturgy are nowhere to be found in the document.

The reforms aimed at emphasizing the communal nature of the liturgy hope to eliminate an individualism in worship and to emphasize unity among the people with one another, their pastor and especially their local bishop and the universal Church.[28] In general, a focus on the communal is to be preferred over "a celebration that is individual and quasi-private."[29] Following the work of the Council of Trent, the Council Fathers state that "a more perfect form of participation" in the Mass is by the reception of the Holy Eucharist; therefore, communion under both species is now encouraged to be granted "when the bishops think fit"[30] not only to religious but also to the laity. In addition, the age-old custom of concelebration of the Mass is to be extended more freely and overseen by the local bishop.[31] Certainly, the common vocal acclamations, prayers, gestures and the use of the vernacular, as proposed by the Council Fathers, would all contribute to the communal nature of the liturgy.

To Adapt the Liturgy Appropriately to the Cultures & Peoples of Mission Territory

The Council Fathers state: "Even in the liturgy, the Church has no wish to impose a rigid uniformity."[32] Holy Mother Church, who is found spread among all cultures and peoples, respects and desires to foster the talents and customs of various peoples, and therefore she looks with sympathy upon elements of those local artistic expressions "not indissolubly bound up with superstition and error" and at times "she admits such things into the liturgy itself, so long as they harmonize with its true and authentic spirit."[33] One such area that the Council Fathers promote in this regard is the incorporation of local music: "In certain parts of the world, especially in mission lands, there are peoples who have their own musical traditions, and these play a great part in their religious and social life."[34] Once again, the Council Fathers express concern for the universality of the Church while maintaining the integrity of tradition and its organic development. It is worth noting that proposals open to more thorough adaptations of the Roman rite appear to be limited to mission territories.

Lumen Gentium
The Dogmatic Constitution on the Church
Promulgated by Pope Paul VI On November 21, 1964

The mission of the Church, proclaim the Council Fathers, is to be, as Christ, "a Light to the nations," and therefore "to bring the light of Christ to all men."[35] The Church acts like a "sacrament" to the entire world, and aims, through the sacred Council, to more fully reveal her "inner nature and universal mission" to draw all men to herself.[36] The unique and universal face of the Church is presented to man: every culture, race and nation are represented by the Church's members. This is important because the Council Fathers want to recognize the global outreach of the Church's mission more fully and emphasize that her focus is beyond Europe and her traditional expression reaches beyond that of the Roman Church.

Throughout this *Constitution*, the Council Fathers refer to the Church by many names (old formulae and new formulae), ostensibly to reveal more fully the connection *all* men have to the Church and her mission of salvation.[37] For instance, the Church is called a "Body" and a "People." These two titles, albeit used somewhat interchangeably in *Lumen gentium*, appear to indicate the implicit and explicit membership of this "People of God" which appears to be a new focus of interest for the Council Fathers. The Council Fathers appear to want to emphasize that though some men may not be Catholic, Christian, or even believe in a god at all, they are, by the interconnected nature of man created by the one and true God, still part of His family, albeit broken. The Council Fathers emphasize that among the "People of God," the one, holy, catholic and apostolic Church on earth and in heaven play a special role in the salvation of all men, forming "one complex reality which coalesces from a divine and human element."[38]

The document reaffirms the traditional teachings on the hierarchical make-up of the visible Church, but it also importantly clarifies the four marks of the Church (one, holy, catholic and apostolic) and how outside elements of Christian truth relate to these essential marks within her. The sacred Council's expression "*subsists in* the Catholic Church"[39] indicates that elements of truth can be found in various ways outside the Catholic Church proper, but those elements of truth are derived from or "subsist in" the heart of the Catholic Church. In other words, other Christian communities or churches may contain or exhibit various marks of the Church as well as elements of truth in teaching, but the merit of those qualities most fully and properly derive from the Catholic Church.[40] The statement likewise indicates that truth, albeit lacking or fragmented, can be found in other religious beliefs outside of Christianity, but again, the merit of any truth found there derives from and "subsists in" the Church. This is a new approach in that it acknowledges the goodness found in others as opposed to the error.[41]

Paragraph 14 of *Lumen gentium* addresses the question of the salvation of all men: "All men are called to be part of this catholic unity of the people of God... for all men are called by the grace of God to salvation. [...] Basing itself upon Sacred Scripture and Tradition, [the Council] teaches that the Church... is necessary for salvation."[42] The *Dogmatic Constitution* also addresses ecumenism and inter-religious dialogue (paragraphs 15-17), restating age-old Church teaching with regard to non-Christians: "Those also can attain to salvation who through no fault of their own do not know the Gospel of Christ or His Church, yet sincerely seek God and moved by grace strive by their deeds to do His will as it is known to them through the dictates of conscience... Whatever good or truth is found amongst them is looked upon by the Church as a preparation for the Gospel."[43] The Council Fathers, preferring the expression "separated brethren,"[44] praise Protestants' consecration and unity with Christ in Baptism, and note that some "churches" or "ecclesiastical communities" celebrate some or all of the other sacraments, emphasizing that those who share all seven sacraments and devotion toward the Virgin Mother of God with the Catholic Church are even more closely linked in the Holy Spirit.[45]

The chapter concerning the hierarchical organization of the Church (paragraphs 18-23), reaffirms Vatican Council I's teaching on papal infallibility as well as the structure of the hierarchical Church and her offices. Perhaps in response to some needed clarification after Vatican Council I, sections 23-28 address the authority of individual bishops over their particular local churches as opposed to authority over the universal Church given exclusively to the Roman Pontiff. Infallibility is discussed at length and clarified: the pope exercises "the charism of infallibility," not as an individual, but only as supreme teacher of the Universal Church "expounding or defending a doctrine of Catholic faith."[46] The Council Fathers also insist that infallibility "resides also in the body of Bishops, when that body exercises the supreme *magisterium* with the Successor of Peter."[47] Closing out this chapter on the hierarchy is a section dedicated to the renewal of the diaconate in the life of the Latin Church.[48]

Regarding the lay faithful, the Council Fathers clearly wished to promote their dignity and vital role in the life of the Church as "sharers in the priestly, prophetical, and kingly functions of Christ"[49] by their involvement in secular or temporal affairs, bringing Christ out into the world through their example and ordering it to the plan of God. Not only was the dignity of the lay faithful underlined, but also their "true equality"[50] to those in the clergy and religious life. The Council Fathers point out and admonish the lay faithful to remember that no secular work or business is below or withdrawn from God's dominion, attacking the notion of living a divided life between the sacred and the secular. The laity are asked to pray for their shepherds and recognize a renewed enthusiasm through dialectic and cooperation: "In this way, the whole Church, strengthened by each one of its members, may more effectively fulfill its mission for the life of the world."[51]

Having discussed the unique roles and responsibilities of the laity and hierarchy, the sacred Council honors the unique charism, life and contributions of religious. Unlike the laity whose role is in the temporal or secular order, "the religious state," note the Council Fathers, "whose purpose is to free its members from earthly cares, more fully manifests to all believers the presence of heavenly goods already possessed here below... in a striking manner daily."[52] The Council Fathers emphasize the great responsibility of all the faithful to live a life of holiness: to be saints. They declare: "all the faithful of Christ of whatever rank or status, are called to the fullness of the Christian life and to the perfection of charity... Every person must walk unhesitatingly according to his own personal gifts and duties in the path of living faith, which arouses hope and works through charity."[53]

The Church on earth is not alone in the struggle for sanctification and salvation. The Council Fathers turn to the earthly Church's connection with the elect in heaven, the Church Triumphant. Reminding readers that the ultimate goal is heaven, the Council Fathers reaffirm that the Church is in exile and awaiting the Lord in hope.

For now, the faithful must constantly be vigilant and "put on the armor of God" to "stand against the wiles of the devil and resist" in order to avoid the "eternal fire."[54] Catholics are not alone in this struggle because Mary, the angels and the saints all ceaselessly intercede on their behalf. In addition, Catholics pray for the dead, the Church Suffering, for it is "holy and wholesome"[55] to do so. In the final chapter of *Lumen gentium*, the Council Fathers clearly wish to re-present the Catholic devotion to Mary to the entire world in order to rebuff confusion about or misrepresentation of the Catholic cult of Mary and to promote her as a spiritual Mother *of all men*.

The Blessed Virgin Mary's integral role in the life of the Church is described by the Council Fathers in four parts:
1) Her role in the economy of salvation;
2) Her role in the Church;
3) The cult of Mary in the Church;
4) Mary as a sign of hope.

Dei Verbum
The Dogmatic Constitution on Divine Revelation
Promulgated by Pope Paul VI On November 18, 1965

The Council Fathers beautifully open this *Dogmatic Constitution* by stating that they follow "in the footsteps of the Council of Trent and the First Vatican Council... to set forth authentic doctrine on divine revelation and how it is handed on, so that by hearing the message of salvation the world may believe, by believing it may hope, and by hoping it may love."[56] The purpose of clarifying the deposit of revelation is for the salvation of souls. Once again, the sacred Council presents the Church at the service of humanity.

God made Himself known to men, "invit[ing] them into fellowship with Himself" in order that they may "share in the divine nature."[57] The Council Fathers offer a most lofty invitation to all men to enter more fully into the People of God, the Church.

The *Constitution* focuses on divine revelation but also offers key maxims about natural revelation and man's ability to apprehend and to know truth, for instance: "God... can be known *with certainty* from created reality by the light of human reason."[58]

The Council addresses the omnipresent existential questions: "How do we know?" and "By what authority do we know?" Jesus, the fullness of divine revelation, "commissioned the Apostles" and gave them His Holy Spirit in order to hand on, with authority, His message of salvation to all generations.[59] This "handing over" by the Apostles was accomplished "by their oral preaching, by example, and by observances handed on" through their successors, the bishops.[60] Therefore, the doctrine of the Church can simultaneously be preserved and continue to develop "as the centuries succeed one another, the Church constantly moves forward toward the fullness of divine truth."[61]

Sacred Scripture, a vital element of divine revelation, is the authentically inspired word of God, for God chose men and "while employed by Him, they, as true authors, consigned to writing everything and only those things which He wanted." Therefore, the Sacred Scriptures are authoritative and "must be acknowledged as teaching solidly, faithfully and without error the truth which God wanted... for the sake of salvation."[62] An important aim of this *Dogmatic Constitution* was to address new concerns surrounding the interpretation of revelation as well as that of Biblical authority and exegesis. It is essential, according to the Council Fathers, to carefully interpret God's message through various means. First of all, the Council Fathers state, it is important to respect the original intention of the sacred writers as well as to pay attention to "literary forms," recognizing that "truth is set forth and expressed differently in texts which are variously historical, prophetic, poetic, or of other forms of discourse."[63] In addition, the "particular circumstances" of the sacred writer must be investigated for they inform the "styles of feeling, speaking and narrating which prevailed at the time."[64]

Equally important is the fact that Scripture must be read and interpreted with attention to the "content and unity of the whole of Scripture if the meaning of the sacred texts is to be correctly worked out."[65] Scriptural exegetes are to read the texts through these hermeneutical lenses in order that the Church's understanding of the Scriptures may mature; ultimately, it is the responsibility of the living teaching office of the Apostolic See to judge the authenticity of interpretations.[66]

In addition to exegetical concerns, the Council Fathers promote the importance of the Old Testament in order that it not be fully eclipsed by the proclamation of the New Testament. The Old Testament Scriptures "show us true divine pedagogy,"[67] for the two Testaments complement one another: "the books of the Old Testament... acquire and show forth their full meaning in the New Testament and in turn shed light on [the New] and explain [the New]."[68] Without a proper appreciation of the Old Testament, the Council Fathers advise, the New Testament cannot be fully understood.

Reaffirming the Church's veneration of the Sacred Scriptures, the Council Fathers wish to promote, "through the reading and study of the sacred books...a new stimulus for the life of the Spirit from a growing reverence for the word of God."[69] In order to realize this goal, the Council Fathers promote "easy access" to the Scriptures for all the faithful, seeing to it that Church authorities provide "suitable and correct translations into different languages" and even prepare editions of Scripture for the use of non-Christians.[70] The sacred synod also encourages "the study of the holy Fathers of both East and West and of sacred liturgies"[71] for these writings help expound upon the meaning of the Scriptures.[72] All the Christian faithful are to study the Scriptures through frequent reading for, as St. Jerome wrote, "ignorance of the Scriptures is ignorance of Christ."[73]

Gaudium et Spes
The Pastoral Constitution on the Church in the Modern World
Promulgated by Pope Paul VI on December 7, 1965

Part I: "The Church & Man's Calling"

As the opening remarks state, the Council Fathers not only wish to speak to the sons of the Church, but they also wish to address "all who invoke the name of Christ" and "the whole of humanity."[74] This Christocentric document expresses the solidarity of the Council Fathers with "the entire human family"[75] in a conversation about "the current trend of the world"[76]: man's hopes, griefs and anxieties as well as the "ultimate destiny and reality of humanity."[77]

According to the Council Fathers, the Church has always "had the duty of scrutinizing the signs of the times and of interpreting them in the light of the Gospel."[78] With that, the Council Fathers briefly highlight the astounding changes and advances man experienced in the preceding century: technological advancements, proliferation of wealth and resources, the spread of freedom, and a deepened global awareness.[79] These changes can be seen in the growth of the industrial society, the pursuit of city living, new efficiencies in media and social communication, and an explosion in immigration.[80] Likewise, there is a new awareness of the freedoms won by nations in the post-colonial age, the rights and opportunities for workers and equality for women; all are seen as issues of great import for the Council Fathers.[81]

Yet, it is observed, that with these changes and advances new and grave problems have arisen such as the distrust of accepted values and moral norms, the denial of God or of religion, and the subjugation of virtually all areas of study by atheistic or materialistic philosophies.[82] In addition, the Fathers observe that "an imbalance [has arisen] between a concern for practicality and efficiency, and the demands of moral conscience... an imbalance between specialized human activity and a comprehensive view of reality."[83] Of these problems, man is both "the cause and the victim."[84]

The Council Fathers wish to point out the deep longing of all of humanity, thirsting for "a full and free life worthy of man,"[85] but warn that man will not solve the problems of the world "solely by human effort,"[86] excoriating materialistic philosophies which are "blinded against any sharp insight into this kind of dramatic situation."[87] Instead, the Church proposes that the key to unlocking the mysteries of the human heart lies "in her most benign Lord and Master... the focal point goal of man, as well as of all human history."[88] With that, the Council wishes to share its perspective on the mystery of man's being and propose solutions to the vexing problems of the age, guided by the light of Christ.[89]

Properly ordering such an important conversation is a comprehensive presentation of the Church's philosophy of the human person and his relation to the created world. According to Holy Mother Church, man is aided by his conscience, which is capable of detecting the Natural Law, one which "holds him to obedience," and turns him "aside from blind choice" toward "objective norms of morality."[90] In addition, the Council Fathers propose, he is able to gain true wisdom through the aid of faith and the Holy Spirit.[91] The Church believes she is well equipped to speak to all men about the dignity of the human person and the unity of mankind for several reasons: (1) "Christ, to be sure, gave His Church no proper mission in the political, economic or social order;"[92] (2) the Church's purpose is religious: "to structure and consolidate the human community according to the divine law;"[93] (3) the Church can promote unity since "in virtue of her mission and nature she is bound to no particular form of human culture, nor to any political, economic or social system... by her very universality can be a close bond between diverse human communities and nations."[94]

In light of this, the Council Fathers wish to exhort all Christians to reject any division between the "faith which they profess and their daily lives" for it "jeopardizes [their] eternal salvation," and this false division is "to be counted among the more serious errors of our age."[95]

The Council Fathers also consider atheism to "be accounted among the most serious problems of this age."[96] The Church recommits herself to repudiating these "poisonous doctrines" and she believes that the remedy of such errors "is to be sought in a proper presentation of the Church's teaching as well as in the integral life of the Church and her members."[97] In this statement, the whole purpose of the Council can be seen: not necessarily to define any new teaching on faith and morals, but to re-present the Church and the splendor of what God offers to all of humanity. As previously stated, the Church sees herself at the service of humanity, not just of her members.

The unity and common destiny of man is further underlined by Sacred Scripture's call to love God and neighbor, but, as the Council Fathers point out, "the love of God cannot be separated from love of neighbor."[98] The Gospel has and continues to arouse in man's heart the "irresistible requirements of his dignity" and "this Council lays stress on reverence for man; everyone must consider his every neighbor without exception as another self."[99] This radical call to solidarity and self gift motivated by the Gospel, points out "the growing awareness of the exalted dignity proper to the human person" and the basic rights of man.[100]

The chapter entitled "Man's Activity Throughout the World" is largely concerned with bridging the gap between faith and reason and recognizing the temptations of human progress. The work of man, from family life to politics to manual labor, can be seen as participating in the "unfolding of the Creator's work"[101] and therefore labor is to be understood to have great dignity; the "triumphs of the human race are a sign of God's grace and the flowering of His own mysterious design" not in any way opposed to God's power.[102] In academic inquiry, truth cannot contradict truth, no matter how it was discovered and any attitudes or habits of mind – whether from Christians or others – which promote a division between faith and science, the Council Fathers say, "we cannot but deplore."[103] By praising the accomplishments, culture and progress of the sciences by the work of men throughout the world and in ages past, the Council Fathers remind readers that the Church has "learned to express the message of Christ with the help of the ideas and terminology of various philosophers,"[104] many of whom were not Christian. So, too, today, the Church "can and ought to be enriched by the development of human social life"[105] in order to "express [Christ's message of salvation] better, and adjust it more successfully to our times"[106] for "the Church admits that she has greatly profited and still profits from the antagonism of those who oppose or persecute her."[107]

Though dialogue is given special regard and emphasis throughout the document, the Council makes sure to note that "this love and good will, must in no way render us indifferent to truth and goodness" and that error "always merits repudiation," though "the person in error... never loses the dignity of being a person even when he is flawed by false or inadequate religious notions."[108]

Part II – "Some Problems of Special Urgency"

The second part of *Gaudium et spes* aims to apply Catholic social teaching and the exhortations found in *Part I* to a number of modern issues that "go to the roots of the human race": marriage and the family (ch. 1), human progress (ch. 2), life in its economic, social and political dimensions (ch. 3), the bonds between the family of nations (ch. 4), and peace (ch. 5).[109] With the exception of the chapter on marriage, many of the proposals given are to be entrusted to prudential judgment and to be measured against the Church's moral and social teaching. With this in mind, the document at times sounds like it is guilty of prescribing utopia or that it is naïve about the fallenness of man; perhaps these are fair criticisms, but the reader must recall that the pastoral constitution clearly assumes that implementation will not break with Church teaching, applying appropriately the Council's recommendations to local situations.

The Council Fathers are concerned with economic development because modern technology has "increased man's dominion over nature"[110] and expanded global trade. This has provided many advancements in the standard of living among developed countries, but has also presented challenges such as economic inequity among nations, ideologies "ruled by economics," and "extravagance and wretchedness [existing] side by side" among many others.[111]

With regard to the welfare of the political order, the Council Fathers are concerned about the proper organization of the political community toward the greatest promotion of human freedom, the dignity of the human person and the promotion of the common good. The Council Fathers point out that there is a growing desire to include as many citizens as possible in the political process, and, especially today, extend to minorities of race and of religious beliefs the exercise of personal rights given to all citizens.[112]

Regarding the relations between Church and state, the Council Fathers remark: "The Church, by reason of her role and competence, is not identified in any way with the political community nor bound to any political system. She is at once a sign and a safeguard of the transcendent character of the human person. The Church and the political community in their own fields are autonomous and independent from each other."[113] Though the political order and the Church ought to remain in fruitful dialogue for the promotion of the common good, the Church "does not place her trust in the privileges offered by civil authority. She will even give up the exercise of certain rights which have been legitimately acquired, if it becomes clear that their use will cast doubt on the sincerity of her witness or that new ways of life demand new methods."[114]

Lasting peace, insist the Council Fathers, rests on a firm resolution "to respect other men and peoples and their dignity, as well as the studied practice of brotherhood."[115] The fifth chapter of *Part II*, entitled "The Fostering of Peace & Promotion of a Community of Nations," is divided into two sections: section one on avoiding war and section two on establishing an international community. Great urgency marks the tone and message of section one, for it is understood that man possesses new weaponry through the advances of modern science by which he can destroy the world many times over. Although the Council Fathers uphold just war theory by way of "legitimate defense,"[116] nevertheless they underline that war is to be avoided if possible due to the "horror and perversity of war [which are] immensely magnified by the addition of scientific weapons."[117] Section two of chapter five encourages nations to gather in international bodies in order to collaborate and cooperate with one another and to work toward the equitable management of the world's resources in order to promote peace, equity, and the dignity of all peoples.[118]

Gaudium et spes, the last of the four constitutions promulgated by the Council, ends with the following prayer: "Now to Him who is able to accomplish all things in a measure far beyond what we ask or conceive, in keeping with the power that is at work in us – to Him be glory in the Church and in Christ Jesus, down through all the ages of time without end. Amen. (*Eph.* 3:20-21)"[119]

All quotations from Vatican II documents are from http://www.vatican.va/archive/ hist_councils/ii_vatican_council/index.htm

ENDNOTES

1.   Pope Benedict XVI, Address to the Roman Clergy, February 14, 2013. Vatican Radio text: http:// en.radiovaticana.va/news/2013/02/14/pope_benedict's_last_great_master_class:_vatican_ii,_as_i_ saw_ it_%5Bfull/en1-665030

2.   *SC*, 2.

3.   *SC*, 21.

4.   *Ibid.*

5.   *SC*, 3. Though focused on the Roman rite, the Council Fathers pointed out that "all lawfully acknowledged rites are to be of equal right and dignity" (*SC*, 3).

6.   *SC*, 4.

7.   *SC*, 25.

8.   *SC*, 23.

9.   RCIA is a catechetical program for adult converts that spans the liturgical calendar, including initiation rites throughout the year culminating in the Easter Vigil.

10. *SC*, 88.

11. *SC*, 36.

12. *SC*, 54.

13. In all cases, use of the vernacular is clearly "extraordinary" or not simply the norm. That said, it is up to the judgment of the local ordinary to decide if the vernacular is permitted at all.

14. *SC*, 116.

15. *SC*, 120.

16. *SC*, 116.

17. *SC*, 123.

18. *Ibid.* 19 . *SC*, 48. 20. *SC*, 62. 21. *SC*, 34. 22. *SC*, 50.

23. "Extreme Unction may now more fittingly be called 'Anointing of the Sick'" (*SC*, 73).

24. *SC*, 107.

25. *SC*, 108.

26. *SC*, 106.

27. *SC*, 30.

28. *SC*, 41.

29. *SC*, 27.

30. *SC*, 55.

31. *SC*, 57-58.

32. *SC*, 37.

33. *Ibid.*

34. *SC*, 119.

35. *LG*, 1.

36. *Ibid.*

37.   Other titles: The Church is called a "Temple", for in her dwells the Holy Spirit; she is called "our mother," implying guide and teacher; she is called "the spotless spouse of the spotless Lamb," meaning the "Bride of Christ" for whom our Lord delivered Himself up that He might sanctify her; she is called "a sheepfold" as she gathers the lost ones for her Master.

38. *LG*, 8.

39. *Ibid.* (my emphasis) The full statement is worth quoting: "This is the one Church of Christ which in the Creed is professed as one, holy, catholic and apostolic, which our Saviour, after His Resurrection, commissioned Peter to shepherd, and him and the other apostles to extend and direct with authority, which He erected for all ages as 'the pillar and mainstay of the truth'. This Church constituted and organized in the world as a society, subsists in the Catholic Church, which is governed by the successor of Peter and by the Bishops in communion with him, although many elements of sanctification and of truth are found outside of its visible structure. These elements, as gifts belonging to the Church of Christ, are forces impelling toward catholic unity" (*LG*, 8). The "subsists in" distinction also helps to clarify how, according to the Council Fathers, the Church is the "visible sacrament of this saving unity" and "transcends all limits of time and confines of race" and acts as a servant by outpouring the riches of its graces upon all men in a mystical and mysterious way, drawing together (and emphasizing the more broad use of the expression) "the People of God."

40.   *LG*, 8.

41. Further reading: *Dominus Iesus*, August 6, 2000 (Congregation for the Doctrine of the Faith); "Responses to Some Questions Regarding Certain Aspect of the Doctrine on the Church," June 29, 2007 (Congregation for the Doctrine of the Faith).

42. *LG*, 14. In addition, the notion of *Baptism of desire* is reaffirmed by the Council Fathers for catechumens who die prior to formal entrance into the Church.

43. *LG*, 16.

44. *LG*, 67.

45.   An important distinction: some non-Catholic groups are "churches" proper and others are simply "ecclesiastical communities" with regard to the four marks of the Church.

46. *LG*, 25.

47. *Ibid.*

48. *LG*, 29. The Council Fathers state: "the diaconate can in the future be restored as a proper and permanent rank of the hierarchy... this diaconate can, in the future, be conferred upon men of more mature age, even upon those living in the married state. It may also be conferred upon suitable young men, for whom the law of celibacy must remain intact."

49. *LG*, 31.

50. *LG*, 32.

51. *LG*, 37.

52. *LG*, 46.

53. *LG*, 41.

54. *LG*, 48.

55. *LG*, 50.

56. *DV*, 1.

57. *DV*, 2.

58. *DV*, 6. (my emphasis)

59. *DV*, 7.

60. *Ibid.*

61. *DV*, 8.

62. *DV*, 11.

63. *DV*, 12.

64. *Ibid.*

65. *Ibid.*
66. *Ibid.*
67. *DV,* 15.
68. *Ibid.*
69. *DV,* 26.
70. *DV,* 22; 25.
71. *DV,* 23.
72. *Ibid.* This move "back to the sources" has been dubbed *ressourcement* in the post-conciliar period.
73. *DV,* 25.
74. *GS,* 2.
75. *GS,* 3.
76. *Ibid.*
77. *Ibid.*
78. *GS,* 4.
79. *Ibid.*
80. *GS,* 6.
81. *GS,* 9.
82. *GS,* 7.
83. *GS,* 8.
84. *Ibid.*
85. *GS,* 9.
86. *GS,* 10.
87. *Ibid.*
88. *Ibid.*
89. *Ibid.*
90. *GS,* 16.
91. *GS,* 15.
92. *GS,* 42.
93. *Ibid.*
94. *Ibid.*
95. *GS,* 43.
96. *GS,* 19.
97. *GS,* 21.
98. *GS,* 24.
99. *GS,* 27.
100. *GS,* 26; 29.
101. *GS,* 34.
102. *Ibid.*
103. *GS,* 36.
104. *GS,* 44.
105. *Ibid.*
106. *Ibid.*
107. *Ibid.*

108. *GS*, 28.

109. *GS*, 46.

110. *GS*, 63.

111. *Ibid.*

112. *GS*, 73.

113. *GS*, 76.

114. *Ibid.*

115. *GS*, 78.

116. *GS*, 79.

117. *GS*, 80. As an American, I found it of particular interest to read the stiff condemnation in paragraph 80, presumably in reference to the use of the atomic bomb: "Any act of war aimed indiscriminately at the destruction of entire cities of extensive areas along with their population is a crime against God and man himself."

118. *GS*, 84.

119. *GS*, 93.

MICHAEL ADKINS is Academic Dean and faculty member of St. Agnes School (K-12) in St. Paul, Minnesota. He has taught various areas of the Humanities in Junior and Senior High School for over a decade, and he currently works on curriculum development and institutional advancement as well as serving as an educational consultant to other schools. A member of the Classical Association of Minnesota and the American Numismatic Association, Adkins holds a Bachelor's Degree in Honors Classics and a Master's Degree in Catholic Studies; he composed his Master's essay on Pope John XXIII's Apostolic Constitution, *Veterum sapientia*, and the importance of the Latin language. He and his wife, Cynthia, have six children and attend the Church of St. Agnes in St. Paul, Minnesota.

Worship Is Our Most Important Calling

By Fr. John T. Zuhlsdorf

Our liturgical worship is probably the most important thing we do as Catholics. The **virtue of Justice** orders all our relationships so that we give to each person what is his due. God, however, is at the top of the hierarchy of all our relationships with persons. God is qualitatively different from all other persons with whom we have a relationship. Thus, giving to God what is God's due concerns its own virtue, the **virtue of Religion**. The first one to whom we owe something is God and the first thing we owe to God is worship, both as individuals and collectively. If our relationship with God is disordered, all our other relationships will be disordered. If we do not worship God and worship Him properly, we have a hard time living properly in relation to everyone else.

Because we are wounded by Original Sin, it is hard for us to fulfill the virtues of Justice and Religion. And because we are limited mortals, we cannot offer God the worship that is His due. Our worship of God is, itself, a gift from God. God makes it possible for us to worship Him in a way that is pleasing to Him. He gave us His Holy Church, upon whom He bestowed His own authority to determine how we, the members of the Church, worship Him and therefore order our lives properly. Christ, the God-Man, the one Mediator, the true Head of the Church, founded His Church on Peter, upon whom He bestowed the special role of exercising the highest authority in the Church in teaching and in worship. By the virtue of Religion and by our professed identity as Catholics we follow the Church's sacred liturgical rites in order to reinforce, strengthen and preserve us and our Faith as we strive in this earthly pilgrimage – strive also against the world, the flesh and the devil – to come to the joy of heaven with as many of us in tow as possible.

So, in short, if we screw up our worship, we screw up our Catholic faith and our Catholic identity. In the last decades after the Second Vatican Council, we screwed up our liturgical worship. Connect the dots.

How did this happen?

Ignoring the Council

We first got off track by not doing what the Fathers of the Second Vatican Council actually asked for.

The bishops gathered in the Council in the early 1960s mandated liturgical reform in a document called *Sacrosanctum concilium*. The document is large and sweeping, but if you read it closely, there are actually very *few* things that the Council Fathers required be done to reform our liturgical worship, which had been stable for centuries. They decided that some few things ought to be done to help people worship in a world that was rapidly changing. I repeat: *some few things*. One author who has explained well the difference between what the Council ordered and what we actually got is Fr. Joseph Fessio, SJ. Fr. Fessio has written and spoken about nine things the Council Fathers determined should be done regarding liturgical worship in "The Mass of Vatican II" (www.ignatiusinsight.com).

However, those who were tasked with implementation of the Fathers' mandates went way beyond those few things. For example, consider that the Council Fathers determined that while there could be some limited use of the spoken languages of the people, Latin was to be retained in the Latin Church. Instead, having Latin in the Mass quickly became a distant memory in most churches. Another example: Gregorian chant was to have pride of place for liturgical music. Again, chant was relegated to the bottom of the organ bench, if, in fact, the churches ever turned on the organ, what with tambourines and guitars and maracas the new instruments of choice. There was nothing in any of the Council's documents about many of the things we saw done to our church buildings, our altars, or to the rites themselves.

What resulted is that, despite the requirement of the Fathers that the nothing be changed unless it was truly for the good of the people and that changes had to come organically from previous forms, a great deal was changed that was not actually for the good of the people and there was a sharp break with continuity through the imposition of new rites composed by liturgy scholars.

Rupture of Ritual

Effectively, after the Second Vatican Council there was a rupture in ritual, of our worship of Almighty God. A selective reading of the conciliar documents by liturgists who were less inspired by what the documents actually said than by a vague and iconoclastic "spirit" of the Council led to the de-emphasis of some very important elements while other important aspects were entirely ignored. As Joseph Cardinal Ratzinger described, the liturgical reforms did not grow organically out of previous forms. Instead, they were artificial developments that grew more out of scholars at their desktops. This caused a rupture in the Church's worship that jarred many Catholics. This rupture in our worship created a "knock on effect," which continues to our day.

As we move in time away from the Second Vatican Council, as a new generation not burdened with a spirit of discontinuity begins to look at the Council more objectively, we are again seeking more connection with our traditions and seeking to clarify who we are as Catholics.

If in the 1960s and 1970s the spirit of revolution dominated, and people were perhaps a little drunk on changes, today we are sobering up on collapsing numbers within the Church and a growing measure of persecution from without. In the past few years we have been given some tools and sign posts for a revitalization of our liturgical worship, for our Catholic identity and for our role in post-Christian society.

First, the liturgical style of Benedict XVI himself inspired a different attitude toward worship. By patient example, not by imposition, he inspired a greater interest in what we have lost since the Council. He gave us the example of distribution of Holy Communion on the tongue to people who kneel. He rearranged the candles and Crucifix of the altars for his Masses to place Christ Crucified again as our common focus. This is a transitional arrangement, pointing us back to *ad orientem* worship. He fostered a shift in sacred music for papal ceremonies, integrating more of the treasury of our Latin sacred music.

While not prescriptive, Benedict's changes were deeply suggestive of a new vision for liturgical worship that is more transcendent, less self-enclosed and constricted.

Furthermore, during the pontificate of Benedict XVI, a new English translation of Roman Missal was completed. While the 2011 translation is not perfect, and no translation is, it is nevertheless a vast improvement over the translation in use since 1973. While it can be a little clunky in places, the new wording renders more accurately what the prayers in the Missal really say in the Latin. The 1973 version did not. Because of the inaccuracies, the whole Church suffered. Our faith and identity were weakened. The new translation allows Christ to speak more clearly in our prayers. This greater clarity will have an effect in the years to come, just as the old translation had its enervating effect over many years.

The true actor and the true speaker at every Mass is Christ the High Priest. His are the gestures and the words enacted and pronounced through the human agency of His ministers and through the baptized in the congregation. Holy Church acts and speaks with Christ's own hands and words. The prayers the Church gives us to pray are Christ praying. If we deviate from those words, we impose ourselves inappropriately on the rite and usurp the Church's role. Thus, it is of great importance that our translations be, in the first place, accurate. All translations deviate somewhat from the original language, but clearly some translations are good and some bad. Some convey what the prayers really say and some don't, all along a spectrum. With the new translation, we are nearer by far the accurate end of that spectrum. The style of the new translation reminds us that what we are doing in church is not our usual, secular activity. The content of the prayers, which is Christ speaking words that transform us, rings more clearly.

We Pray What We Believe

There is a reciprocal relationship between how we pray and what we believe. Change the one, and you change the other. Therefore, having a new translation is a change to our liturgical worship which is positive. It will influence belief and it follows that belief will influence our lives and culture.

Another great change and boon for our Catholic identity was the gift of Benedict XVI's *Summorum pontificum*. The 2007 motu proprio *Summorum pontificum* is a kind of "emancipation proclamation" for the use of the older, traditional, pre-Conciliar form of the Roman Rite for Mass and all the other sacraments.

In this document Benedict did not solve the historical or theological arguments about whether or not the *Novus Ordo* constituted a break in continuity. Instead, Benedict established *juridically* that the Roman Rite has two forms, "extraordinary" and "ordinary," that is, the traditional form and the newer, post-conciliar form. People can and should have access to both. They now have the right to request the older form. Priests have the right to use them without special permissions. In short, the older, traditional forms can enter more easily into the mainstream of Catholic worship and exert again their influence on our identity. The use of the older form of Holy Mass and sacraments alongside the newer forms will exert a gravitational pull on the newer forms, attracting them back into greater continuity with how Catholics prayed – and believed – for centuries.

Another advantage will be the influence that use of the older forms will have on all priests. Once younger priests learn to celebrate the Extraordinary Form of the Roman Rite, they do not celebrate the newer, *Novus Ordo,* in the same way ever after. The older forms have a different emphasis. They teach the priest things about who he is at the altar in a way that the newer forms do not. Learning the older form changes the priest's *ars celebrandi*, his "art of celebrating," as Benedict described the whole style and ethos of liturgical worship in his apostolic exhortation, *Sacramentum caritatis* (February, 2007).

As the priest's self-perception changes, as the way his saying Mass changes, a knock on effect will be produced in the congregations for whom he says Mass and to whom he preaches. The priest acts in Christ's place and Person during Holy Mass as the Head of the Body the Church, raising prayers and sacrifice to the Father. Much depends on his way of saying Mass. The use of the older forms will produce a pull, like that of gravity, which is slow but steady, thus allowing us over time to recover much of what was essential through the centuries in the shaping of a more complete and robust Catholic identity.

Our liturgical rites make a difference. Even small things have their influence. If we really believe what we say about what happens during Mass, if we really believe that the Office is the Church's official prayer, Christ the High Priest acting and praying through our words and gestures, then how can what we do, liturgically, not have a ripple effect through the whole Church (*ad intra*), through the whole world (*ad extra*)?

These two new factors which are in play, the new English translation and the growing availability of the traditional liturgical forms, will produce over time a salutary effect on our Catholic identity, especially because they will aid what the Council asked for: a greater, stronger, healthier "full, conscious, and active participation" *(SC* n.14). They will stimulate also greater interest in our traditions and our treasury of sacred music. When Latin was improperly jettisoned after the Council, contrary to what the Council required, one effect was the immense treasury of sacred music was slammed shut and locked up tight. We are again, in a sober way, taking stock of what we have lost and recovering it to our great advantage.

A new generation is coming into their moment. Younger people, younger committed Catholics who simply don't get why so much was taken away. They are not involved emotionally and in their own identities with the baggage of those halcyon days of Vatican II. They want the faith taught to them and because of their faith, they want their worship of God to be pure and sublime.

The positive process underway is slow, there will be bumps and detours and regressions, but there will be no turning back.

FR. JOHN T. ZUHLSDORF is a convert from the Lutheran religion. After obtaining degrees in theater and classical languages, he earned his STB from the Pontifical Lateran University and his STL in Patristic Theology from the Augustinianum in Rome. Ordained in 1991 by Pope John Paul II for the diocese of Velletri-Segni in Italy, Fr. Zuhlsdorf is a former collaborator in the Pontifical Commission Ecclesia Dei and has served in parishes both in Italy and the U.S. He has appeared on EWTN's *The Journey Home*, Fox News, and has written for *Sacred Music, Catholic World Report* and other periodicals. He contributes weekly to *The Catholic Herald* in England, and for over a decade wrote a column for *The Wanderer* newspaper entitled "What Does The Prayer Really Say," which was also the name of his popular and award winning internet blog (wdtprs.com) now known as Fr. Z's Blog. It has been listed as one of the ten top Christian blogs in the world. Fr. Zuhlsdorf has addressed National Wanderer Forums, gives retreats, and speaks at conferences. He currently works in Madison, Wisconsin.

The Liturgy: Our Connection With the Divine

By Cindy Paslawski

The first inkling many Catholics had of the impact of the Second Vatican Council on ordinary people came through the changing Liturgy. The documents of the Council were not readily available nor read by the people in the pews. That older generation of Catholics from the days of the Council had mostly been brought up with a mentality that "the pastor will take care of things."

In 1966, three years after the *Constitution on the Sacred Liturgy* was issued, the people at my parish received a little pamphlet containing a very correct English translation of the people parts of the Mass. It was approved by the Bishops' Commission on the Liturgical Apostolate of the United States and carried an imprimatur of Bishop Gorman of Dallas/Fort Worth. This was a most welcome change. People liked it.

Meanwhile, the new church for the parish was under construction, to be dedicated in January, 1967. When presenting the design, circular with the free-standing altar up front facing the people and seating three-fourths of the way around it, the pastor said he'd heard it was the "new way" the Council wanted churches to be built. There were questions, many didn't like the new style, but the parish council approved it because the pastor, who was in charge of church things, said it was correct.

Other changes began to show up: laymen giving out the Holy Eucharist; guitar Masses and teen Masses; using French bread for Communion and newspaper articles for Scripture at the University Newman Center; liturgical dance at the Offertory. These are things which were introduced in the 10 years after the issuance of the *Constitution on Sacred Liturgy*. Were they what the Council asked for as well?

What exactly did the Second Vatican Council say about the Mass? And now, fifty-plus years later, does it make a difference? Anyone born after the Council years has grown up with the changes – right or wrong – which were implemented. Enough so that when my grandson's Catholic school class was learning to sing the "*Ave Maria*" this year, he asked where the Latin had come from.

Vatican II's *Constitution on the Sacred Liturgy* was released on December 5, 1963. It is relatively short, only seven chapters, covering topics from the nature of the Liturgy and the Mystery of the Eucharist to sacraments, sacramentals, the Divine Office, the liturgical year, sacred music and art, and furnishings. Regarding the Liturgy, the Council stated:

In the earthly liturgy, we take part in a foretaste of that heavenly liturgy which is celebrated in the Holy City of Jerusalem toward which we journey as pilgrims, where Christ is sitting at the right hand of God, Minister of the holies and of the true tabernacle. With all the warriors of the heavenly army we sing a hymn of glory to the Lord; venerating the memory of the saints, we hope for some part and fellowship with them; we eagerly await the Savior, Our Lord Jesus Christ, until He, our Life, shall appear and we too will appear with Him in glory (*SC*, n.8).[1]

This is very traditional, almost sublime. Considering the Liturgy, our public worship, connects us with the divine, these words prepare the mind to step into a sacred place. Later on the document stated:

In order that the Christian people may more certainly derive an abundance of graces from the sacred liturgy, Holy Mother Church desires to undertake with great care a general restoration of the liturgy itself. For the liturgy is made up of unchangeable elements divinely instituted and of elements subject to change. These latter not only may be changed but ought to be changed with the passage of time, if they have suffered from the intrusion of anything out of harmony with the inner nature of the liturgy or have become less suitable. In this restoration both texts and rites should be drawn up so as to express more clearly the holy things which they signify (*SC*, n.21).

Thus it is pointed out,

Regulation of the sacred liturgy depends solely on the authority of the Church, that is on the Apostolic See, and, as laws may determine, on the bishop (*SC*, n. 22.1). In virtue of power conceded by law, the regulation of the liturgy within certain defined limits belongs also to various kinds of bishops' conferences, legitimately established, with competence in given territories (*SC*, n.22.2). No other person, not even a priest, may add, remove, or change anything in the liturgy on his own authority (*SC*, n.22.3).

...There must be no innovations unless the good of the Church genuinely and certainly requires them, and care must be taken that any new forms adopted should in some way grow organically from forms already existing (*SC*, n.23).

The next paragraph calls for more use of the Sacred Scripture (*SC*, n.24) and further on, "a more ample, more varied, and more suitable reading from Sacred Scripture should be restored" (*SC*, n.35.1). Of particular interest is a section on language at Mass:

The use of the Latin language, with due respect to particular law, is to be preserved in the Latin rites (*SC*, n.36.1).

But since the use of the vernacular, whether in the Mass, the administration of the sacraments, or in other parts of the liturgy, may frequently be of great advantage to the people, a wider use may be made of it, especially in readings, directives, and in some prayers and chants (*SC*, n.36.2).

The third sentence, however, holds the key to the changes that occurred over the next several years:

These norms being observed, it is for the competent territorial ecclesiastical authority mentioned in Article 22.2 to decide whether, and to what extent, the vernacular language is to be used. Its decrees have to be approved, that is, confirmed, by the Apostolic See. Where circumstances warrant it, it is to consult with bishops of neighboring regions which have the same language (*SC*, n.36.3).

Translations from the Latin for use in the liturgy must be approved by the competent territorial ecclesiastical authority already mentioned (*SC*, n. 36.4).

Substitute the words *music, art, buildings, liturgy* for *vernacular language* in the paragraph above citing Article 22.2 in the *Constitution* and you can see a large loophole in the Vatican Council document. This is the first reference of many in various liturgical documents to "Article 22.2" giving power to bishops' conferences. And the bishops' conferences acted on this power. Instructed to appoint commissions (*SC*, n.44, n.46) for all of the areas listed above, they did so, of course using the "experts" who were at the Council and who seemed so knowledgeable.

Here is a synopsis of the actual decrees from the *Constitution on the Sacred Liturgy*:

- The rite of the Mass was to be revised in such a way that the nature and purpose of its parts would be highlighted. It was thought that such a revision would assist "devout and active participation by the faithful." Rites were to be simplified, due care being taken to preserve their substance. Parts which were duplicated, or of little benefit would be omitted and parts lost would be reinstated (*SC*, n.50).
- More Scripture was to be used over year-long cycles (*SC*, n.51).
- The mysteries of the faith and principles of Christian life were to be taught in the homilies (*SC*, n.52).
- The "prayers of the faithful" were to be restored (*SC*, n.53).
- Vernacular could be allowed in readings and common prayers in the people parts. Article 36 of the *Constitution* gives the situations for this. However, it was mentioned the faithful should be able to say or sing in Latin (*SC*, n.54). Article 40 is cited for locations, *especially in mission lands*, where greater adaptation of the liturgy in the vernacular is needed. Article 40 refers back to territorial ecclesiastical authority (Article 22.2!) for consideration of which local traditions might be admitted to worship.
- Reception of the Lord's Body should be from the Species consecrated at the same Mass (*SC*, n.55).
- The two parts of the Mass, the Liturgy of the Word and the Eucharistic Liturgy are "but one single act of worship" (*SC*, n.56).
- Concelebration of the Mass is discussed in paragraphs 57 and 58.

Regarding music, art, and churches, the *Constitution* said

> The musical tradition of the universal Church is a treasure of inestimable value, greater even than that of any other art. The main reason for this preeminence is that, as a combination of sacred music and words, it forms a necessary or integral part of the solemn liturgy (*SC*, n.112).

> The treasury of sacred music is to be preserved and cultivated with great care... and...pastors of souls must take great care to ensure that whenever the sacred action is to be accompanied by chant, the whole body of the faithful may be able to contribute that active participation which is rightly theirs...(*SC*, n.114).

It went on:

- The church recognizes Gregorian chant as being specially suited to the Roman liturgy (*SC*, n.116).
- Religious singing by the faithful is to be fostered (*SC*, n.118).
- A suitable place should be given to local musical traditions in mission lands (*SC*, n.119).
- The pipe organ is to be held in high esteem in the Latin Church... but other instruments also may be admitted for use in divine worship, in the judgment and with the consent of the competent territorial authority [Article 22.2 again!] (*SC*, n.120).

Regarding sacred art and furnishings:

- In the course of centuries [the Church] has brought into existence a treasury of art which must be preserved with every care (*SC*, n.123).
- The practice of placing sacred images in churches so that they be venerated by the faithful is to be maintained (*SC*, n.125).

That is all the *Constitution on the Sacred Liturgy* from the Second Vatican Council decreed. It also called for revision of rites for various sacraments to make their meaning more clear, and after the *Constitution* was promulgated, Pope Paul wrote a few clarifying documents, two of note: In his *Motu Proprio on Sacred Liturgy, Sacram liturgiam* (January 25, 1964), Pope Paul VI announced the creation of the Consilium for the Implementation of the *Constitution on the Sacred Liturgy* to fill in the working details of the *Constitution* with Archbishop Annibale Bugnini as secretary. In that document the Holy Father also noted that his use of the word "territorial" regarding episcopal conferences meant at that time "national" conferences of bishops. Pope Paul also wrote the *Apostolic Constitution on the Roman Missal* (April 9, 1969) on the Mass and its rubrics.

However over the next ten years after the *Constitution* was written, until 1974, there followed several instructions, decrees, and declarations, nearly 120 of them[2] issued by the Sacred Congregation for Rites, the Consilium for the Implementation of the Constitution on the Sacred Liturgy, and the Congregation for Divine Worship, which was created in 1969 and used members of the Consilium to continue the reform of the Liturgy.[3] These instructions tweaked, fine tuned, and tweaked some more, referenced their own documents in covering everything from administering Communion in hospitals to church building decisions, group Masses, reception of Communion, and Children's Masses. Sometimes, by the time the later documents were issued, what was written by the Council in the *Constitution* was watered down or negated. A few examples will suffice.

Music

Chapter 6 of the *Constitution* speaks of the "treasury of sacred music" (*SC*, n.114), polyphony and Gregorian chant's pride of place (*SC*, n.116), the encouragement of the faithful to sing (*SC*, n.118), the pipe organ and a general statement about other instruments which can be used during worship (*SC*, n.120), and composers (*SC*, n.121).

In 1967, the Sacred Congregation for Rites issued the *Instruction on Music in the Liturgy*. It defined sacred music as Gregorian chant, sacred polyphony, music for the organ, and sacred popular music. It called for the format of the celebration and degree of participation to be varied as much as possible (*IML*, n.10); singing of the entire Mass by the choir was not recommended (*IML*, n.15c); use of vernacular and how much of it in the Mass was left to the territorial ecclesiastical authority (Article 22.2 again!) to decide (*IML*, n.47); ecclesiastical authority would also decide if vernacular texts from the past could be used (*IML*, n.55); other instruments to be permitted, with an exclusion for instruments of secular use.

By the *Third Instruction on the Correct Implementation of the Constitution on the Sacred Liturgy* by the Sacred Congregation for Divine Worship (1970), things had changed:

> All means must be used to promote singing by the people. New forms of music suited to different mentalities and to modern tastes should also be approved by the episcopal conference. The conference should indicate selections of hymns to be used in Masses for special groups, e.g. for young people or children; the words, melody and rhythm of these songs, and the instruments used for their accompaniment, should correspond with the sacred character of the Mass and the place of worship.
>
> Though the Church does not exclude any kind of sacred music from the liturgy, not every type of music, song, or instrument is equally capable of stimulating prayer or expressing the mystery of Christ. ... Episcopal conferences will determine more particular guidelines for liturgical music, or, if these do not obtain, local bishops may issue norms for their own dioceses. Great care should be given to

the choice of musical instruments; these should be few in number, suited to the place and the congregation, should favor prayer and not be too loud (*TICI*,n.3,c).

Not only was chant absent by this time, but Latin hymns had almost completely disappeared as well as traditional English hymns in favor of more folksy tunes with guitar accompaniment, which my convert father would call Hootenanny[4] Masses. "Bring on the chips and beer," he'd say after attending a "contemporary" Mass.

Buildings

Another example: In 1964, the *Instruction on the Proper Implementation of the Constitution on the Sacred Liturgy*, September 26, 1964, by the Sacred Congregation for Rites started laying the groundwork for the renewal of the liturgy. The document, approved by Pope Paul VI, covered liturgical commissions, liturgical formation of the spiritual life of clergy, the vernacular. Chapter 5 discussed designing churches and altars to facilitate active participation of the people. Erik Bootsma has aptly described what the Council wanted and what we people received in his chapter, "The Cult of the Ugly and Vatican II" in this volume.

By the time the *Instruction on the Worship of the Eucharistic Mystery* came along (May 25,1967), things had changed a bit:

> The place in a church or oratory where the Blessed Sacrament is reserved in the tabernacle should be truly prominent. It ought to be suitable for private prayer so that the faithful may easily and fruitfully, by private devotion also, continue to honor our Lord in this sacrament. It is therefore recommended that, as far as possible, the tabernacle be placed in a chapel distinct from the middle or central part of the church (*IWEM*, n.53).

How – within the same paragraph – did "truly prominent" in church become a "chapel distinct from the middle or central part of the church"?

Many parishes removed the tabernacle from the altar to a side altar; others to a back room "chapel" that was hardly prominent. Most prominent is in or very near the sanctuary so that the Real Presence is associated with the Mass, not off to the side. In one church, the tabernacle was off to the side and hung from the ceiling. While awaiting the baptism of a new niece, my children and I toured the church. My son saw the dangling tabernacle and threw his arms around it. "An amplifier!" After a quick look around and seeing kneelers two inches from the golden receptacle, I realized it was the tabernacle and pried him away from it.

Receiving the Body of Christ

This *Instruction on the Worship of the Eucharistic Mystery* also discusses the way of receiving communion,

> "...communion may be received by the faithful either kneeling or standing. One or the other way is to be chosen, according to the decision of the Episcopal Conferences, bearing in mind all the circumstances, above all the number of the faithful and the arrangement of the churches. The faithful should willingly adopt the method indicated by their pastors so that communion may truly be a sign of the brotherly union of all those who share in the same table of the Lord." (*IWEM*, n.34)

Once again, this appears to be the decision of the episcopal conferences (yet again, *SC* n.22.2). Kneeling was rarely seen and in fact in some places kneeling communicants were criticized in front of the congregation! One diocese in the state of Virginia went so far as to forbid kneeling to receive Holy Communion in all circumstances as late as 2002-2003.[5]

In the *Instruction on the Manner of Distributing Holy Communion* (May 29, 1969), by the Sacred Congregation for Divine Worship, Communion in the hand was discussed and the process of voting on it in some episcopal conferences was recorded. The Holy Father decided not to allow the practice.[6] But a few years later, the *Instruction on Facilitating Sacramental Eucharistic Communion in Particular Circumstances* (January 1973), indicated that the faithful should be instructed on proper reception and piety when receiving Communion in the hand. That document also stated that the local ordinary could permit suitable people to be appointed as Eucharistic Ministers of the Eucharist, if the congregation is too large, the priest incapacitated, for giving Communion to the sick, and other situations. The priest could also be designated by the Ordinary to appoint Eucharistic Ministers (*IFSE*, n.1)

Many people were unhappy over laymen becoming Extraordinary Ministers of the Holy Eucharist. Generations prior to Vatican II were taught not to touch the Sacred Species or even the sacred vessels. How could an unconsecrated person touch the Host? And then there arose the question of who would be worthy to do so. Several people could be seen at Masses crossing over to the priest's Communion line to avoid the Extraordinary Minister. At our parish, the trustees and other committee heads were appointed. But my father, who worked with many of them on church projects took particular issue with Mr. O. "What's he doing touching the Host. He's not worthy. I'm never going to have him give me Communion."

As luck would have it, Mr. O was the Extraordinary Minister for our side of the church that Sunday. We crawled over my dad's feet as we got in line. To my surprise, he hesitated and came out of the pew behind me.

"I thought you wouldn't receive Communion from Mr. O, Dad," I said. "I decided I wasn't going to hell because of him." It was a compromise, one of many we all made with Vatican II.

Back when the topics of Communion in the hand and standing for Communion were initiated, the faithful were told it was befitting their dignity to receive the Holy Eucharist in these ways. An adult feeds himself; receiving Communion on the tongue was being fed. The whole concept of reverence was left out of the conversation on standing for Communion, and the words of Indiana Jones – "the penitent man is humble before God, penitent man is humble...*kneels* before God"[7] – ignored.

Reforming the Reform

It is interesting to note that before not too many years went by, a few corrections needed to be made. On April 27, 1973, the Sacred Congregation for Divine Worship issued a *Circular Letter on the Eucharistic Prayers*. It seems that although Pope Paul VI's revision of the *Missal* had a wider choice of texts for scripture, chant, prayers, acclamations and even four Eucharistic prayers instead of one, some priests, in many countries, began composing and using their own Eucharistic prayers. Permission was asked by the episcopal conferences to allow this deviance. The Holy Father turned down the request.[8]

On May 24, 1973, the Sacred Congregation for the Clergy and the Sacred Congregation for the Discipline of the Sacraments issued the *Declaration on First Confession and First Communion*, requiring the practice of First Confession before First Communion. For 2 years there had been experimentation on having First Communion before Penance until children were a few years older than age 7, but at this point, all were urged to follow Pope St. Pius X's decree *Quam singulari* (1910).[9] The reason given for the deviation in the first place was that young children could not commit mortal sin and thus need not confess. Age 9 or 10 was thought more suitable. No mention of the need for grace. Even as late as 2001, Confession before Communion was still being challenged. "We follow the Bishops Conference in this country, not the Vatican," a sacramental coordinator was heard to say when corrected on the proper order of First Penance and First Communion.[10]

According to the *Letter to Bishops on the Minimum Repertoire of Plain Chant*, (April 14, 1974), the Sacred Congregation for Divine Worship created a booklet, *Jubilate Deo*, which contained a selection of sacred chants the Holy Father wanted sent to every diocese. The Pope had asked again and again that the faithful should know some Latin Gregorian chants. While stating "liturgical reform has opened up new perspectives for sacred music and for change," nonetheless, "liturgical reform does not and indeed cannot deny the past." It should "preserve and foster it with the greatest care."[11] That letter also contained the following:

> "In presenting the Holy Father's gift to you, may I at the same time remind you of the desire which he has often expressed that the Conciliar *Constitution on the Liturgy* be increasingly better implemented."[12]

In other words, the reform was beginning to need reform. The words of the Council had been morphed into a whirlwind of exceptions, with episcopal conferences (territorial ecclesiastical authorities) requesting change after change to the original decrees, until there was no way for the people in the pews to tell what beneficial changes the Council had asked for versus what was reformed using the Council as an excuse.

And then there was the translation of the Sacred Liturgy into the vernacular.

Translation

"You mean the Mass was in a different language?" the young woman asked. She had never heard of such a thing, but, at age 25, how could she? When she said this, it had been almost 40 years since the *Constitution on the Liturgy* had been issued by the Second Vatican Council and "the use of the Latin language...is to be preserved in the Latin Rite (*SC* n.36.1) was gone with the wind.

Please understand, those who attended Mass pre-Vatican II were not sitting in the pews speechless. There were *Sunday Missals* and *Daily Missals* – most popular being the St. Andrew or St. Joseph versions – which had the Latin and an excellent English translation side by side. People knew what the priest was saying and understood what they responded to his words.

The updating and shortening of the prayers of the Mass in the *Novus Ordo* (New Order) of the Mass required a new translation. In 1963, the bishops representing 10 (later 11) English speaking conferences began planning for the International Commission on English in the Liturgy (ICEL) which would be charged with making English texts from the *Novus Ordo* of the Mass. The translated texts would be presented to respective bishops' conferences for approval and then sent to Rome for final approval.

In 1964, experts, lay people and priests were invited to be members of an oversight advisory committee: liturgists, classical scholars, patrologists, English scholars, musicians, and biblical scholars.[13] Commentary was invited on the first samples of translation in 1966 and 1967 from "all who are interested in the liturgy, not only Roman Catholics, but also members of other Christian bodies."[14]

The translations gained a life of their own under ICEL. While *SC*, n.23 spoke of "no innovations unless the good of the Church genuinely and certainly requires them, and care must be taken that any new forms adopted should in some way grow organically from forms already existing," others had a different idea.

Anscar J. Chupungco, OSB, former president of the Pontifical Liturgical Institute in Rome, pointed out: "Fidelity to the original refers to the content or meaning of the text, not to the form or component words and phrases. That is why a word-for-word translation is not a guarantee of fidelity to the text" (Newsletter of the Federation of Diocesan Liturgical Commissions, December 1994).[15]

It may be an apocryphal explanation, but the reason given at the time was the early translators felt Americans did not, could not, understand the Mass if properly translated to English. We could not understand some of the words because we don't use them. In the eyes of the scholars then, the translation had to be as simple as possible and in some places these scholars made up a freestyle translation, a "dynamic equivalence" by detaching the content from the original form.[16]

Is that why the opening *"Credo"* (I believe) in the Nicene Creed became "We believe"? Not to mention *we* is a community word people can hide behind and *I believe* shifts responsibility directly to the person standing there and professing it.

Or consider the traditional response to the *Dominus vobiscum* (The Lord be with you) which became "And also with you" even though the Latin still said "*Et cum spiritu tuo*" (And with your spirit). The spirit got left out of that translation and years into it, "And also with you" became as meaningful as the automatic "Have a nice day," "You, too" dialogue.

At some time during these years, the gender neutral movement entered the picture, claiming God could be a he or a she. In the Creed, people hissed (some still do) through "for us men (meaning all mankind) and our salvation" with a unique "for ussssss and our salvation."

Several references to God as *He* were slowly deleted from hymns, which accounts for the clumsiness of the some of the songs which repeated "God" over and over when "He" was more appropriate. For example, Psalm 34 (#47 in the *Gather* book[17]):

verse 1, line 1: I will bless the Lord at all times, God's praise ever in my mouth.

verse 2, line 2: Glory in the Lord with me, let us together extol God's name.

But the *New American Bible*[18] renders it:

34:2, line 1: I will bless the Lord at all times, his praise shall be ever in my mouth.

34:4, line 1: Glorify the Lord with me, let us together extol his name.

The most controversial translation came in the actual words of consecration, the words of Jesus Christ. In the consecration of the wine, Christ said, "This is the chalice of My blood which will be given up for you and for many for the forgiveness of sins." The word *multis* was present in the Latin and is translated *many*. But the *Novus Ordo* translation was rendered "This is the chalice of My blood which will be given up for you and for all for the forgiveness of sins." There is a difference between the words *many* and *all*, *multis* and *omnis*, theologically speaking.

The ink was hardly dry on the early translation before people began to complain that it wasn't accurate, that it affected the meaning of the Mass and its validity. Change for the sake of change was the frequent charge against the 1969 translation. And many people left the Church, which holds the means to salvation in her sacraments, because of it.

When Pope John Paul II came to office in 1978, he came as one intimately connected with the Second Vatican Council and the meaning of the *Constitution on the Liturgy* which called for renewal. He travelled widely, he had been to our country more than once; he saw and heard the Mass as it had been given to us by our leaders. It wasn't as if in 2001 he got up one day and decided to order a new translation. He recognized the loss of language, the loss of faith, and began in various writings years ahead of time to set the stage for a change back to authentic texts, a reform of the reform, so to speak. The Congregation for Divine Worship and the Discipline of the Sacraments undertook the writing of a document mandating changes to the translation of the Mass in use. In February of 2001, Pope John Paul II approved the document, *Liturgiam authenticam* by the Congregation. Early in that document, written by Jorge Cardinal Medina Estevez, it says:

> It has been noted that translations of liturgical texts in various localities stand in need of improvement through correction or through a new draft. The omissions or errors which affect certain existing vernacular translations – especially in the case of certain languages – have impeded the progress of the inculturation[19] that should have taken place. Consequently, the Church has been prevented from laying the foundation for a fuller, healthier and more authentic renewal.
>
> For these reasons, it now seems necessary to set forth anew, and in light of the maturing of experience, the principles of translation to be followed in future translations – whether they be entirely new undertakings or emendations of texts already in use – and to specify more clearly certain norms that have already been published, taking into account a number of questions and circumstances that have arisen in our own day" (*LA*, n.6-7).[20]

A more interesting question to ask is why it took until 2011 to effect the changes asked for. The countries were given 5 years to come back with the new translations, to come back with musical settings for the parts to be sung. And for the added 5 years? Translation drafts went between the Vatican and various bishops' conferences (Article 22.2 again!) in an effort to get the correct words. Back and forth, back and forth.

The Vatican Council had called for renewal and many people, priests and religious included, adopted the do-your-own-thing mantra. Teaching the Mass and its history and meaning had no place in this venue where we gathered around the table with the presider for the meal instead of attending the Sacrifice of Calvary reenacted. How many children learned that in the Mass Jesus offers Himself to the Father through the action of the priest?

As a result, an entire generation lost the concept of Mass as something special, a holy experience, not just something you do on Sunday morning or Saturday night if more convenient. A generation lost the language of the Church, the church words that were different enough that they meant something special in the Mass: "beseech," "glorify," "holy," "soul" come to mind. The word "host" in the *Sanctus*, as in "Lord God of hosts," means God commands an army. That's a different idea of God from the benevolent, noninterventionist old man in many people's minds.

What We Believe

As James May writes in *The Wanderer Forum* magazine,[21] "What we habitually pray must reflect correctly and clearly what we believe, for the more we hear or recite a text, the more it becomes part of us interiorly." For example, there are continuous references to the Body of Christ as bread, just bread, blessed bread. The hymns at Mass have contributed to this problem. If you say bread over and over, that's what becomes ingrained in the mind, and belief in the fact that Jesus Christ is present under the ap*pearance* of mere bread slowly disappears.

The discussions about *Liturgiam authenticam* centered upon correct translation. Some insisted prayer should be the way we ordinarily talk to people.[22] Others felt that the words we pray have meaning. If that meaning is lost, the faith could be lost.

In 2002, Susan Reilly, the U.S. delegate to the International Center for Liturgical Studies (CIEL) noted a survey at the time which showed that only 30 percent of Catholic Americans believed in the Real Presence of Christ in the Eucharist. The survey showed a much lower percentage of belief in the Real Presence for those under 40, meaning those who grew up since Vatican II. "Most people attend the *Novus Ordo*, so it's important," she said, that the translation be accurate.[23] Can anyone say that the percentages have reversed in the ensuing years?

What did the Second Vatican Council say about the Liturgy? Does it matter?

Indeed, it matters what Vatican II said. Our Liturgy, our worship of God today is the means of our salvation. It is in line with what the Council requested to reach out in modern times: simplicity of meaning, plentiful Scripture and Psalms for meditation, prayers of the faithful, the Offering, Consecration and Communion with the Divine Host of the eternal banquet. The actions are more visible, the language is more precise and uplifting. Changes were made so many years ago to effect the holiest of changes in us today.

ENDNOTES

1. All document quotes in this chapter are from Austin Flannery, O.P., editor, *Vatican Council II, Vol. I, The Conciliar and Post-Conciliar Documents* (Costello Publishing Company, Northport, NY., 1996).

2. Flannery, Appendix, p.38

3. *Ibid.,* Footnote b, p.42.

4. Hootenanny was a word to describe a gathering of guitar strumming, tambourine banging folk singers popular in the 1960s and war protest days. There was also a television series by that name (www.google.com).

5. Events described occurred during the National Wanderer Forum in 2002 or 2003, in Sterling, Virginia. Of course the Forum provided a *prie dieux* for reception of Communion by participants.

6. Flannery, p.151.

7. *Indiana Jones and the Last Crusade*, film, 1989.

8. Flannery, p. 233-235. *Circular Letter on Eucharistic Prayers.*

9. Flannery, p. 241. *Sanctus pontifex.*

10. This comment was made to me after an instruction on First Penance and Eucharist by this coordinator.

11. Flannery, p. 273-275. *Voluntati obsequens.*

12. *Ibid.,* p. 275.

13. International Commission on English in Liturgy (ICEL), *New Catholic Encyclopedia,* 2003. http://encyclopedia.com/religion/encyclopedias-almanacs-transcripts-and-maps/interenational-commission-english-liturgy-icel.

14. *Ibid.*

15. Most Rev. Donald Trautman, "Rome and ICEL," *America,* March 4, 2000.

16. Most Rev. Arthur Roche, in address to the Canadian Conference of Catholic Bishops, September, 2014, as quoted in "Pope Francis Has Ordered a Review of the New Mass Translation Rules," Gerard O'Connell, *America,* January 26, 2017. https://www.americamagazine.org/faith/2017/01/26/pope-francis-has-ordered-review-new-mass-translation-rules.

17. *Gather Comprehensive* (GIA Publications. Chicago, IL 1994).

18. *New American Bible* (Catholic Book Publishing, New York, NY 1970). Confraternity of Christian Doctrine (Washington, DC 1970).

19. Inculturation means that the Liturgy and Catholic practice influence and reform society. Many of a progressive bent take it to mean society influencing and reforming the Church.

20.   *Liturgiam authenticam, On the Use of Vernacular Languages in the Publication of the Books of the Roman Liturgy.* 2001. http://www.vatican.va/roman_curia/congregations/ccdds/documents/rc_con_ccdds_doc_2 0010507_liturgiam-authenticam_en.html.

21.   Dr. James May, "Basic Principles of Translation and the Art of Compromise," *Bellarmine Forum* (Bellarmine Forum, Hudson, WI   2011).

22.   Most Rev. Donald Trautman quoted in "Lost in Translation," John Burger, *Crisis* (Morley Institute, Washington, DC 2002). https://www.catholicculture.org/library/view.cfm?recnum=4264.

23.   Susan Reilly quoted in "Lost in Translation," John Burger, *Crisis* (Morley Institute, Washington, DC 2002). https://www.catholicculture.org/library/view.cfm?recnum=4264.

CINDY PASLAWSKI holds a B.A. in Journalism from the University of Minnesota. She has been active with the Wanderer Forum Foundation almost since its inception, while working as a reporter for *The Wanderer* newspaper and then as Secretary of the Foundation since 1995. She has also worked on the front lines as a church secretary and most recently as a freelance book editor. As the Wanderer Forum Foundation/Bellarmine Forum's executive secretary and publication editor, she has overseen production of the *Forum Focus* and the *Bellarmine Forum* magazines, and publication of both *Saving Christian Marriage* (2007) and *Slaying the "Spirit" of Vatican II With the Light of Truth* (2017). From 2001-2004, she coordinated all regional and national forums and Focus on Faith retreats. She and her husband have six grown children.

The Cult of the Ugly and Vatican II
By Erik Bootsma

Since the close of the Second Vatican Council, the Catholic Church has seen a revolution in sacred architecture. In parish after parish, the refrain was the same, the reforms of Vatican II "required" that every church be renovated for the new Mass. Churches that people loved and cherished were all given over to radical transformation. Altars were removed and replaced with "communion tables"; statues of saints were tucked away into the basement or tossed into the trash; and beautiful painted ceilings and walls, filled with symbolism and devotional images, were whitewashed. Altar rails were torn out as a relic of the dusty old days of clericalism and the tabernacle, supposedly a sign of superstition, was tucked away into a corner.

What happened during Vatican II that made our church architecture so terrible? The common belief about Vatican II holds to the following narrative. In the 1950s, the Catholic Church was in its prime, and, while far from a golden age like the Renaissance in terms of art and liturgy, people in general found beautiful, solemn and sacred art in their churches. Whether in the smallest of parishes or a great cathedral, the Church still was the patron of beauty in art. Then, in 1962, the Second Vatican Council was called and suddenly instituted sweeping changes to the Mass, and mandated a sea change in the styles and forms of architecture and art.

Since all of this was done by pastors, priests, and bishops in the name of Vatican II, it is easy to understand how people began to believe that the Council was to blame for the destruction of beauty in their churches. But this conclusion, though it may seem to be consistent with both what people really saw at the time and what the liturgical and architectural experts said, happens to be almost entirely false.

In fact, there was not a single decree of Vatican II that mandated any of the many travesties visited upon so many historic and beautiful works of architecture. Instead, the occasion of the Council, through its desire to be general rather than specific and leaning toward a tendency to be vague, offered the liturgical and architectural agendas already at work in the Church an opportunity to push for aggressive modernist forms of architecture.

The "Mandates" of Vatican II

Studying the documents of Vatican II, particularly *Sacrosanctum concilium*, the *Constitution on the Sacred Liturgy*, one begins to discover that the Council as a whole was a much more conservative event than most believe. In every example where change is called for, it is only in a general sense, and always with a note of caution that changes should be made only where the Church "genuinely and certainly requires them."[1] Concerning sacred art and architecture itself, very little is actually said, but for a small section of *Sacrosanctum concilium*. There, the Council contents itself to make only general recommendations and not a trace of the mandates commonly thought to exist, such as calls for ripping out altar rails, centralized churches in the round, Jacuzzi style baptismal fonts etc., are present in any way.

Instead, the directives are for the most part general, such as the direction to revise "the canons and ecclesiastical statutes which govern the provision of material things involved in sacred worship,"[2] the only direction that is given is to bring things "into harmony" with the reformed liturgy and "active participation," leaving only a vague notion what those changes should be. Looking at these general principles in *Sacrosanctum concilium* raises the question of whether or not they in any way justified the litany of abuses visited upon our venerable old churches.

General Principles of Art in Sacrosanctum Concilium

Chapter VII of *Sacrosanctum concilium* lays down the "ground rules" for the necessary reforms of sacred art. First, the Council notes that sacred arts are those which are "oriented toward the infinite beauty of God" and works of art that are to be used for worship should "always be *worthy, becoming and beautiful, [as] signs and symbols of the supernatural world*"[3] (emphasis added). This principle of *sacredness* and divinity, above all others, is to inform and guide any reforms – a point reiterated throughout the text.

The Council then notes that the Church "has admitted styles from every period" and called for "the art of our own days" to be given "free scope in the Church."[4] This second principle holds that there exists worthy and honorable new forms of art that ought to be embraced, with the caveat "*provided* that it adorns the sacred buildings and holy rites with due reverence and honor."[5] The Council does not mean that *all* new art is good, but only that which is good and worthy of reverence and honor. Thus, modern art and architecture is allowed by the Council, but *only* if it adheres to the first principle of sacredness and divinity.

Nothing, though, in this statement implies that *only* modern art is allowed in the church, or that old art should be removed – in fact, quite the opposite. In allowing for "art of our own days" each era can take part in the tradition of the Church and "contribute its own voice to that wonderful *chorus* of praise in honor of the Catholic faith sung by great men in times gone by."[6] The metaphor of the chorus is apt, implying that modern art can be just one voice of many singing the praises of God. If modern art was to be the *only* form of art, to the exclusion of other styles, it would be akin to a single voice trying to take over a choir, and silencing the voices of all others.

Indeed, the Council certainly believed this, as it reminds us of the need to *preserve* as much as add to sacred art, stating that the Church holds a "treasure of art which *must* be very carefully preserved,"[7] and that clerics should "be able to appreciate and preserve the Church's venerable monuments." So rather than mandating that churches be stripped bare of art and ornament and beauty, to look like Protestant churches, the Council expressly forbade it. Though the Council allows bishops to remove those works of art "repugnant to faith, morals and Christian piety," it does so only with a note to do this "carefully."

But, if it did not call for a radical new approach to sacred architecture and art, why was it that before Vatican II we can see beauty and solemnity in sacred architecture, and afterwards only banality and ugliness? Perhaps it would be good then to go just slightly further back in time to look at the state of sacred architecture prior to Vatican II.

Back in Time

In an article in the journal *Sacred Architecture,* titled "Don't Blame Vatican II,"[8] Professor Randall Smith argues that much of the architectural havoc that was unleashed on the Church, particularly in America, began "decades before Vatican II." Examining a popular book called *Speaking of Liturgical Architecture,* published in 1952 by Fr. H.A. Reinhold, professor of Liturgy at the University of Notre Dame, Smith argues as early as the 1950s, Fr. Reinhold and other liturgists began to embrace a doctrine of *liturgical functionalism*, which becomes "a means of forcing all churches to conform themselves to a fundamental principle of modernist design."

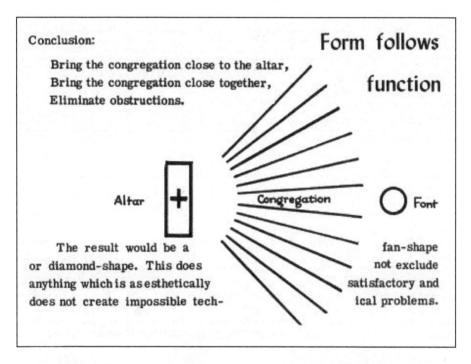

Form follows function is a principle of functionalist modern architecture, not of sacred art. *Speaking of Liturgical Architecture*, Fr. H.A. Reinhold, 1952, as quoted in "Don't Blame Vatican II," Randall Smith, *Sacred Architecture*, Vol. 13, 2007.

One illustration from Fr. Reinhold's book is enlightening. Foretelling buzzwords of contemporary "liturgical design consultants" of today, Fr. Reinhold states, "Bring the congregation close to the altar, Bring the congregation close together, Eliminate obstructions." Even in the 1950s, the end result looked for was clearly "a fan-shaped church." Emblazoned in bold over this illustration, the phrase "Form Follows Function," reveals the true source of Fr. Reinhold's theories, modernist architectural theory. First coined by Louis Sullivan, the mantra, *"form follows function"* became, for modernists, the rationale for stripping architectural decoration and ornament from buildings, leaving only what was "useful."

Looking back further we can see that this functionalist architecture had infiltrated church architecture even earlier than this. From its earliest days, this new modern utilitarian architecture was not just limited to secular architecture, but had its adherents among Catholic architects as well. One particularly prolific architect working in this ideology was Rudolph Schwarz, who designed almost two dozen Catholic churches in Germany, most of which were completed well before Vatican II. One which continues to be praised in modernist textbooks is the parish church of St. Fronleichnam in Aachen. Built in 1930, the church exhibits *par excellence* the sort of whitewashed purity that functionalist architects and liturgists praised.

St. Fronleichnamskirche in Aachen represented the modernist ideal of a church stripped of ornament, symbol and even color. Credit: Norbert Schnitzler, https://commons.wikimedia.org/wiki/File:Aachen-Fronleichnamskirche_Innenraum.jpg

While Schwarz was an early adherent of modernism in Catholic architecture, he was hardly alone. Amongst the most famous modernist churches, LeCorbusier's pilgrimage church of Notre Dame du Haut in Ronchamp was built in 1955 and the Cathedral of Brasilia, designed by atheist and communist Oscar Niemeyer was built in 1958.[9] From Schwarz to Niemeyer, every one of these icons of modernist church architecture was built well before Vatican II.[10]

Built by an atheist and communist modern architect, the Cathedral of Brasilia was as radical as anything found after Vatican II, yet was built in 1958. Credit: B. Gabel, https://commons.wikimedia.org

St. John's Abbey, Collegeville, Minnesota. Credit: Richard Anderson. Used with permission. https://www.flickr.com/photos/32224170@N03/5931443472/in/album-72157627180212948/

Most influential, though, was the Abbey Church at St. John's University in Collegeville, Minnesota, begun by architect Marcel Breuer in 1954. This church was built when the university was the epicenter of a group called the Liturgical Conference, which was massively influential in pushing radical reforms of the liturgy. The Conference, made up of both Catholic priests (including the aforementioned Fr. Reinhold) as well as Lutherans, also pushed for radical reforms in church architecture. Profoundly influenced by modernist architecture, they shaped the form of the Abbey Church and pushed for experimental forms of architecture to symbolize radical notions of the liturgy.

Because of the influence of the Liturgical Conference as well as the dominance in the public mind of modernist architecture, modernist churches were not just limited to commissions from the "starchitects" in the pre-Vatican II era. So pushed by the tides of radical liturgy and architecture, local architects were working almost exclusively in the new functionalist style throughout the postwar years. Indeed one need not look hard, especially in areas that saw expansion in the 1940s and '50s, to find dozens upon dozens of churches in the modernist style, even ones fully in the round.

The Hermeneutics of Rupture

So now, coming back to 1962, to the opening of Vatican II, we find that the state of ecclesiastical architecture was not quite what our common notions had led us to believe. Far from a state of perfection in which the arts were flourishing and creating great and beautiful churches, architecture in the church was defined both by radical pet theories of liturgy, and a barren utilitarianism already seen as part of the culture of Catholicism. As the late Avery Cardinal Dulles noted in an article for the Jesuit magazine, *America*, in 2003,

> The Council occurred at a unique moment of history, when the Western world was swept up in a wave of optimism typified by Pope John XXIII himself. The "new humanism" was confident that if free play were given to human powers and technology, the scourges of poverty, disease, famine and war could be virtually eliminated.... Secular enthusiasts interpreted Vatican II as an invitation for Catholics to jump on the bandwagon....In this atmosphere, early interpreters of the Council suggested that the documents

contained revolutionary implications not apparent on the surface. Some propounded the hermeneutical principle that where there are ambiguities in the Council documents, these should always be resolved in favor of discontinuity. Others used the device of preferring to follow the "spirit of Vatican II" at the expense of the letter.[11]

In other words, radical notions of the liturgy, and of art were already "in the air," so the only task then for modernist architects to do was open the door. And indeed, when the door was opened, despite the fact the Council made only vague and general recommendations, the modern theorists would lay claim to exclusive right to interpret what notions of "noble simplicity" of art would mean, and furthermore claim the exclusive imprimatur of the Council.

This is due to one critical failure of the Council regarding art, a preference to rely upon "experts" to advise the Church on what should be done. Despite the assertion in *Sacrosanctum concilium* that the Church "always reserved the right to pass judgment on art,"[12] the preference for experts would allow the theorists, artists and architects of modernism already well entrenched, to lay claim to be the sole arbiter of all aspects of art and architecture in the Church.

The destruction of beautiful art, in accordance with modernist principles, but in name of the "spirit of Vatican II" quickly commenced. The rapidity and radicality of this destruction was so alarming that the Vatican's Congregation for Clergy felt it necessary to release a letter to bishops in 1971 to halt the wanton destruction of art in Catholic churches. The letter, titled *Opera Artis,* expressed shock that "disregarding the warnings and legislation of the Holy See, many people have made unwarranted changes in places of worship under the pretext of carrying out the reform of the liturgy and have thus caused the disfigurement or loss of priceless works of art."[13] Unequivocally reiterating the words of *Sacrosanctum concilium,* that works of art are "always to be preserved," the letter urges restraint in renovations. Nevertheless, the renovations and experimentations continued apace from the '70s, '80s and beyond.

In America, nothing typified this radical experimentation more than the document released by the Bishop's Committee on the Liturgy, *Environment and Art in Catholic Worship* in 1978. Though never approved by the USCC (renamed the United States Conference of Catholic Bishops in 2001) as a whole, it influenced a generation of bad architecture, promoting an aggressively iconoclastic form of liturgical functionalism. Not surprisingly, it based its authoritative statements on a misinterpretation of Vatican II.[14]

Thankfully however, the USCC released in 2000 a new document on church architecture and art, *Built of Living Stones,* which received full approval of the bishops. Though far from perfect, it replaced the error-filled *Environment and Art,* and laid groundwork for a more authentic interpretation of Vatican II and sacred architecture.

Reasons for Hope

With the publication of *Built of Living Stones,* there was a tangible sign that the sorry state of sacred architecture was beginning to change. Indeed in the past two decades many tangible signs of positive change have occurred.

The pontificate of Pope Benedict XVI had a tremendous effect not only on the appreciation for the beauty of the Mass and church architecture, but also for an authentic understanding of the true meaning of Vatican II. His illumination of the hermeneutics of continuity, versus the hermeneutics of rupture, has laid a positive philosophical foundation for understanding the Council which will bear fruit for generations to come.

Numerous new churches in a traditional style, which are filled with the depth of symbolism, beauty and holiness have been built, such as St. Mary in Aiken, South Carolina, by James McCrery, and the Chapel at Thomas Aquinas College by Duncan Stroik. Traditional churches are being built all over, a testament to the new generation of St. John Paul II and Pope Benedict priests who understand properly the importance of architectural beauty to the liturgy.

In the Church hierarchy itself there are a number of encouraging signs as well. Though certain bishops have recently commissioned expensive and gargantuan modernist cathedrals, there is a new generation of bishops with more traditional tastes. Dedicated in 2017, Holy Name of Jesus Cathedral in Raleigh, North Carolina, was built in an entirely traditional style.[15] Designed by O'Brien and Keane Architects, it is among the largest new classical churches built since World War II. In Knoxville, Tennessee, a new Cathedral by McCrery was also finished in 2017, and numerous other cathedrals are being "de-wreckovated," removing unfortunate renovations which took place in the iconoclasms of the '60s, '70s, and '80s.

Holy Name Cathedral, Raleigh, North Carolina
http://www.holynamecathedralnc.org/wp-content/uploads/2107/06/Flyboync.
come-09015-copy.jpg

In the professional sphere there are signs for encouragement as well. As late as the 1990s, a cleric looking to build a traditional church would be hard-pressed to find a classically trained architect to build it for him. But today, the number is large and growing. Along with well known architects like Duncan Stroik and Thomas Gordon Smith, a new generation of architects like Domiane Forte are creating beautiful churches worthy of the sacredness of God.

In painting and sculpture, talented artists such as Anthony Visco,[16] have been joined by younger artists like James Langley,[17] who decorated the chapel of the New York Opus Dei center. Neilson Carlin[18] has painted devotional images for the Shrine of Our Lady of Guadalupe in La Crosse, Wisconsin and the image of the Holy Family in Philadelphia for the 2015 visit of Pope Francis. None of these architects, painters and sculptors are stuck in the past like the critics claim, but neither are they stuck chasing a phantom idea of the "spirit of Vatican II."

It should be mentioned, though, that one of the specific goals of the Second Vatican Council regarding sacred art has yet to be implemented, which would provide even greater hope for beauty. Namely the Council recommended that "schools or academies of sacred art should be founded in those parts of the world where they would be useful, so that artists may be trained."[19] Perhaps it's best that this one specific goal of the Council has not so far been realized, as likely the modernist establishment would have dominated and enforced its utilitarian orthodoxy. But now, with experience and maturation of a genuine renewal of the liturgy, the "reform of the reform," a real renaissance in sacred arts can be fostered with such an academy of sacred art, especially here in the United States.

At the very least we should encourage and educate priests to the importance of sacred architecture, as both the Council and Pope Benedict XVI urged, and teach seminarians "the history and development of sacred art, and about the sound principles governing the production of its works."[20] We ought to be training new priests about what the Council actually said, and what the proper theological principles of sacred architecture are. Places like the North American College in Rome, where so many priests are trained, ought to take advantage of being in Rome, the epicenter of sacred arts, to help guide the future leaders of the Church to seek the truly sacred in art and architecture.

We live in a time now when the true spirit of Vatican II in art, architecture, and liturgy is beginning to be understood by the clergy as well as the artists. They are beginning to understand that sacred art must not simply embrace the forms of the art world at large, but as Cardinal Ratzinger put it, "Christian art today… must oppose the cult of the ugly, which says that everything beautiful is a deception and only the representation of what is crude, low and vulgar is the truth, the true illumination of knowledge."[21]

Most of all, we must understand beauty is not just simply added on to sacred architecture like frosting, which can be discarded to find something more pure and authentic, but is something *essential* to the sacred. Feeding and growing that sense of the sacred, which was always the intent of the Holy Spirit working in the Council, is now beginning to be helped rather than hindered by the "art of our age."

ENDNOTES

1. *Sacrosanctum concilium*; 23

2. *SC*, n. 128

3. *SC*, n. 122

4. *SC*, n. 123

5. *SC*, n. 123

6. *SC*, n. 123

7. *SC*, n. 123

8. Smith, Dr. Randall B.; "Don't Blame Vatican II," *Sacred Architecture*, Volume 13; 2007

9. Godfrey, Peter, *"Swerve with verve: Oscar Niemeyer, the architect who eradicated the straight line"*. *The Independent (London)*; April 18, 2010   http://www.independent.co.uk/arts-entertainment/architecture/swerve-with-verve-oscar-niemeyer-the-architect-who-eradicated-the-straight-line-1944761.html

10. See Duncan Stroik's book for a fuller list: Stroik, Duncan; *The Church Building as a Sacred Place*; *Beauty, Transcendence and the Eternal;* Hillenbrand Books, Chicago/Mundelein, Illinois; 2013

11. Avery Cardinal Dulles; "Vatican II: The Myth and the Reality," *America* Feb. 24, 2003

12. *SC*, n., 122

13. *Opera artis*, Circular Letter on the Care of the Church's Historical and Artistic Heritage, Congregation for the Clergy - April 11, 1971   http://www.adoremus.org/Opera_Artis.html

14. Stroik, Duncan; "Environment and Art in Catholic Worship - A Critique," *Sacred Architecture*, Volume 2; 1999

15. http://www.dioceseofraleigh.org/news/view.aspx?id=1233

16. http://www.anthonyvisco.org/

17. http://www.langleyart.com/

18. http://www.neilsoncarlin.com/

19. *SC*, n. 127

20. Pope Benedict XVI; *Sacramentum charitatis, Post-Synodal Apostolic Exhortation;* February 22, 2007

21. Joseph Cardinal Ratzinger; Message sent to a meeting of the ecclesial movement Communion and Liberation in Rimini, Italy; August 2002 http://www.crossroadsinitiative.com/library_article/601/contemplation_of_beauty_cardinal_joseph_ratzinger.html

ERIK BOOTSMA is an architect practicing in Richmond, Virginia. He holds a bachelor's degree from Thomas Aquinas College, where he concentrated on theology and philosophy and he holds a Master of Architecture from the University of Notre Dame. His firm concentrates on Catholic sacred architecture and liturgical design. He has written for numerous publications and speaks throughout the country on the theology and philosophy of sacred architecture. He co-runs *Aedificare Sacra*, a program for the training of priests in the principles and practice of sacred architecture.

God in Touch With His Children

By Frank Morriss

(Editor's Note: This eloquent discussion of *Dei verbum* is from the *Divine Epic*, written by Morriss as the script for a church history radio program aired in 1973.)

What loving parent, having the power to stay in touch with his children in some distant land, would leave them without word? And were those children inclined to foolishness, excess, imprudence – or even worse, darkness and error – think how such a parent would attempt to instruct them, guide them, turn their eyes to him, share his wisdom with them!

God has never disappointed His children in that regard. He has never left us in darkness about His will; He has told us all we need to know for our happiness and salvation. In short, He has revealed Himself to us so not the most stubborn or blind of us can fail to see Him if we wish to do so, not the deafest of us can fail to hear Him if we wish.

Then, placing our First Parents on earth, God, almost we might say like a man who has his first child, never is far away from them. He walks with Adam in Eden, somehow speaking to this son those things that are for his welfare. It was Adam, not God, who chose to break off the conversation, and to flee in shame from the sound of God's voice. And but for God's infinite mercy and love, there in silence and darkness man might have dwelt forever. But God refused to be shut out of man's affairs. He chose to keep in touch.

The climax of God's will in this matter is, of course, Christ – God's very own Word made flesh. God showed Himself in various ways, as we shall see, but only fully in Christ, who actually is God Incarnate. All revelation before Christ's Incarnation was preparation for that event. The records of the Evangelists after Christ's death and Resurrection reflect back to the Incarnation. Beyond this there is to be no further public revelation, because it is completed and perfected. In Christ we have all we need to know of God. He is God's only – and therefore final – Word. The palaver is finished.

We may take it or leave it, either to our joy or our damnation, but God will not provide some other way, Christ is not a halfway station in some evolving movement. He is God uttering Himself to men – not a mirror of God, but God Himself; not a prophet or an evangelist, but the object of all the prophets' foreseeing and the subject of all evangelical teaching; the Alpha and the Omega, the Creator and the End to which all creation must come.

The Catholic Church's appreciation of this is expressed in the Second Vatican Council's *Dogmatic Constitution on Divine Revelation, Dei verbum.* Revelation is the one and indispensable source of our faith, for it is God as He Himself chose to show Himself to His children. In Revelation, the Council says, the pilgrim sees God as in a mirror, until that time when we shall see God face to face.

Revelation flows to us in two streams, rising as it were from a single spring – God Himself. Those are parallel streams, destined to meet where they began, streams we follow as one might seek a way out of a dark forest by walking along a river so that we shall find our way home. The streams are that of Scripture, the words that were put down in written form by men God commissioned to be His secretaries, as it were, although His words were communicated to them by inspiration rather than by actual dictation; and that of Tradition, the teaching kept and handed down by Christ's official appointed teachers in the Church itself. As the Council puts it, there was a time when the early Church did not have the written New Testament – a period of at least fifty or sixty years after Christ's death. Nor, when the Evangelists recorded their versions of the Gospel, did they claim or pretend to have included all of the teachings Christ handed to His Apostles to treasure and transfer through all generations. And so the apostolic preaching, which is expressed in a special way in the inspired book, was to be preserved by a continuous succession of preachers until the end of time. Therefore, the apostles, handing on what they themselves had received, warn the faithful to hold fast to the traditions which they have learned either by word or by letter and to fight in defense of the faith handed on once and for all (n.8).

It is quite clear from this that there cannot be any new things essential to the Christian faith. In regard to our faith it is not disgraceful or unperceiving to insist that what we believe is the same old thing, in other words to be judged conservative. "Keep the faith" is not just an adage, it is the soundest of theological truths, and is reiterated here by the most modern of the Church's Ecumenical Councils. And, just as nothing new can be added to Revelation, nothing can be subtracted from it either. That which Revelation has told us insults God, is sinful and dangerous for man, cannot in our day become pleasing to God and harmless for us to practice.

Keeping the Faith

True, each age may bring deeper and more complete understandings of what is in Scripture and Tradition. Revelation is imbedded in history, and takes some mining to extract. Among the professional miners, we might say, are theologians and exegetes, scripture scholars and the rest. They are not to rule on the worth or value of what they find; only the official Church teaching may do so, for it is those teachers Christ commissioned to keep the stream pure and full and fresh as when it flowed from Him.

Tradition and Scripture make up the single deposit of faith which the Church guards. This conservatory note is strong in the Council's constitution:

> Holding fast to this deposit, the entire holy people united with their shepherds, remain always steadfast in the teaching of the apostles, in the common life, in the breaking of the bread, and in prayers, so that in holding to, practicing, and professing the heritage of the faith, there results on the part of the bishops and the faithful a remarkable common effort (n. 10).

For the most part, God chooses to speak to men in their own language. The divine message is there, and it is only that which is important; but it is in human packaging, either the words used by the men of the time when it is delivered or the teaching of the Church, always placed in the language of the time.

This being the case, the Second Vatican Council reminds us of the vital value of scholarship designed to dissect that human packaging, unwrap it and unravel it so that the divine message may be obtained in its fullness. Thus it is permissible, says the Council, to make study of the literary forms in which the message has been placed in the Scriptures. Such a study of course, will make use of all the canons of literary scholarship that might apply to any document – to Shakespeare, or Chaucer, or Dante. This involves a great range of scholarship, including the language, the customs, the manners of ancient peoples, their very psychology and mentality. It is because of scholarship we know, for example, that when Christ said to Mary, "What is that to you and to me, woman," He was not treating her coldly because the term "woman" was not a formal and contemptuous use by the Jews of Christ's time, though it is for us today. We likewise know that reference to Christ's brothers and sisters does not necessarily mean Mary had other children (which she could not have had and been ever-virgin) since those terms in Christ's time embraced relatives we call cousins, nieces, nephews.

To Serve Faith

There is an inherent temptation in all scholarship, and that is to make one discipline of the scholar supreme, decisive, and definitive. It is a type of obsession that we sometimes see, for example, in a scholar who judges all things by law; or an economist whose view of all things – government, politics, society – is only in terms of economics; or a psychologist whose total view of humanity is subject to that science. So the Scripture scholar sometimes forgets his science is designed to serve faith, and that when it seems to lead him in the opposite direction, it is no longer trustworthy.Scripture scholarship is subject to the Church. The Council says:

> The living tradition of the whole Church must be taken into account along with the harmony which exists between elements of the faith. It is the task of exegetes to work according to these rules toward a better understanding and explanation of the meaning of Sacred Scripture, so that through preparatory study the judgment of the Church may mature. For all of what has been said about the way of interpreting Scripture is subject finally to the judgment of the Church, which carries out the divine commission and the ministry of guarding and interpreting the Word of God (n.12).

The Council explains how the written account of the Gospel of Christ came about:

> The sacred authors wrote the four Gospels, selecting some things in view of the situation of their churches, and preserving the form of proclamation but always in such a fashion that they told the honest truth about Jesus. For their intention in writing was that either from their own memory and recollections, or from the witness of those who themselves "from the beginning were eyewitnesses and ministers of the Word" we might know "the truth" concerning those matters about which we have been instructed (n.19).

The Council's words are also important in view of the recent [Editor's note: in the decade after the Council] spate of Jesus literature – particularly dramatic art – that presents a picture of Christ peculiarly at odds with that of the New Testament itself, i.e., the play and movie *Jesus Christ Superstar.* In the New Testament we have always an image of Christ as one in command, quite certain of His divine nature and willing to do all He can to lead men to freely admit that fact of His Divinity, sure of His mission to lead all men to Himself by being lifted up upon the Cross. Now, this is the picture of the Gospels, and if we are to accept Vatican II, we must accept it as "the honest truth about Jesus." But it is the opposite of the Christ as almost entirely human, with only a few longings or stirrings of Divinity; confused, thwarted, frantic, not sure enough of His mission to really abandon it; driven, compelled, and finally overwhelmed by the world.

It is half Melville, half Joyce, with large dashes of Sartre, Camus, Bonhoeffer, Heidegger, and the host of existentialists who see mankind in essentially the same fix as Jesus. Jesus is superman in that He embodies all mankind's inadequacies; and He is superstar in the existential manner because He has endured them to death, which is the existential manner of heroism.

[At the time] many young Catholic nuns and priests saw such dramatics as important and instructive; a sure indication they were not very appreciative of the truth of the New Testament, and hardly well acquainted with the teaching of Vatican II about the New Testament. Their inadequacy points out the inadequacy of their own education. One reason for this is that the words of the Council were not heeded:

> Sacred theology rests on the written word of God, together with sacred tradition, as its primary and perpetual foundation. By scrutinizing in the light of faith all truth stored up in the mystery of Christ, theology is most powerfully strengthened and constantly rejuvenated by the word. For the Sacred Scriptures contain the word of God; and so the study of the sacred page is, as it were, the soul of sacred theology. By the same word of Scripture the ministry of the word also takes wholesome nourishment and yields fruits of holiness. This ministry includes pastoral preaching, catechetics, and all other Christian instruction, among which the liturgical homily should have an exceptional place(n. 24).

It is unfortunate, therefore that so much of today's catechetics and preaching is shaped more by new books, by agenda-driven theologians and scholars than by the old and only books of the New Testament. There is a decided lack of inspiration in most of the modern theological writing. Much of it is not in harmony with the spirit or the word of the Gospels. And yet it has become gospel itself for many.

By Their Fruits You Will Know Them

Vatican II says the fruits of holiness come from the words of Scripture. We have seen the fruits of unholiness come from the words and speculations of the new *periti*. Vatican II says Scripture should be the soul of theology. Yet the new theology rather than tending to strengthen faith and to uphold Scriptures, seems dedicated to undermining both. Some new versions of the Scripture, especially in their explanatory notes, actually seek to impose a completely new understanding contrary to the old truths.

While not discussing this problem directly, Vatican II does hint at an answer. It concludes its chapter on Revelation thus:

> It devolves in the bishops, "who have the apostolic teaching," to give the faithful entrusted to them suitable instruction in the right use of the divine books, especially the New Testament and above all the Gospels, through translations of the sacred texts (n.25).

Let us be mindful of the premise of this humble article: God in touch with His children, not His children telling Him the way they want life to be.

FRANK MORRISS, J.D., was a graduate of Regis College, Denver, received his Juris Doctorate from Georgetown University School of Law. He also holds a degree in philosophy. Since returning from Army service in the Philippines and Japan in 1945, Morriss devoted his talents to Catholic journalism. He is a former news editor of the *Denver Catholic Register,* a founding editor of *Twin Circle,* editorial writer and contributor to *The Wanderer,* and the author of a number of works, including *The Catholic as Citizen, A Little Life of Our Lord, The Divine Epic, Saints in Verse,* and *Two Chapels,* a treatment of Cardinal Newman and the Oxford Movement. Morriss' most recent book is *Francis Thompson - A Reflection on the Poetic Vocation.* In addition, he has authored several historical fiction books for children. Morriss has twice earned the George Washington Medal given by the Freedom Foundation of Valley Forge. In 2003, Morriss was awarded the Bl. Frederic Ozanam award by the Society of Catholic Social Scientists. He was co-editor and writer of the Wanderer Forum's *Forum Focus* magazine and a member of the Board of Directors of the Wanderer Forum Foundation/Bellarmine Forum. Morriss passed from this life on January 25, 2014.

The Quest for Christian Unity

By James Likoudis

It is a matter for profound examination of conscience, after almost 50 years of ecumenical activity by Catholics sparked by the *Decree on Ecumenism*, to study the success of such efforts.

The decree, *Unitatis redintegratio (Restoration of Unity)*, was formulated during the Third Session of the Second Vatican Council and released on November 21, 1964. Pope Paul VI, bishops, and theologians devoted themselves to determining how the Catholic Church could take positive steps to achieve that unity among Christians which it had always desired in conformity with Our Lord's words during the Last Supper: "That all may be one...that the world may believe" *(John* 17:21). The Lord's prayer certainly assured to the Church He founded on Peter and the Apostles that substantial visible unity which can never be lost – in spite of the heresies and schisms which would historically tear away millions from her bosom.

Exhorting all Catholics to take an active and intelligent part in the work of ecumenism and to "gladly acknowledge the truly Christian endowments for our common heritage which are found among our separated brethren," the Council Fathers took some practical measures to facilitate greater understanding and friendship with them: the encouragement of theological dialogues, cooperation in dealing with social problems, and joining in common prayer as a "very effective means of petitioning for the grace of unity" (*UR*, n.4, 8). There is the admonition (often ignored afterwards) that " Nothing is so foreign to the spirit of ecumenism as a false irenicism which harms the purity of Catholic doctrine and obscures its genuine and certain meaning" (*UR*, n.11).

And Now, Fifty Years Later?

Well-known Catholic author Kenneth D.Whitehead, one of the best informed writers dealing with texts of Vatican II controverted by critics, observed:

Agreement is far from universal among Catholics themselves whether the new Catholic emphasis on ecumenism adopted by Vatican Council II has been an entirely good thing for the Church. Among the various misunderstandings and confusions that followed in the wake of the Council, those related to the question of ecumenism have in fact seemed to be especially acute. And this is not just because of the apparent lack of success to date of the really extraordinary ecumenical efforts the Church has made in the post-conciliar years. For after more than 40 years of such ecumenical efforts, there is scarcely a single case of completely restored Christian unity; nor, in spite of widely publicized ecumenical meetings between Church leaders, extensive dialogue by theologians, numerous agreed statements, many and regular joint prayers for Christians to be united, along with much talk on all sides about how Christians ought to be united, there still does not seem, any time soon, to be much of a real prospect for actual Christian reunification, or restoration of communion between formally separated Christian bodies.[1]

At the beginning of the Church's *Decree on Ecumenism* (*UR*) that was promulgated in public session by Pope Paul VI on November 21, 1964, one reads:

The restoration of unity among Christians is one of the principal concerns of the Second Vatican Council. Christ the Lord founded one Church and one Church only. However, many Christian communions present themselves to men as true inheritors of Jesus Christ; all indeed profess to be followers of the Lord but they differ in mind and go their different ways, as if Christ Himself were divided. Certainly, such division openly contradicts the will of Christ, scandalizes the world, and damages that most holy cause, the preaching of the Gospel to every creature (*UR*, n.1).

Mr. Whitehead noted that in view of the distortions that would be committed by trendy theologians concerning the nature and identity of the Church, "It is perhaps more than a little ironic that Vatican II's strongest and most insistent reiteration of the Church's traditional claim to be the one, true Church founded by Jesus Christ should have come, of all places, in its *Decree on Ecumenism*." [2]

For the *Decree* declared with no equivocation:

It is through Christ's Catholic Church alone, which is the universal help toward salvation, that the fullness of the means of salvation can be obtained. It was to the Apostolic College alone, of which Peter is the head, that we believe Our Lord entrusted all the blessings of the New Covenant, in order to establish on earth the one Body of Christ into which all those should be fully incorporated who belong in any way to the People of God. (*UR*, n.3)

As the obstacles to perfect ecclesiastical communion are overcome, all Christians will be gathered, in a common celebration of the Eucharist, into the unity of the one and only Church, which Christ bestowed on His Church from the beginning. This unity, we believe, subsists in the Catholic Church as something she can never lose, and we hope that it will continue to increase until the end of time (*UR*, n.4).

The *Decree on the Catholic Eastern Churches* (*Orientalium ecclesiarum-OE*) which was promulgated on the same day as that on Ecumenism, also noted the unicity of the true Church of Christ by stating:

The holy Catholic Church, which is the Mystical Body of Christ, is made up of the faithful who are organically united in the Holy Spirit by the same faith, the same sacraments and the same government (*OE*, n.2)...These individual Churches, both Eastern and Western, while they differ among themselves in what is called "rite," namely in liturgy, in ecclesiastical discipline and in spiritual discipline, are none the less all equally entrusted to the pastoral guidance of the Roman Pontiff, who by God's appointment is successor to Blessed Peter in primacy over the Universal Church. Therefore these churches are of equal rank, so that none of them is superior to the others because of its rite. They have the same rights and obligations, even with regard to the preaching of the Gospel in the whole world (cf. *Mark* 16 :15), under the direction of the Roman Pontiff (*OE*, n.3).

The above quotations from the decrees on Ecumenism and the Eastern Catholic Churches simply repeat in succinct fashion the words of Vatican II's most important document, *Lumen gentium* (*Dogmatic Constitution on the Church*), the most magnificent ecclesiological exposition of the nature of the Church in 2000 years of the Church's history:

This is the sole Church of Christ which in the Creed we profess to be one, holy, catholic and apostolic, which our Savior, after His Resurrection, entrusted to Peter's pastoral care (*John* 21: 17), commissioning him and the other Apostles to extend and rule it (cf. *Matt.* 28:18, etc.) and which He raised up for all ages as "the Pillar and Mainstay of the truth" (*1 Tim.* 3:15). This Church, constituted and organized as a society in the present world, subsists in the Catholic Church, which is governed by the successor of Peter and by the bishops in communion with him. Nevertheless, many elements of sanctification and of truth are found outside its visible confines. Since these are gifts belonging to the Church of Christ, they are forces impelling towards Catholic unity (*Lumen gentium*, n.8).

Vatican II insisted, moreover, on the Petrine ministry of the Pope as essential to the hierarchical structure and spiritual mission of the Church as Evangelizer of the nations.

One sees the Second Vatican Council guided by the Holy Spirit reaffirming in the strongest terms the teaching on Papal supremacy and infallibility found in Vatican I, a Council particularly disliked and calumniated in the writings of Liberal/Modernist theologians and writers. In the last 50 years critics of such traditional Catholic doctrines have been a major factor contributing with their anti-Catholic errors and their anti-Papal complex to the crisis in the Church. Clearly, the crisis that appeared after the Council reflected a great loss of faith aided by intellectual elites (clerical and lay) who had lost sight of the divine and supernatural character of the Church. They neglected the Church as the divine work of Christ. For five decades the Congregation of the Doctrine of the Faith issued repeated instructions for fidelity to Catholic truth and censures of heterodox views and writings to remind bishops and laity that Our Lord Jesus was the one Savior of the world and that the Catholic Church is His one Church.

Yet egregious "misinterpretations" of the teachings of Vatican II continued, especially regarding the nature and identity of the Church – the heart of the crisis that the Church finds itself in. The blurring of the identity of the Church due to a false irenicism and the obscuring of Catholic doctrinal distinctiveness made the reason for being or remaining Catholic less compelling. It also led to the sorry diminution of missionary activity and zeal for the salvation of souls.

Misinterpretations

Distortion of the ecclesiology of Vatican II, moreover, led to hostility towards the exercise of the Petrine ministry of the Roman Pontiff. Disobedience to the Popes' teachings and directives would characterize what would be termed by journalists an "American Church", whose rebellious "Liberal Establishment" hung loose to Rome. Such bishops resistant to Roman Curial correction would prove to have failed time and again to safeguard the "One Lord, one Faith, one Church".

The resultant offenses against Catholic doctrine have been outrageous and have resulted in much damage to the Church. This has been the judgment of Popes and Bishops across the post-conciliar years, with Pope Benedict XVI especially denouncing the gross error that dogma and doctrine had been changed by Vatican II. The spread of this error resulted in an "hermeneutic of rupture and discontinuity." One of the most serious denials (explicit or implicit) of Catholic doctrine was that which denied "the Catholic Church to be Christ's one and only Church." Vatican II's *Decree on Ecumenism* was, in effect, manhandled by subtle dissenters as was *Lumen gentium's* use of the word "*subsistit*" ("Christ's Church subsists in the Catholic Church" *LG*, n.8) which was twisted to mean that the Church of Christ is wider and broader than the Catholic Church.

Thus, for example, the scholarly Jesuit Fr. Robert Taft, perhaps the world's leading expert on the Byzantine Liturgy, could actually write in open contradiction to Vatican II's *Decree on Ecumenism* and other documents:

> The new Catholic "Sister Churches'" ecclesiology describes not only how the Catholic Church views the Orthodox Churches. It also represents a startling revolution in how the Catholic Church views itself; we are not the only kid on the block, the whole Church of Christ, but one Sister Church among others. Previously, the Catholic Church saw itself as the original one and only true Church of Christ from which all other Christians had separated for one reason or another in the course of history, and Catholics held simplistically, that the solution to divided Christendom consisted in all other Christians returning to Rome's maternal bosom (*Catholic World Report*, 5/2/2013).

Fr. Richard McBrien who dominated the theology department at Notre Dame for many years (and termed by fellow faculty member/ philosophy professor Dr. Ralph McInerney as "the worst thing that ever happened to the University of Notre Dame") was known for his rages and invectives against the Vatican and the Papacy. His view of the Church and his doctrinal dissent on many issues was disseminated in books, columns in diocesan papers, and church bulletins throughout the U.S. and Canada for many years. For Fr. McBrien and his followers,

> The expression "one, true Church of Christ" is misleading and it should be avoided...The Body of Christ is larger in scope and extent than the Church by itself...Were a Catholic to shift his own place within the Body of Christ (by moving from one Christian community to another), one cannot speak of that Catholic as one who "has lost the faith" (cf. *Catholicism*, McBrien, 1994, pp. 684, 732, 735).

Another well-known writer, Fr. Ben F. Meyer, eventually left the priesthood but not before misrepresenting Conciliar teaching:

> By "Church" throughout my study is meant the one Church of Christ, which as the Council put it, subsists in the Roman Catholic Church, and as the Council left to understand...subsists also in the Orthodox, Anglican, and Protestant Churches.

Eastern rite Catholics were not immune from the dissenters' new ecclesiology. Ukrainian Catholic Fr. Victor Posipishil wrote:

> [Vatican II introduced] the distinction between the Church of Christ and the Catholic Church. To the first belong all baptized persons; to the second belong those who have subjected themselves to the primatial authority of the bishop of Rome (*Diakonia*, no.3, 1987, p. 146).

Even the noted Dominican spiritual writer Fr. Jordan Aumann was influenced to state in his book *On the Front Lines: the Lay Person in the Church After Vatican II*:

> We have made a distinction between membership in the "Church of Christ" and in the Catholic Church. All validly baptized Christians, whatever their religious affiliation, are members of the Church of Christ.

Even Catholic parish bulletins would question the identity of the Catholic Church as the one true Church and the Mystical Body of Christ:

Each year from January 18-25, Christians around the world observe the Week of Prayer for Christian Unity. This was formerly known as the Chair of Unity Octave, when we Catholics prayed that the Protestants would soon see the light and return to the one true Church. Today, we look at that a little differently. There is no one true Church. Truth is never found just in a Church. Truth is found in Jesus (*St. Luke's Parish Bulletin*, Two Rivers, Wisconsin, January 25. 1987).

Many other quotations could be given showing the confusion generated by theologians, catechists, and certain lay and clerical ecumenists regarding the identity of the one true Church of Christ, i.e., the Catholic Church. This misrepresentation of the Council's teaching was even found in the catechisms of elementary school children.

It may be pointed out briefly here that:

1. The documents of Vatican II nowhere uses the expression "Roman Catholic Church" to describe itself. It always refers to itself as "the Catholic Church," period. That Catholic Church is Christ's "one and only Church."

2. Catholics are those who are in full communion with the Successor of Peter, the visible head of the visible Church.

3. Baptized non-Catholics may be said to be "joined in many ways" and to possess a certain belonging to the Catholic Church but only Catholics are "fully incorporated" in the Church and thus the "members of the Church." Non-Catholics, i.e., Protestants, Eastern Orthodox, and Oriental Orthodox, are all "called to this Catholic unity" (*LG*, 13, 15).

4. Unlike the separated Eastern Churches, Protestant denominations lack the Apostolic Succession of Bishops, and thus are not called by Vatican II "churches" but rather "ecclesial communities."

5. As the distinguished Catholic theologian and Servant of God, Fr. John Hardon, S.J., explained in *The Catholic Catechism*: "That which constitutes the one true Church – its churchiness, so to speak –

not merely exists but it subsists in the Catholic Church, which is governed by the Successor of Peter and by the bishops in communion with him. Behind the carefully chosen verb 'subsists' stands the affirmation that the objective fullness of Christ's heritage to the Church – totality of His Revelation, totality of His Sacraments, and totality of authority to rule the People of God in His Name – resides in the Catholic Church, of which the bishop of Rome is the visible head" (p. 213).

The Church's teaching is unequivocal but through the deliberate misinterpretation of the Council by those who passed their own opinions off as truth, decades of ecumenical work became nothing but futile wheel spinning. Unity with Peter was not discussed as the ultimate goal.

Is There Hope for the Future?

Despite the attempts to obscure the unique nature of Christ's Catholic Church and to wreak confusion among the faithful, it would be a profound mistake to believe that the *Magisterium* of Holy Church had abandoned that central tenet of the Faith: the Catholic Church is the one true Church Christ founded.

Erroneous views promoting religious indifferentism, false ecumenism, and universal salvation were the constant object of concern and vigilance as reflected in the addresses of Pope Paul VI and his successors throughout the post-conciliar period. The refutation of serious errors and even revived heresies occupied a host of documents issued by the Congregation for the Doctrine of the Faith (CDF), all striking at the hydra-head of the theological Leviathan seeking to destroy the Church in the name of "renewal." Major dissenters were applauded by the world press for their efforts to dismantle the hierarchical structure of the Church and to render irrelevant the "deposit of faith" confided by Christ to the Apostles with Peter at their head. Censures and excommunications of those media darlings who tore at the teachings of the Church from inside her ranks were decried as injustice. The distortion of doctrine continued.

But while the Catholic Church was being battered with serious losses of largely poorly catechized members, the ongoing disintegration of doctrinal Protestantism would attract many Evangelicals, Anglicans, and those of other denominations *to* the Catholic Church.

In the spiritual wasteland of modern society plunging into moral relativism and barbarism, the Catholic Church was viewed increasingly to be that visible society and spiritual Kingdom against which the Gates of Hell could not prevail. For all the liturgical and disciplinary changes that proved troubling, the Catholic Church held to its dogmatic and doctrinal patrimony. Amidst the severe storms raging against the Barque of Peter, the Catholic Church had proved to be not a "house built on sand" but rather a House built on the enduring Rock of Peter.

It is to be noted that it was in the post-conciliar period marked by disorders in the Church that the "best and brightest" of Protestants, Scott Hahn, Graham Leonard, William Oddie, Thomas Howard, Kenneth Howell, became Catholics. Then, too, there have been the agnostic seekers of truth who (like Malcolm Muggeridge) were revolted by modern nihilism to become Catholics. Anglican congregations have become increasingly interested in becoming Catholic and the Church has allowed them to do so with their own rites.

The warming of relations between Eastern Orthodox and Catholics with Orthodox prelates and bishops engaging in visits to Rome also represents one of the fruits of Vatican II's "spiritual ecumenism," preparing the way for the long-hoped Reunion of the Churches. Nor can one overlook the spiritual heirs of the greatest of Russian philosophers, Vladimir Soloviev, in Russia and Romania. Influenced by Vatican II's outreach to the East and by Soloviev's ecumenical writings, work is going on quietly for the ending of the Byzantine Greco-Slav Schism.

ENDNOTES

1. Whitehead, Kenneth D., *The New Ecumenism* (St. Paul/Alba House, 2009; 214 pages), p. 3-4.
2. *Ibid.*, p. 31.

JAMES LIKOUDIS is a nationally known writer and lecturer on catechetics, sex education and liturgy. He is president-emeritus of Catholics United for the Faith (CUF), a lay Catholic organization formed in the wake of the Second Vatican Council to promote the truths and doctrines of the Church. A convert to the Catholic Church from Greek Orthodoxy in 1952, Likoudis has devoted a great deal of his efforts to foster the reunion of the Orthodox churches with Rome, and is the author of three books on the subject. Likoudis also co-authored *The Pope, The Council, and the Mass*, a defense of Pope Paul VI's *Ordo Missae* and liturgical reforms. *L'Osservatore Romano* wrote that "this book has been sorely needed for well over a decade." It was reprinted in 2006. Likoudis was the 2002 recipient of the Blessed Frederick Ozanam Award for Catholic Social Action of the Society for Catholic Social Scientists.

Vatican II – The Most Verbose Council on Mary, the Mother of the Church

By John B. Manos

In 1995, the spring edition of *The Marian Library Newsletter*[1] stated: "Reports about the rosary's demise are premature." The article went on to explain that Vatican II did not put a halt to Marian devotion. I remember reading the article around that time; I think it was given to me by someone who attended several prayer cenacles a week and always had a rosary in hand. "See, it's turning around!" I was told.

The attitude towards Mary in the Church at large is a bell weather, after all. The logic of this approach is sound: If people were willing to come back to Mary, then they may be willing to believe in the sacraments again, especially the Blessed Sacrament. Ironically, the flux of alleged Marian apparitions around the Cincinnati area had many praying their rosaries, if for nothing else, in the hopes that Mary would come in apparitions to them, too.

Vatican II is blamed for destroying Marian devotion. In my own experience, there was sharp contrast between how I heard Mary referred to in various places. At home and among people that attended Latin Mass at Old St. Mary's parish, where numerous statues and paintings of Mary abounded, including a statue that carried an indulgence from Pope Leo XIII, the Blessed Mother was clearly venerated. At school and in catechetical settings, Mary was treated as a vestige. She was sort of mentioned as a necessary character of the nativity scene, but that's as far as it went in catechesis. Never mind that nearly every other parish across our town, in fact across the country, is named for her, Our Lady of Victory, Our Lady of Visitation, Our Lady of Lourdes, Old St. Mary's, and on and on. Despite this fact and the *sensus fidelium*, part of the "wreckovations" in the wake of Vatican II – parish RENEW programs and guitar Masses – were a substitution for Marian devotion along with bible studies and groups. Mary was to be minimized, "in the Spirit of Vatican II."

This idea that Mary was minimized was a *cause célèbre* in the sedevacantist and SSPX circles over the years. One of the more sensationalized threads is borne out by a book published in 2012 in Italian titled *The Second Vatican Council: An Unwritten Story.*[2] The author, Roberto De Mattei, presents a story of an epic battle to define Mary in various ways at the Council. It pits Karl Rahner on one side and those who were claimed to be fighting for the title "Mediatrix of All Graces" on the other. I like stories like this because they do bring about the human side of the Church and the characters and persons within. I don't like the way these stories tend to lead people away from the truth, though, for Vatican II did not distort any Marian tradition in any way.

Fr. John Hardon wrote on this very topic of the Second Vatican Council and Mary in 2001. Fr. Hardon's analysis is reliable, given that he had not only written the *Catholic Catechism: A Contemporary Catechism of the Catholic Church* to refute the notorious *Dutch Catechism*, and *The Modern Catholic Dictionary*, but also had taught and he reported the situation succinctly: "Never in the history of Christianity has any general Council spoken at such length and with such depth about Mary as the Second Vatican Council."[3]

So much for the controversy as to how much the Second Vatican Council wrote about Mary: Chapter 8 of *Lumen gentium* is devoted entirely to Our Lady – it is the longest discussion ever. But what did that mean? Did the Council get rid of the Rosary or somehow deprecate Marian tradition? No, and Fr. Hardon tells us that the "Council [...] put this [Marian] devotion into focus and spell[ed] out its doctrinal foundation."

Continuing, Fr. Hardon fleshes out his analysis into explaining directly that the Council exalted and preserved Marian devotions and practices — the exact opposite of what people were being told in post-council years. He says:

The Council "charges that practices and exercises of devotion to her be treasured as recommended by the teaching authority of the Church in the course of centuries." True Marian piety consists neither in fruitless and passing emotion, nor in a certain empty credulity.

Rather authentic devotion to Mary "proceeds from true faith by which we are led to know the excellence of the Mother of God, and are moved to filial love toward our Mother and to the imitation of her virtues" (*Lumen gentium*, n.67-8).[4]

Like so many other false accusations against the Council, we can see that it is true that the rosary is not mentioned by name, but what else is meant by "practices and exercises of devotion to her be treasured?" That doesn't mean having no practice of devotion to her. First of all, it's plural, meaning there are many. Secondly, it's manifold, "practices and exercises." That implies all the variety, Rosaries, cenacles, novenas, flowers on the side altar, statues, pilgrimages, and so much more. Are we to suppose that because the word Rosary does not appear directly that the Council got rid of it? Not at all, yet, it definitely was something the progressives wanted us to believe.

The sentence that is taken out of context is this alarming sounding one from n. 67:

But it exhorts theologians and preachers of the divine word to abstain zealously both from all gross exaggerations as well as from petty narrow-mindedness in considering the singular dignity of the Mother of God.

Abstaining zealously! People thought that meant to abstain from devotion to her. Yet, the sentence just before that one is an exhortation and admonishment that "This most Holy Synod deliberately teaches this Catholic doctrine and at the same time admonishes all the sons of the Church that the cult, especially the liturgical cult, of the Blessed Virgin, be generously fostered[.]" In other words, Vatican II, by general reference, and by observation made by Fr. Hardon, wanted devotion to Mary promoted! They moved Mary from the side altar of casual mention in Church documents to within the very main altar of *Lumen gentium* itself. Now, more like the Eastern practices, Mary is pictured bearing Christ to us, and her role in doing so highlighted at the main altar.

The Council could not possibly enumerate all practices handed by tradition, such as the Rosary, but it did give us a general list that all "the practices and exercises of piety, recommended by the *Magisterium* of the Church toward her in the course of centuries be made of great moment, and those decrees, which have been given in the early days regarding the cult of images of Christ, the Blessed Virgin and the saints, be religiously observed" (n.67). This doesn't sound like the Council was cutting any practice out. In fact, by going all the way back in time, it would seem that they were attempting to include *all* practices!

Did the Council somehow minimize Mary's role? Not in the least. In n. 66, it states clearly:

> Placed by the grace of God, as God's Mother, next to her Son, and exalted above all angels and men, Mary intervened in the mysteries of Christ and is justly honored by a special cult in the Church.

Exalted above all angels and men is not a minimization by any stretch. This same paragraph explains that this special cult of Mary is to her uniquely and distinct from the cult to Jesus, the Holy Spirit, or elsewhere – it is for her.

The Council also gives a practical summary of the benefits of having a Mother in Mary, when it states that this special cult is across the Church and from the beginning.

> Clearly from earliest times the Blessed Virgin is honored under the title of Mother of God, under whose protection the faithful took refuge in all their dangers and necessities (n.66).

These statements are not surprising, and for many readers it may seem an elementary restatement of greater thoughts. They are. The shocker here is what Fr. Hardon observed: the Council appears to have attempted to cram all we know and teach of Mary into Chapter 8 of *Lumen gentium*, something Mother Church hadn't done ever before!

In other words, rather than being a disappointment because the Council didn't name a new thing, create a new label, or deprecate devotion to her, as the critics, revisionists and progressives would tell us, the real genius of the Council is in the subtle change in the Church's manner of declaration. Mary was moved from the side altars and grottos of mere mention in Church documents right up to her rightful place, within the high altar of a *Dogmatic Constitution* itself.

ENDNOTES

1. "The Rosary Since Vatican II" The Marian Library Newsletter (Spring 1995) Marian Research Institute, Dayton, Ohio. (also available online at http://campus.udayton.edu/mary/resources/rosary.html last retrieved September 13, 2013).

2. Roberto De Mattei, *Il Concilio Vaticano II. Una storia mai scritta.* Loreto Publications. January 1, 2010, ISBN: 978-8871808949

3. John A. Hardon, SJ, "The Blessed Virgin in the History of Christianity" *The Catholic Faith Magazine*, July/August 2001. Ignatius Press.

4. Ibid.

JOHN MANOS is currently Vice President, General Counsel, and Corporate Secretary for the Eternal Word Television Network (EWTN). He is also president of the Bellarmine Forum and contributs extensively to the website. Manos is a native of Cincinnati, studied chemical engineering and worked as a consultant analyzing explosions, chemical disasters, and workplace fatalities. He was hired by Mother Angelica to work for EWTN, and later left to be in the inaugural class of Ave Maria School of Law. Subsequently he clerked for Justice Donald C. Wintersheimer of the Kentucky Supreme Court, became an Assistant Attorney General for the State of Michigan, and then returned to EWTN. Manos' practice of law is focused on the needs of EWTN, in nonprofit, media and entertainment, trademark and intellectual property, licensing, as well as international law. He regularly attends a Melkite Church and carefully monitors movements in the eastern Churches.

Vatican II and the Missionary Imperative
by David Paul Deavel

In his apostolic exhortation *Evangelii nuntiandi (EN)*, released in 1975 on the tenth anniversary of the closing of the Second Vatican Council, Paul VI claimed that the objectives of that event could be summed up thus: "to make the Church of the twentieth century ever better fitted for proclaiming the Gospel to the people of the twentieth century."[1] Given that the *Dogmatic Constitution on the Church* was titled *Lumen gentium — Light to the Peoples —* this is not a stretch. Pope Paul's apostolic exhortation was meant to focus the Church on this primary task of going out into all the world and spreading the Good News. Pope John Paul II's encyclical *Redemptoris missio (RM),* promulgated fifteen years later, in 1990, repeated this basic claim about the Council's "missionary nature," noting that this had been based "in a dynamic way on the Trinitarian mission itself. The missionary thrust therefore belongs to the very nature of the Christian life, and is also the inspiration behind ecumenism: 'that they may all be one . . . so that the world may believe that you have sent me' *(John* 17:21)."[2] Pope John Paul himself spoke about a "new springtime of the Church" and a "New Evangelization." American Catholics faithful to the *Magisterium* have often echoed this language, but if this is truly a new springtime, it is April, which T. S. Eliot famously called "the cruelest month."

Best of Times, Worst of Times

These are the best of times and the worst of times. The last forty years have seen a great number of new initiatives among American Catholics, many of which have produced abundant fruit. The numbers of men discerning a vocation to the priesthood have begun to bounce back. Many men's and women's religious orders have sprung up over the last four decades, as have a number of smaller Catholic institutions of higher learning. A number of new apostolates, some specifically dedicated to evangelization, have been formed. A steady stream of educated converts from the academic and ministerial worlds of Evangelical and other Protestant worlds has poured in to much fanfare. Yet looking at the health of the Church in America as a whole forty years after *Evangelii nuntiandi,* the results are, at best, mixed.

For one thing, the Church has hemorrhaged massive enough numbers such that, according to the Pew Research Center's 2009 report, *Faith in Flux,* 10% of Americans are now ex-Catholics.[3] While this is depressing, the New Testament is full of warnings that many would fall away from the truth, and the report indicates that more than half of ex-Catholics have come to disagree with one or more of the Church's teachings before they leave. Whether those people understand the teachings they reject is another question, but what is actually more disturbing is a new Pew study of American religious participation beginning from 1974, the year before Paul VI's exhortation, using data taken from the General Social Survey (GSS), a research tool coming out of the University of Chicago and funded by the National Science Foundation to study American beliefs and habits. What forty years of surveying shows is that while American Evangelicalism has held relatively firm in participation, American Catholicism has seen a continuing precipitous drop in its overall levels of participation in the sacraments and worship, and a precipitous drop in the percentage of Catholics who say they are "strong" Catholics. While 54% of American Protestants say they are "strong," only 27% of Catholics do, the lowest levels of response since the GSS started asking this question. While one might hesitate to take too seriously the question of whether Catholics say they are "strong" or not — after all, didn't Chesterton say that while every Protestant says he is a good Protestant, Catholics always say they are bad Catholics? — the fact is that higher self-identification tracks strongly with higher commitment and belief in Catholic Christian teaching. Among Catholics, for whom attendance at Sunday Mass is a basic obligation, only 24% can be found on any given Sunday, compared to 47% in 1974. Even among those who claim to be strong Catholics, only 53% attend weekly as of 2012, compared with 85% in 1974.[4]

The medieval tag is *nemo dat quod non habet.* No one gives what he does not have. Catholics who cannot even be bothered to participate in what the Second Vatican Council calls the "source and summit" of Christian life – the Eucharist – during an hour a week are unlikely to understand what Christ teaches through the Church, unlikely to attempt to make converts to a religion they do not understand, and thoroughly unlikely to win any converts.

The main problem in American Catholic evangelization is that there are so few people who actually *believe* what the Church teaches. "I'm Catholic, but. . ." is, unfortunately, not the kind of testimony that will win anybody over — especially when the "but" is followed by a list of beliefs that do not just stand on the periphery of Catholic teaching, but all too often come from its core. Is it any wonder that a study of Catholic parishes in the early 2000s found that only 6% of American Catholic parishes affirmed that spreading the faith was a high priority, and only 3% sponsored any kind of evangelistic activity? The late Avery Cardinal Dulles observed that "Converts to Catholicism often report that on their spiritual journey they received little or no encouragement from Catholic clergy whom they consulted....The Council has been interpreted as if it discouraged evangelization."[5]

Leaving it to the Professionals: Old Habits

Before we discuss the interpretations of the Second Vatican Council, it is perhaps useful to remember that even beforehand, neither Catholics as a whole nor American Catholics were necessarily inclined to see themselves as agents of "evangelization" per se. Scott Hahn, the well-known Catholic convert and biblical scholar, notes in a recent article on evangelization that:

> "Evangelizing" is something we had long associated with Protestant groups that send their members door to door. When we Catholics worried about the growth of the church, we thought in terms of missions, which meant, in practical terms, sending a donation to clergy who traveled overseas. The notion of evangelization was foreign to Catholics. Though the term and its near relatives are common in the church's documents from the second half of the 20th century, one has to strain to find it before then. In the documents of Vatican I (1869-70), the word *evangelium* (Latin for "Gospel") appears only once, and only then in reference to the four written Gospels.[6]

Old habits die hard. It is still quite common to find older Catholics who are completely faithful to the Church, who nevertheless blanch at the notion that they might be called to be evangelizers themselves. Paying, praying, and obeying was not always simply a clerical trick to keep power, but it could also be a mechanism for laypeople to avoid the difficulties inherent in sharing faith in a world hostile to it. The attitude often glimpsed is that one should leave it to the professionals, i.e., priests and religious, and perhaps a few laypeople who are into that sort of thing. While there were some parishes that involved parishioners in door-to-door evangelization (see the comments below Hahn's article), this was not the experience of most Catholics.[7] It was the missions that were important, but a sense that each Catholic was ideally a missionary was lacking. After all, the faith was something that was solid, concrete, seen in the teeming numbers of children in Catholic schools and parishes, and in the various Catholic associations that formed Catholic life in America. In a recent article on Catholic parishes taking up "Protestant-style" evangelistic techniques, Fr. Stephen Bevans, SVD, a professor of missions and culture at Chicago's Catholic Theological Union, gave perfect expression to this view. Going door-to-door, he said, "is not really a Catholic practice that we've done often in the past. There have been so many of us we haven't had to do it."

This notion that "we haven't had to do it" has a kind of cultural confidence behind it. But it is the kind of confidence that can easily lead to a fall. What was needed, under this view, was institutional maintenance. Keep the structures of the Church firm, shore up discipline, and things will be all right. We're big enough we don't need to do that Protestant stuff. Clearly something more was needed.

The Council and Its Interpretations

This something more, the notion that every individual Catholic must seek the holiness of Christ and share in His mission to the world in individual ways, not just as a part of a larger Catholic culture that would transmit the faith "by osmosis,"[8] was what was being proposed in the documents of the Second Vatican Council, as evidenced by this new use of the term "evangelization." It was what Paul VI and John Paul II were aiming at in their writings. But they were stymied not just by older Catholic attitudes toward the job of the laity or even by the institutional understandings of the Church since the Counter-Reformation. Instead, they were stymied by that notion of the Council mentioned by Cardinal Dulles: the sense that the Council discouraged evangelism.

One can see that this notion is a large part of the reason John Paul wrote in his encyclical: "Missionary activity specifically directed 'to the nations' (*ad gentes*) appears to be waning, and this tendency is certainly not in line with the directives of the Council and of subsequent statements of the *Magisterium*" (*RM* 2). Further, the reasons for this waning appear to be located in theological questions:

> Nevertheless, also as a result of the changes which have taken place in modern times and the spread of new theological ideas, some people wonder: *Is missionary work among non-Christians still relevant?* Has it not been replaced by inter-religious dialogue? Is not human development an adequate goal of the Church's mission? Does not respect for conscience and for freedom exclude all efforts at conversion? Is it not possible to attain salvation in any religion? Why then should there be missionary activity?

Are Catholics today to give up on the goal of full conversion of individuals to the fullness of truth in Christ and His Church? Should we simply focus on "human development" and "dialogue" with others? This is certainly the idea that is to be had from many Catholic priests and academics. Concerning an exhibition of the work of French painter Georges Rouault, who declared, "My only ambition is to be able one day to paint Christ so movingly that those who see Him will be converted," Peter Gilmour, a professor at the Institute of Pastoral Studies at Chicago's Loyola University offered a word of warning. "Rouault's concept of conversion might be a bit dated for a post-Vatican II Church that recognizes truths in other religions and for a culture that embraces pluralism."[9] Conversion, you see, is "dated" because the Church recognizes truths in other religions. No one need actually convert to Christ and the Catholic Church for any reason. Dominican sister Maureen Sullivan draws out this notion that truth in other religions equals an end to the idea of evangelism leading to conversion, which she attributes directly to Vatican II:

> The underlying assumption [of the Council Fathers] was that if God is the creator of the universe and of all humans, then the presence of God can be found everywhere on earth and in all peoples — reason enough to presume that there is a value in interfaith dialogues. This insight would have a serious impact on the way we understood the church's outreach. No longer would the primary focus of missionary

activity be to simply convert others — not if we truly believed God was present in the world and in humanity. Our task would be to give witness to the world of the universality of Christian redemption, to be a special Christian presence in the world.[10]

A Question of Salvation

The Church, both before and after Vatican II, has always recognized truths in other religions. But it has also recognized the need for conversion. Just because God is present to all does not mean that He is accepted by all, much less that "the universality of Christian redemption" means that everyone, everywhere is saved. But this is the assumption that Sullivan and others have been working with for many decades now. It is significant that in quotations like the above, what Vatican II taught is merely asserted. There is no reference to what is actually said in the documents.

In his recent book, *Will Many Be Saved: What Vatican II Actually Teaches and its Implications for the New Evangelism* (Eerdmans), Ralph Martin of Sacred Heart Seminary (Detroit) has examined what Vatican II actually does teach about the possibilities for salvation, particularly for those not only outside full communion with the Catholic Church, but outside of Christian faith altogether. His focus is *Lumen gentium* which asserted that:

> Those who, through no fault of their own, do not know the Gospel of Christ or His Church, but who nevertheless seek God with a sincere heart and moved by grace, try in their actions to do His will as they know it through the dictates of their conscience — those too may achieve eternal salvation. Nor shall divine providence deny the assistance necessary for salvation to those who, without any fault of theirs, have not yet arrived at an explicit knowledge of God, and who, not without grace, strive to lead a good life (*LG* 16).[11]

What we see here is nothing different from Pius IX's 1863 encyclical *Quanto conficiamur moerore*.[12] It is possible to be ignorant of the truth of Catholic teaching without being culpable. It is possible through adherence to the natural law and the pursuit of the divine will as glimpsed in the conscience to achieve salvation without an explicit faith through divine assistance. *LG* 16's subsequent paragraph, however, is rarely quoted by those who, like Sr. Sullivan, claim that the universality of redemption means that everybody, or almost everybody, is already saved.

LG 16 reads:

> But very often, deceived by the Evil One, men have become vain in their reasonings, have exchanged the truth of God for a lie, and served the creature rather than the Creator. Or else, living and dying in this world without God, they are exposed to ultimate despair. Hence to procure the glory of God and the salvation of all of these, the Church, mindful of the command of the Lord, "Preach the Gospel to every creature," fosters the missions with care and attention.

It is this danger of men succumbing to idolatry and/or ultimate despair — something the Council Fathers describe as happening "very often" — that leads to the quotation from the Great Commission: Preach the Gospel to every creature! The possibility of salvation, interpreted by Sr. Sullivan and others as universal certainty, is actually only a possibility in the text of *Lumen gentium*. And the fact that "very often" this possibility has not been realized, should be the motivator for us to preach the Good News.

Martin goes to great lengths to show that this "dark side" of the Good News is rooted firmly in the biblical worldview of Jesus and the Twelve, not just mean old St. Paul. To preach the good-times Gospel of Sr. Sullivan and others – the news that I'm okay, you're okay – is to betray the Gospel that Jesus preached and to weaken its power on listeners. "Unless we squarely face the bad news — original sin and personal sin have severe consequences — it is impossible really to appreciate the good news (God is rich in mercy; out of the great love with which He loved us we are saved by grace through faith)."[13]

Martin observes that the pastoral strategy in place after Vatican II, of emphasizing only the positive side of the equation, has also been a failure in producing Catholic evangelists. Even for those who haven't embraced the universalism of Sr. Sullivan, the reticence about speaking about those severe consequences — aka hell — has led to a truncated message, even from bishops and popes. Inspiring as Paul VI and John Paul II's encyclicals on evangelization were, "neither one addresses extensively one of the primary underlying reasons for the waning of the mission *ad gentes* or the lack of any significant embrace of the call to the 'new evangelization' or 're-evangelization' (*RM* 33) of those who perhaps have been baptized but are far from the faith. Neither one elaborates on why 'very often' the possibility of people being saved without hearing the gospel is not realized."[14] Catholics can be told to evangelize, but without a sense that their message has anything to do with the eternal destiny of its hearers, the likelihood of their doing so is remote at best. And American Catholics haven't beaten the odds with this strategy. We need to preach the Bad News and the Good News. Only that is effective. Only that is Catholic.

ENDNOTES

1. *Evangelii nuntiandi*, 2. Available at http://www.vatican.va/holy_father/paul_vi/apost_exhortations/documents/hf_p-vi_exh_19751208_evangelii-nuntiandi_en.html.

2. *Redemptoris missio*, 1. http://www.vatican.va/holy_father/john_paul_ii/encyclicals/documents/hf_jp-ii_enc_07121990_redemptoris-missio_en.html

3. See the Pew Research Center's *Faith in Flux* report for details on changing religious identity for Catholics. http://www.pewforum.org/faith-in-flux.aspx

4. http://www.pewforum.org/Christian/Catholic/Strong-Catholic-Identity-at-a-Four-Decade-Low-in-US.aspx.

5. Avery Dulles, foreword to Timothy E. Byerley, *The Great Commission: Models of Evangelization in American Catholicism* (New York: Paulist Press, 2008), ix. The statistics cited are from Nancy T. Ammerman, *Pillars of Faith* (Berkeley: University of California Press, 2005), 117, 134.

6. Scott W. Hahn, "Mass Evangelization," *America Magazine*, April 22, 2013. http://americamagazine.org/issue/mass-evangelization

7. Tim Townsend, "Catholics Take Up Protestant-Style Evangelism," *Christianity Today* blog, May 2, 2013.

8. George Weigel, *Evangelical Catholicism* (New York: Basic Books, 2013), 16.

9. Peter Gilmour, "The Art of Evangelization," *US Catholic* 72:2 (December 2007): 11.

10. Maureen Sullivan, *101 Questions and Answers on Vatican II* (Mahwah, N.J.: Paulist Press, 2002), 60.

11. Available at http://www.vatican.va/archive/hist_councils/ii_vatican_council/documents/vat-ii_const_19641121_lumen-gentium_en.html

12. For an English translation of the encyclical, see http://www.papalencyclicals.net/Pius09/p9quanto.htm The relevant section is #7: "There are, of course, those who are struggling with invincible ignorance about our most holy religion. Sincerely observing the natural law and its precepts inscribed by God on all hearts and ready to obey God, they live honest lives and are able to attain eternal life by the efficacious virtue of divine light and grace. Because God knows, searches and clearly understands the minds, hearts, thoughts, and nature of all, his supreme kindness and clemency do not permit anyone at all who is not guilty of deliberate sin to suffer eternal punishments." In #8 Blessed Pope Pius IX emphasizes that those who are "stubbornly separated" from the Church cannot, however, achieve salvation.

13. Ralph Martin, *Will Many Be Saved? What Vatican II Actually Teaches and its Implications for the New Evangelization* (Grand Rapids, Mich.: Eerdmans, 2012), 201.

14. *Ibid.*, 198.

DAVID PAUL DEAVEL is editor of *Logos: A Journal of Catholic Thought and Culture* and visiting assistant professor of Catholic Studies at the University of St. Thomas (Minnesota). He has a Ph.D. in theology from Fordham University. He is the vice president of the Newman Association of America and a contributing editor for *Gilbert*, the magazine of the American Chesterton Society. He has published over 250 articles, essays, and reviews in a number of books as well as a wide variety of popular and scholarly journals including *America, Books & Culture, Catholic World Report, Chesterton Review, Christian Century, Commonweal, First Things, National Review, Journal of Markets and Morality, New Blackfriars, Nova et Vetera,* and *Touchstone.* In 2013, the Acton Institute presented him with the Novak Award for promising scholarship on the connections between religion and economic liberty. He lives in St. Paul, Minnesota, with his wife Catherine, an associate professor of philosophy at the University of St. Thomas, and their seven children.

Heralds of Christ in the Marketplace
by Frank Morriss

(Editor's Note: This discussion of *Apostolicam actuositatem*, the *Decree on the Apostolate of Lay People*, is from the *Divine Epic*, written by Morriss as the script for a church history radio program aired in 1973.)

The Sunday Christian is no real Christian at all. The Christian vocation is a seven-days-a-week, 365-days-a-year one. The men and women of God's People are called to do whatever they can do in service to Christ and His Church. Marking their labors with the highest virtues their faith inspires, they carry Christ wherever they go, including the marketplace of everyday life which is the special realm of the laity. It is impossible truly to keep God's day holy if one does not attempt to sanctify the weekdays which belong to the world and its cares.

Apostolican actuositatem, promulgated on November 8, 1965, makes it very clear the lay person must help build up the Church, adding glory to Christ's very body. The Second Vatican Council is quite harsh regarding those who will not accept this obligation:

> Indeed, so intimately are the parts (that is, of Christ's body) linked and interrelated in this body (cf. *Eph.* 4:16) that the member who fails to make his proper contribution to the development of the Church must be said to be useful neither to the Church nor to himself (n.2).

Apathy to the affairs of the Church, its welfare, the afflictions it bears, the import of what it teaches indicates that a flame which should burn with intensity in the Catholic's heart is instead burning low, or perhaps gone out entirely. Abortion threatens the life of the unborn, and many Catholics are unmoved to action. Contraception has become an American way of life, and Catholics side with those who are untaught in this matter. Injustice is imposed upon the weak, and Catholics respond no quicker than those unconcerned about justice. The elderly are in need of help, and Catholics turn their backs along with their fellow citizens. Basic rights of individual action are curtailed by government, pressure groups, fear, political movements, and Catholics shrug their shoulders. Atheistic governments deprive their citizens of freedom, and support similar atheistic revolutions around the world, and Catholics join the cry not for justice, but for American unconcern. "What is that to us?" they ask as readily as any other persons.

This obviously shows no understanding of the duty defined by Vatican II, for that Council called for a display on the part of laity of "honesty, justice, sincerity, kindness, and courage." These are virtues, incidentally, that suit any way of life, any calling. If enough persons put them into daily practice, the world would be instantly changed and God's purposes served far better than now, when these virtues are in such short supply (n.4).

But it is primarily in direct regard to the faith that the Catholic lay person should be concerned. If the Church is rendered ineffective, crippled by disloyalty, weakened by disregard, then Christ's message is in effect hidden, the duty He imposed upon His followers delayed in fulfillment.

Such a condition is implicitly warned against by Vatican II:

> Since in this age of ours, new problems are arising and extremely serious errors are gaining currency which tend to undermine the foundations of religion, the moral order, the human society itself, this sacred Synod earnestly exhorts laymen, each according to his natural gifts and learning, to be more diligent in doing their part according to the mind of the Church, to explain and defend Christian principles, and to apply them rightly to the problems of our era (n.6).

Unfortunately, too few lay persons have been able to recognize some of these dangers that the Council speaks about. And, in fact, some clergymen, the officers of the Church, have been no more sensitive to error and danger, no better equipped by their priestly formation to deal with philosophic peril than lay persons. The successful invasion of Catholic education by behaviorist psychology and evolutionary biology over the years is ample proof of this.

The existence of lay organizations, lay-edited newspapers which are openly contemptuous of the Pope and his teaching authority, the hierarchy, Catholic schools (not just in their inadequacies, but in their very theory) also reveals a mentality unappreciative of Vatican II. When a false liberty is proclaimed by the secularists, these spokesmen applaud it; when the Church cautions against such libertarianism, these spokesmen label the Church insensitive and old-fashioned. When an exaggerated humanism asserts its rights contrary to the natural law and the rights of individuals, these same spokesmen side with humanism, and against the supernaturalism of the Church. They have done so for 50 years, unabated.

Silence and Apathy

Population alarmists seize the reins of state authority, and impose their immoral solutions to unproven problems, even forcing their way between child and parent, and there is a stunning silence on the part of most Catholic lay persons. Those who dare point out the implications are called alarmists, if not unbalanced.

Gnosticism in the guise of interest in Oriental religion is pushed at Catholic students in Catholic colleges and universities, and the laity is silent. Immoralists are invited to Catholic campuses, and the laity is silent. Religious education teachers present confusion instead of doctrine in regard to religious belief and the laity was silent for years, the very laity whose own children's faith became endangered. Theologians attack the permanency of marriage [Note: and now, whether marriage pertains to a man and a woman or anyone as a spouse] and the laity is silent, either overawed by the credentials of those making this attack, or else indifferent to the very institution that has sustained Western civilization.

None of this silence and apathy then or now shows any appreciation for the laity's duty and rights as outlined by Vatican II. And yet strangely those most inclined to accept those dangers, and in fact to see them as simply enlightenment, are the very ones ready to claim Vatican II as their Bible. It is clearly an unread and misunderstood Bible, if indeed those persons are sincere at all.

The Council makes specific reference in some of the areas just mentioned:

> It has always been the duty of Christian couples, but today it is the supreme task of their apostolate, to manifest and prove by their own way of life the unbreakable and sacred character of the marriage bond, to affirm vigorously the right and duty of parents and

guardians to educate children in a Christian manner, and to defend the dignity and lawful independence of the family. They and the rest of the faithful, therefore, should cooperate with men of good will to ensure the preservation of these rights in civil legislation, and to make sure that attention is paid to the needs of the family in government policies, regarding housing, the education of children, working conditions, social security, and taxes; and that in decisions affecting migrants, their right to live together as a family is safeguarded (n.11).

Yet we see laws of the contrary – anti-family laws, anti-child laws – proposed regularly, often in the name of population control or ecology, and only a few lonely voices are raised in protest. In fact, some of those supporting these very evils are Catholic legislators themselves!

As Catholic education declines, the Catholic parent more and more loses his best means of protecting his child from a completely secular education. Soon the combination of this country's compulsory education laws, court decisions barring anything but the secular from public schools, and the shutdown of parochial schools will mean the parent will have only his own resources with which to rear a child with a sense of the sacred and the supernatural – provided the parent has preserved this sense within.

An interest in this problem on the part of enough Catholic lay persons could bring about a profound change – it could keep truly Catholic schools open, or else open ones directed by loyal Catholic lay people; it would change the composition of legislatures and school boards, thus helping end agnostic or atheistic secularism where it exists in public education. But all of this takes an interest and an activity of the kind called for by Vatican II.

The Council does not call only for defensive action. Rather it points to the duty to take the offensive for truth:

This apostolate should reach out to all men wherever they can be found; it should not exclude any spiritual or temporal benefit which can possibly be conferred. True apostles, however, are not content with this activity alone, but look for the opportunity to announce Christ to their neighbors through the spoken word as well. For there are many persons who can hear the gospel and recognize Christ only through the laity who live near them. (n.13)

A vast field for the apostolate has opened up on the national and international levels where most of all laity are called upon to be stewards of Christian wisdom. In loyalty to their country and in fulfillment of their civil obligations, Catholics should feel themselves obliged to promote the true common good. Thus, they should make the weight of their opinion felt, so that civil authority may act with justice and laws may conform to moral precepts and the common good (n.14).

The modern Catholic is inclined to feel he has no right to intrude moral precepts, the teachings of religious truth he has received from his Church, into public matters. There is a false idea that it is improper to fight for or against anything because one has learned to be for or against it from his faith. This is not only wrong, it is specifically rejected by Vatican II as the passage above clearly shows. Indeed, the first virtue that needs rehabilitating among the laity today is that of courage – courage concerning the faith. To be a true Catholic, a conciliar one heeding the teaching of Vatican II, is to be a courageous Catholic, one who is known and heard in regard to his beliefs.

When active, militant persecution attacks the Church, the laity are allowed the opportunity for special service. In every persecution, Catholic lay persons have suffered and died assisting the clergy. At one time, every Catholic knew stories of these saints, from Tarcisius who carried the Eucharist to prisoners until he was discovered and martyred, to St. Margaret Clitheroe, who during the terrible persecution under the Tudor monarchy, died for concealing priests and providing a place for Holy Mass to be celebrated. She not only died a martyr for her faith, but a martyr for the idea there are limitations to the jurisdiction of the state. We need more martyrs today for that latter idea, for it is under attack everywhere the state purports to legalize immorality or allows interference with the parental right to decide what a child shall be taught regarding the use of sex, or determining the right to contraceptive information and devices for twelve-year olds.

Where were the protests on the part of Catholic authorities and legislators and laypersons against these immoral laws?

St. Robert Southwell, SJ, wrote from prison, "When we come to the service of Christ, we come to a rough profession." That could well be the keynote, the theme for the laity, especially in our day. It is no easy profession, not if it is taken seriously and fulfilled as Vatican II wishes.

It can bring the contempt of the world, the loss of friends, even among those who should be joined hand-in-hand for the battle; it can bring loneliness, slander, anonymity, poverty, and the appearance of defeat. Martyrs of old at least had the consolation of an unclouded vision of the unshaken majesty and certainty of the Church. Today the clouds of dubious teaching by those who should be defenders of the faith obscure that vision and it is almost as if the defenders of the faith battle alone on the issues of the day, cut off from help, supplies, the chance to retreat to the calm of the Rock which is the Church.

Modern persecutors do not rage. What they attempt to do is weary us to death. They will overwhelm us with sweet reasonableness, ignore us because of our foolish involvement with the emphemerality of faith, ridicule us as old-fashioned, dismiss us because – crime of crimes! – we are not part of the consensus. It is a persecution perhaps more terrible to face than the fangs of hungry lions or the whips and hooks of more honest pagans compared to the those who run the affairs of government and even religion in our day.

That, however, merely makes it all the more important for lay persons to speak, when priests are silent; to teach, when nuns grow weary of teaching or there are no nuns to teach; to adore, when theologians suggest there is nothing there in the tabernacle to adore and hide it from view; to defend, when the timid say it is improper to speak up; to organize, when the defeatists say nothing can be accomplished by numbers; to pray, when our enemies insist that action is all important; to act, when others succumb to the temptation to believe that all action is hopeless.

Things have not changed in 50 years.

In a word, though, it is time for resurrection. The time is here to be a Catholic as Confirmation calls us to be – a soldier of Christ – and a herald of Christ everywhere we go, as the Second Vatican Council tells us we must be. It is always when the battle is in doubt, that the devil whispers, "The new Catholic is not militant, aggressive; he does not flaunt to the world his beliefs; he does not intrude where he is not appreciated. You dare not call abortion murder, for that is to be uncharitable to those who see it differently; you dare not call sin a sin, for that is to give a guilt complex to those who do what you think is sinful. Best be silent and let the world have its way."

Let The World Have Its Way?

None of this finds any echo or excuse in Vatican II. Here, for example, is what the Council says about the lay apostolate in those parts of the world where the freedom of the Church is restricted:

> There is an imperative need for the individual apostolate in those areas where the Church's freedom is seriously hampered. In such difficult circumstances, the laity take over as far as possible the work of priests, jeopardizing their own freedom and sometimes their lives; they teach Christian doctrine to those around them, train them in a religious way of life and in Catholic attitudes, encourage them to receive the sacraments frequently and to cultivate piety, especially Eucharistic piety. The Council renders God most heartfelt thanks that even in our own times He is still raising up laymen with heroic courage in the midst of persecutions; the Council embraces them with gratitude and fatherly affection (n.17).

The Catholic mentality which the Council speaks of is every bit as endangered in the so-called free world as it is under Communism. As error infects the fields of Catholic action ever more deeply, it becomes more and more difficult to distinguish the Catholic from any other person – Christian or pagan. This, some progressives feel is desirable. It proves the Catholic emergence from the ghetto, his acceptance of the world and its problems, his emancipation from a divisive and separatist psychosis.

The answer, following the Council, must be this: If there is a Catholic mentality, which there must be since Vatican II speaks of it with praise, then certainly it must be recognizable. Surely having a Catholic mentality makes a difference.

It is ironic when racial minorities are quite correctly recognizing the pride that should mark their differences and culture, that Catholics, who are or should be fundamentally different, are being told it is wrong to take pride in that fact. It is time for Catholic pride – Catholic power. That power should not be to rule, to deprive anyone of right or conscience; that power should be to serve. Catholic power can serve society, truth, and Christ by upholding those things that are for society's good, those things that reflect Christ's light rather than the pagan darkness. The pagans do not hesitate to assert their power. They will harry, hack, push, pull, bulldoze, coerce, wheedle their views into laws through committee, legislature, court, until paganism in regard to life, sex, conduct becomes the rule of the land [Note: prophetic words in light of the efforts on behalf of homosexual 'marriage.']. We need not imitate their methods; but we should learn from their worldly wisdom, their guile in support of what they believe, or more properly, disbelieve.

If it is Catholic power to stand in their way, to recite the natural and divine laws which they transgress, to challenge their right and their jurisdiction, then it is time for Catholic power to be used. What body of men has the jurisdiction to sit in judgment over whether the unborn are to be protected by the state or to be turned over to the executioner? That is arrogance in the extreme, and Catholic power should have labeled it so. What legislature or court has the jurisdiction to grant anyone immunity for the taking of innocent life simply because it had grown old and foolish? Yet that battle is upon us. When lawmaker, judge and executive can claim to have originated and given the life, then we should heed their claim to power over that life. But since they cannot make such claim, we should stand between their assertion of power and the object of its deadly intent. If we are persecuted for doing so, if we are jailed for doing so, if we are executed for doing so, it will be an honor and a defense in the only court and before the only Judge and Lawgiver who really counts.

The Catholic Church may be the only reality left which recognizes this fact and which is capable of doing anything about it. And Catholic laity surely should be in the front lines when the battle is ultimately joined on the spiritual, legal, and juridical fields in our time. If we understand our vocation and take pride in what Vatican II teaches about our duties, we would want it no other way:

> The Council, then, makes to all laity an earnest appeal in the Lord to give a willing, noble and enthusiastic response to the voice of Christ, who at this hour is summoning them more pressingly, and to the urging of the Holy Spirit. The younger generation should feel this call to be addressed in a special way to themselves; they should welcome it eagerly and generously. It is the Lord Himself, by this Council, who is once more inviting all the laity to unite themselves to Him ever more intimately, to consider His interests as their own (cf. *Phil.*2:5), and to join in His mission as Savior. It is the Lord who is again sending them into every town and every place where He Himself is to come (cf. *Luke* 10:1). He sends them on the Church's apostolate, an apostolate that is one yet has different forms and

methods, an apostolate that must all the time be adapting itself to the needs of the moment; He sends them on an apostolate where they are to show themselves His cooperators, doing their full share continually in the work of the Lord, knowing that in the Lord their labor cannot be lost (cf. *Cor.* 15:58) (n.33).

This document of the Council on the Laity calls for witness, there is no other way about it if one signs himself with the Cross of Christ.

FRANK MORRISS, J.D., was a graduate of Regis College, Denver, received his Juris Doctorate from Georgetown University School of Law. He also holds a degree in philosophy. Since returning from Army service in the Philippines and Japan in 1945, Morriss devoted his talents to Catholic journalism. He is a former news editor of the *Denver Catholic Register*, a founding editor of *Twin Circle*, editorial writer and contributor to *The Wanderer*, and the author of a number of works, including *The Catholic as Citizen, A Little Life of Our Lord, The Divine Epic, Saints in Verse*, and *Two Chapels*, a treatment of Cardinal Newman and the Oxford Movement. Morriss' most recent book is *Francis Thompson - A Reflection on the Poetic Vocation*. In addition, he has authored several historical fiction books for children. Morriss has twice earned the George Washington Medal given by the Freedom Foundation of Valley Forge. In 2003, Morriss was awarded the Bl. Frederic Ozanam award by the Society of Catholic Social Scientists. Morriss was co-editor and writer of the Wanderer Forum's *Forum Focus* magazine and a member of the Board of Directors of the Wanderer Forum Foundation/Bellarmine Forum. Morriss passed from this life on January 25, 2014.

The Truth Shall Make You Free

By Frank Morriss

(Editor's Note: This discussion of *Dignitatis humanae*, the *Declaration on Religious Liberty*, is from the *Divine Epic*, written by Morriss as the script for a church history radio program aired in 1973.)

Freedom is perhaps the most misunderstood term of our time. So when the Second Vatican Council issued *Dignitatis humanae*, the *Declaration on Religious Freedom* (December 7, 1965), it became probably the most misunderstood document of that Council. The general idea of those who do not really understand what the Council said was that this document set people free to believe anything they wish about religious matters, to do whatever they want if their conscience says it is okay. If *Dignitatis humanae* had done that, of course, it would only have made men slaves. For we know Christ said, "If you abide in My word, you shall be My disciples indeed, and you shall know the truth and the truth shall make you free."

His Jewish hearers had just about the same misunderstanding of freedom as do moderns. They thought it meant being free of political domination, clear of imposition of laws not of their own choice. "We have never been slaves of anyone," was their answer to Christ's words. Then Our Lord made clear the true nature of liberty: It is an abiding in goodness, a freedom from sin. That is the liberty Christ brought – the liberty of human fulfillment; that man is most free who most conforms to his nature, is most respectful of that nature. The free man walks in sanctity unchained by evil. The slave does not abide in the house forever, Christ told His listeners, but the Son does. "If therefore the Son makes you free, you will be free indeed." Freedom means being with Christ. Slavery means being without Him.

Those who have never actually studied Vatican II, but proclaim what they call "the spirit of the Council," will be shocked to learn the *Declaration on Religious Freedom* opens with an assertion of the truth of the Catholic Faith as the one true religion and the duty of all men to seek out that truth and accept it (n.1). The right of men to be free from coercion by any force or power in matters of religion, does not relieve their consciences of the need of accepting the true Faith, the Council says. Religion itself, as the word implies, is a matter of being tied – tied back to God. The Christian paradox is that man finds true liberty by submission. When he puts his will with Christ's, man is freed for he is in possession of that truth which is liberty itself. Freedom, therefore, does not exist in the possibility or capability of rejecting truth, of believing whatever one wants, of acting in any way one chooses (n.1).

However, the right and duty to choose the truth demands freedom from coercion. To be forced to accept the truth is actually to be denied the right to choose it; what one *must* accept one does not *choose*. On the other hand, to be denied the right to choose truth is also an invasion of liberty, for man in that manner cannot make the submission to the truth that frees – or at least cannot enjoy the fruits of that submission (to which he has a right), that is, the fruits of religious practice, piety, prayer, the Mass.

Vatican II confronts modern man with an unpalatable paradox. Freedom consists in acceptance of law. Modern man, of course, would rather think that freedom means an escape from law.

Man is not without norms regarding that which is suitable to his humanity, that is, things that truly fulfill him, make him more human. Those norms rest in the divine law which is of God's nature. God conceived man as a free creature, but not one without direction. The wanderer is often perceived by men to be a free creature. He comes and goes as he wishes, without any reference to some home from which he came or some home to which he is going. Yet if we think about such a person it becomes apparent he is not essentially different from someone who is lost in a desert or in a forest. A person who is lost is not free. He is a victim of ignorance. God chose not to leave man – His greatest material creation – simply a wanderer, a victim of ignorance. Instead, God created a polar star – the divine law – and gave to man a compass designed to point out that law, the compass being man's conscience. Vatican II expresses it more formally:

> On his part, man perceives and acknowledges the imperatives of the divine law through the mediation of conscience. In all his activity a man is bound to follow his conscience faithfully, in order that he

may come to God, for whom he was created. It follows that he is not to be forced to act in a manner contrary to his conscience. Nor, on the other hand, is he to be restrained from acting in accordance with his conscience, especially in matters religious (n.3).

Properly understood, freedom of conscience is simply the duty and freedom to accept God's law. Unfortunately, many have it exactly backward. They believe freedom of conscience involves the right to reject all law and duty – man's or God's. How often do we hear freedom of conscience described in words something like these, to defend a diversity of religious faith: "We're all headed toward the same place but on different paths." Implied in this is the right of conscience to set its own path, choose its own manner of spiritual progress.

The Straight Path

But conscience is not a pathmaker – it is a pathfinder. It is obliged to seek out the steps of God, which in history are the steps of God's Son, Jesus Christ. If Christ has walked only a single path – which certainly is so – then conscience must put man on only a single path. "I am *the* Way," Christ said – not "*a* way." "Come, follow *Me*," Christ said – not "Go, follow your conscience." The path is one, it is straight, it is marked.

It is not, however, the prerogative of civil government to decide where that path is laid, what turns it takes, and who must walk upon it. This, again, is the prerogative of conscience. Government may hinder no one from finding the path, should put no obstacles in the way, penalize no move in the direction conscience points. This does not mean that conscience is above or beyond civil law. One may not shirk civic duty and claim a right of conscience. Only when conscience performs its duty is it immune from interference. When it becomes the excuse for lawbreaking, when it seeks to write a writ of exception from civil law, then conscience must be suspect. The object of conscience is God and His path. Walking that path does not lead men *away* from civil order, but on the other hand, conforms man *to* proper civil order.

No claim of conscience can, for example, seek to deprive society of its rights. No claim of conscience can strip a nation of its right and power to defend itself against aggression. No claim of conscience can deprive persons of their right to own property. No claim of conscience can ignite class warfare, bind men to a conduct that is not dictated by God's own law. Conscience does not impose personal belief on any person. Its works can be recognized in the fact it respects all rights, and does not seek to dictate anything on the basis of opinion – political, sociological, or economic. The appeal of conscience is to truth. It is not a rabble rouser. It does not call out the action of mobs or conspirators. It does not dictate one wrong to right another. Vatican II recognizes this fact:

> ...Society has the right to defend itself against possible abuses committed on the pretext of religious freedom. It is the special duty of government to provide this protection. However, government is not to act in arbitrary fashion or in an unfair spirit of partisanship. Its action is to be controlled by juridical norms which are in conformity with the objective moral order (n.7).

The Council lays a duty upon educators in this regard:

> This Vatican Synod urges everyone, especially those who are charged with the task of educating others, to do their utmost to form men who will respect the moral order and be obedient to lawful authority. Let them form men too who will be lovers of true freedom – men in other words, who will come to decisions on their own judgment and in the light of truth, govern their activities with a sense of responsibility, and strive after what is true and right, willing always to join with others in cooperative effort (n.8).

It should be questioned, therefore, if what is happening on many college campuses – including Catholic ones – is in conformity with this doctrine of Vatican II. First we have the production of young non-conformists who are told that the most grotesque individualism is a sign of liberty. All that is bizarre in behavior and appearance is praised as an outward sign of some inner liberation. Restraint is considered wrong; self discipline and self-sacrifice are discounted as foolish. Self-expression, on the other hand and no matter how vulgar, is the beginning of wisdom. Youths are encouraged in the idea that anything anyone does is somehow in the realm of praiseworthy achievement.

Out of Control

When this individuality is combined into mass action, it is called social or artistic awareness. Educators, law authorities, parents are expected to stand in awe of great gatherings where youths sleep together on the ground, bathe together *au naturel*, smoke pot together in a search for some pseudo-mystical experience, and hear illiterate leaders shout *cliches* about the tyranny of institutions. (Note: Now, 50 years later, the college dorms provide the togetherness, cocaine and alcohol are the drugs of choice, and the illiterate leaders whipping up the students of the past have become the college professors who, with their proteges of yesteryear, now rule strong in the ivory halls, still preaching their libertine enslavement.)

Whatever this type of society is – it is not a society of freedom. When expression and experience are considered superior to thought and artistry, when sociology is valued more than philosophy, when behavioristic psychology is considered the replacement for religious ethics – then we are not raising up a generation of free people, but a generation of automatons, all trained to react even if the reaction is chaotic, all conditioned to respond to the Pied Pipers of the "new times" and "new things." These are not schools for liberty but rather schools for slavery.

Dante, I believe, has those souls – consigned to the Inferno because of lustful lives on earth – tossed about by eternal winds. They are out of control, as their actions were out of control when they lived. Conscience and law did not restrain them on earth; now they are doomed to an eternity of buffeting – merely the extension of that type of life they once chose.

The same might be said of modern intellectual man, who has chosen to take the path of eternal questioning, which in a sense is an eternal intellectual lust. Those who serve the flesh are never satisfied; each sensation must be followed by another; each experience must be supplanted by a new one. Those who serve the new philosophy are never satisfied; each attempt at an answer merely increases their appetite for knowledge, so that a new question must be attempted. They are driven by the ancient intellectual lust called gnosticism – the appetite to know things beyond even God's own Revelation, to experience intellectual delights somewhat similar to the delights of the flesh that always attract, but never satisfy, the libertine. Freedom has escaped such persons.

The free man, with his mind not scandalized by any assertion, weighs that which confronts it and makes judgments. The intellectual slave becomes enthralled with whatever confronts his mind, since he has been conditioned to make no judgments. The Pavlovian dog slavers at the ringing of a bell. The Pavlovian man's mind excites at – not truth – but simply the claim to truth.

Philosophic and religious demagogues shout out that they have found a new way and a new truth (or a new theology) – and the modern product of education answers "Alleluia." He will shout the same thing to the next demagogue who claims to have the truth, and the next.

"Oh, do not ask what is it?" they say with Eliot's J. Alfred Prufock. "Let us go and make a visit." Taking intellectual trips is the greatest enjoyment of the modern pretender to scholarship. He is on a continual Cook's Tour, seeking out new excitements and new intellectual vistas. Cut off by a contempt for history from any return home, he is deprived of the greatest truth in the world – the object of travel is to make one more appreciative of home; the object of study is to make one more appreciative of truth.

The truly free man is not excited by each new philosophy. He delights only in some new appreciation or explanation of truth. He is free because he knows about home and its delights; his reference is always here, where the heavenly Father dwells in the constant light of truth that emanates from Divinity.

Vatican II was speaking to and about such free persons when it gave the Catholic understanding of freedom of conscience:

> In the formation of their consciences, the Christian faithful ought carefully to attend to the sacred and certain doctrine of the Church. The Church is, by the will of Christ, the teacher of the truth. It is her duty to give utterance to, and authoritatively to teach, the Truth which is Christ Himself, and also to declare and confirm by her authority those principles of the moral order which have their origin in human nature itself. Furthermore, let Christians walk in wisdom in the face of those outside, "in the Holy Spirit, in unaffected love, in the world of truth" (II *Cor.* 6:6-7). Let them be about their task by spreading the light of life with all confidence and apostolic courage, even to the shedding of their blood (n.14).

How different such persons are from those who will not even accept the Church's teaching at the risk of loss of human respect, of worldly acclaim. How different such persons are from those who will withhold the application of truth for political reasons, or academic ones.

No Weathervane

Confidence, courage, serenity mark the free man. He is not a weathervane, reflecting the changes of philosophic wind. He does not reject truth because it is difficult; he would rather be right and free, than enslaved by conformity to anything less than the truth. He never succumbs to the argument that a thing cannot be true if it is demanding. All truth is demanding, for it calls man from a realm beyond himself, from a court that judges all intellectual and moral decisions.

The greatest modern religious scandal has been over a misunderstanding of "religious" liberty and it was set off by the promulgation of *Humanae vitae* in 1968. If the Church teaches what is true and the world teaches in contradiction to it, an acceptance of the world's teaching is an enslavement to error. Scholars and Catholics judged *against* the Church's teaching on contraception on the basis of its difficulty, rather than judging *for* it on the basis of its truth. Their actions told the world that there are "Catholics" who would rather have an easy enslavement than a difficult liberty.

God is the master artist in the creation of life. He knows surely what is good for mankind. Man, in the use of sex, is merely an apprentice. He elevates himself by joining his talent for procreation to the knowledge, wisdom, charity, and energy of God. Contraception is merely man's attempt to do things his own way, even if it means enslavement.

The new theologians [after Vatican II] refused to tell Catholics the truth about this matter. Mini-theologians argued that the Pope didn't know what he was talking about, as if he could teach on such a grave matter of morals without the divine guidance, which as it happens, Pope Paul VI actually invoked in the very words of *Humanae vitae*. They attempted to justify man's own will in a matter obviously intended to serve God's will first. They used *Dignitatis humanae* as justification. Man himself and newly "liberated" women, led by the lure of the flesh, listened as these prophets of a "new theology" twisted the document's call for religious freedom from government interference into freedom to decide what is right and wrong for oneself. The new theologians invented situational ethics, in which the situation determines rightness or wrongness of an act. Thus one could fornicate, but in a situation in which one is acting with "loving concern" it would not be sinful. They preached the commission of mortal sins was not damning because sin did not mean a person had turned completely, and fundamentally, from God. The theologians invented and invented and taught and taught their tainted view of freedom, of man telling conscience what is right and wrong, not the other way around. Without the true teachings of the

Church front and center, Catholic life eroded publicly and privately. And those Catholics, with itching ears for new, easier obligations, or none at all, accepted unquestioningly what was told to them.

From that point, there was no stopping the black gates from opening. So complete was the misdirection of Catholic life that nary a Catholic voice was raised when state legislators passed laws allowing the invasion of children's lives by contraceptive experts, population alarmists, assorted secular *periti,* and sex educationists. Here was a definite assault on freedom of conscience as the Council understood it, the right of children to be guarded from error and to follow only the truth. Here the government took factional sides in a matter definitely basic to human life and liberty, a direct invasion of the Catholic conscience, and yet the Catholic voice was muted because the experts of error had twisted Catholic teaching. And lest one bold soul would go forth to do battle and speak the truth, the same prophets of "new theology" whispered, "Do not assert Catholic teaching, for to do so is to impose on the beliefs of others." The beliefs of others could not be infringed upon, even if it meant trampling the beliefs of Catholics, all in the name of religious freedom. Yet the Council had stated mankind must be free from government interference *to seek the truth found in the Catholic Faith.*

The truth is not compartmentalized. There is not a secular truth over and against a religious truth. All things rest in the divine and natural laws, which are in effect one and the same. It is not liberty to allow the desertion of these laws in the name of the Constitution or some imagined constitutional rights. That path leads to enslavement and man will find himself enslaved if he forgets he alone does not form his conscience, God does in truth. Not the government, surely not the President or Prime Minister or Supreme Court. The *truth* makes man free, not the choice to participate in uninhibited and uncontrolled behavior.

Only Christ is the way, the truth, and the life, the only source of freedom we must follow.

FRANK MORRISS, J.D., was a graduate of Regis College, Denver, received his Juris Doctorate from Georgetown University School of Law. He also holds a degree in philosophy. Since returning from Army service in the Philippines and Japan in 1945, Morriss devoted his talents to Catholic journalism. He is a former news editor of the *Denver Catholic Register*, a founding editor of *Twin Circle*, editorial writer and contributor to *The Wanderer*, and the author of a number of works, including *The Catholic as Citizen, A Little Life of Our Lord, The Divine Epic, Saints in Verse*, and *Two Chapels*, a treatment of Cardinal Newman and the Oxford Movement. Morriss' most recent book is *Francis Thompson - A Reflection on the Poetic Vocation*. In addition, he has authored several historical fiction books for children. Morriss has twice earned the George Washington Medal given by the Freedom Foundation of Valley Forge. In 2003, Morriss was awarded the Bl. Frederic Ozanam award by the Society of Catholic Social Scientists. Morriss was co-editor and writer of the Wanderer Forum's *Forum Focus* magazine and a member of the Board of Directors of the Wanderer Forum Foundation/Bellarmine Forum. Morriss passed from this life on January 25, 2014.

Humane Vitae: Completion of Vatican II

By Charles E. Rice, J.S.D.
Professor Emeritus, Notre Dame Law School

In December 1965, in *Gaudium et spes*, the *Pastoral Constitution on the Church in the Modern World*, the Second Vatican Council built a bridge. That bridge connected the unbroken Christian teaching on contraception to the courageous reaffirmation of that teaching by Pope Paul VI, less than three years later, in *Humanae vitae*. In 2013, the 45th anniversary of *Humanae vitae*, it is good to remind ourselves of the continuity of that encyclical with Vatican II. This is especially important because the teachings of that Council have been "hijacked" by some who would make of them a mandate not for conversion of the world but for surrender to it.

An entire chapter of *Gaudium et spes* is devoted to "The Dignity of Marriage and the Family." You will search in vain through that chapter – and all the documents of Vatican II – for any statement or implication that the unbroken teaching on contraception has somehow become optional. Here, specifically, is what the Council said:

> Married people should realize that in their behavior they may not simply follow their own fancy but must be ruled by conscience – and conscience ought to be conformed to the law of God in the light of the teaching authority of the Church, which is the authentic interpreter of divine law....[T]here can be no conflict between the divine laws governing the transmission of life and the fostering of authentic married love.... In questions of birth regulation the sons of the Church, faithful to these principles, are forbidden to use methods disapproved of by the teaching authority of the Church in its interpretation of the divine law.[1]

Truth has nothing to fear from authentic science.

By order of the Holy Father, certain questions requiring further and more careful investigation have been given over to a commission... in order that the Holy Father may pass judgment when its task is completed. *With the teaching of the Magisterium standing as it is*, the Council has no intention of proposing concrete solutions at this moment.[2]

That advisory commission was created by John XXIII in March 1963. Paul VI confirmed and enlarged it but properly declined to be bound by its conclusions.

When Paul VI issued *Humanae vitae* on July 25, 1968, he confronted a disintegrating culture with the truth that "each and every marriage act... must remain open to the transmission of life."[3]

Humanae Vitae warned that with the acceptance of contraception, "how wide and easy a road would thus be opened up toward conjugal infidelity and the general lowering of morality."[4]

Paul VI predicted that, "the man, growing used to...contraceptive practices, [would] lose respect for the woman and...come to the point of considering her as a mere instrument of selfish enjoyment, and no longer as his respected and beloved companion."

Finally Paul VI voiced a concern that we see validated in the Health and Human Services Health Care Mandate, government imposition of contraception and abortion in health care policies and as a condition of foreign aid, and other abuses:

[A] dangerous weapon would...be placed in the hands of... public authorities who take no heed of moral exigencies. Who could blame a government for applying to the solution of the problems of the community those means acknowledged to be licit for married couples in the solution of a family problem? Who will stop rulers from...even imposing upon their peoples...the method of contraception which they judge to be most efficacious?[5]

"If Paul VI were right about so many of the consequences deriving from contraception," said Archbishop Charles Chaput, "it is because he was right about contraception itself."[6]

Truth, with a capital T, we can never forget, is a person, Jesus Christ. As Paul VI said in 1964, "It is indeed Christ who lives in the Church, and through her teaches, governs and sanctifies."[7]

The trajectory from Vatican II to *Humanae vitae* and beyond is a straight line. We hope and pray that the 50th anniversary of *Humanae vitae*, in 2018, sees a renewed appreciation for the reality that the answer to the problems of our culture will be found only in the moral and social teachings of the Catholic Church – and in prayer.

ENDNOTES

1. *Gaudium et spes*, no. 50-51; *Casti connubii, AAS* 22, p. 559-561.
2. *Gaudium et spes*, footnote 14 to n. 51 (emphasis added).
3. *Humanae vitae*, n.11.
4. *Ibid.*, n. 17.
5. *Ibid.*, n.17.
6. Pastoral, *On Human Life*, July 22, 1998.
7. *Ecclesiam suam* (1964), n. 35.

CHARLES E. RICE received his B.A. degree from the College of the Holy Cross, J.D. from Boston College Law School, and the LL.M. and J.S.D. from New York University. He served in the United States Marine Corps and was a Lieutenant Colonel in the Marine Corps Reserve (Ret.). Rice practiced law in New York City and taught at New York University Law School and Fordham Law School before joining the law school faculty at Notre Dame University in 1969. His areas of specialization were constitutional law and jurisprudence. From 1981 to 1993, Professor Rice was a member of the Education Appeal Board of the U.S. Department of Education. He served as a consultant to the U.S. Commission on Civil Rights and to various Congressional committees on constitutional issues as well as editing the *American Journal of Jurisprudence*. Rice has authored several books, including *Freedom of Association*; *The Vanishing Right to Live*; *The Winning Side: Questions on Living the Culture of Life*. His latest books are *Where Did I Come From? Where Am I Going? How Do I Get There?* (2nd ed.) co-authored with Dr. Theresa Farnan; *What Happened to Notre Dame?*; *Right or Wrong, Forty Years Inside Notre Dame*; and *Contraception & Persecution*, all published by St. Augustine's Press. Rice served as Chairman of the Board of Directors of the Wanderer Forum Foundation/Bellarmine Forum from 1993 until his passing to eternity on February 25, 2015.

A Question of Experts

By John M. DeJak

A mark of humility is not seeking fame. It is a temptation for the best of us to be recognized by others and receive accolades. I've long thought that those who seek the approval of the media and the ruling class are ones not to be trusted – especially experts.

Fr. Francis X. Murphy was born to Irish immigrants in 1915 and raised in the "Irish Bronx" in New York City. Like many of his generation, he was raised in a thoroughly Catholic culture and found a vocation to the priesthood. He took vows as a Redemptorist in 1935 and was ordained in 1940. The order recognized his intellectual talents and he was sent for further studies, eventually obtaining a Ph.D. from the Catholic University of America in 1945. Subsequent to receiving his degrees, he served as a military chaplain and in 1959 was assigned as a professor at the Pontifical Lateran University. That same year, Pope John XXIII issued both *Veterum sapientia* (the apostolic constitution that called for and mandated proficiency among seminarians and priests in Latin and Greek to better understand the Church's theology) and the decree initiating the call for the Second Vatican Council. Being in Rome, Fr. Murphy had a front row seat to the ecclesiastical event of the century.

Back in the United States, it seemed that every newspaper and periodical was covering the Council. The high-brow literary magazine, *The New Yorker*, was no different. Founded in 1925, the original conception of its being a periodical for the *literati* and *glitterati* has not changed to this day, its sophistication designed for the "upper crust" and intelligentsia. Thus, to provide its own coverage of the Council, *The New Yorker* called upon the services of Fr. Murphy in Rome. Writing under the pseudonym "Xavier Rynne," Fr. Murphy's column was entitled "Letter from Vatican City" and gave updates on the Council's happenings and some "juicy" insider gossip.

A perusal of the columns during this time is fascinating reading and it does not take long for one to realize the posture of Fr. Murphy. From the very first column, there is a definite sense that Murphy is anti-hierarchical, indeed anti-Roman. He highlights the centralizing tendencies of the Roman Curia which he finds to be stifling – especially in the intellectual sphere. Likewise, he highlights throughout his series of articles certain frictions that developed between some of the Council participants and the Roman Pontiff. His preference no doubt is for a progressivist Council, a remaking of the Church, a new Church. As he wrote in one of his last columns covering the Council, "More important than the documents, the Council has consecrated a new spirit, destined in the course of time to remake the face of Catholicism."[1] Indeed, the "Council of the Media" in America had its spokesman and he was a Catholic priest.

Fr. Murphy's correspondence from Rome during these years did much to shape public opinion in the United States on the Council, its aims, and its supposed theology. Several years after the close of the Council, Fr. Murphy penned another item in *The New Yorker* offering the orthodox position of Manhattan's Upper East Side. This column was in the November 2, 1968 edition of the magazine and was an attack on Pope Paul VI's encyclical *Humanae vitae*, which was just issued the previous July. Fr. Murphy laments that "As far as the encyclical is concerned, Vatican Council II might just as well never have occurred. The Pope has taken a first important step toward repudiation of the Council."[2] The column was written in a smug and condescending tone in the manner of the orthopraxis of the Manhattan elite.

In practical terms, Xavier Rynne *was* the *Magisterium* in the United States. His was the lens through which the Second Vatican Council – even more, Catholic teaching generally – was seen. It did not take long for Catholic intellectuals, university presidents, politicians, bishops, and parish priests to fall under the seductive whisperings of the rather obscure Irish priest who wrote daily dispatches from Rome and was buttressed through the influence of his wealthy and *avant-garde* friends. Professor Charles Rice nailed the situation well in these initial years after the Council:

> [T]hat disorder [in the Church] is the product of two dangerous trends with the Church. One involves the rejection of authority. The other arises from a widespread absorption of relativist and secularist principles of theology and philosophy. Although both trends have deeper origins in a loss of faith, they work on each other as cause and effect....Both trends, the rejection of authority and the acceptance of the new morality, secularism, and a New Modernism,

have contributed to a growing spirit among Catholics of compromise with the standards of a secular and sensual society.[3]

That's why the name Monsignor Rudolph Bandas is not well known. Msgr. Bandas was a *peritus* (expert) at the Second Vatican Council assisting the Archbishop of St. Paul. In the mid-to-late sixties, the more well-known *periti* were the darlings of the media and propagated the so-called cutting-edge of "theology" of the likes of Schillebeeckx and Rahner. In addition, a certain American *peritus* named Fr. John Courtney Murray, S.J. was also the talk and toast of the town – largely because what he was alleged to promote fit a preconceived template of those who would diminish the power and authority of the Church. Implicit in this talking and toasting was the notion that the theologians and/or *periti* were the true authority and interpreters of the Council, but as the story of Msgr. Bandas will show, only certain *periti* were the "authority" of the Council.

Msgr. Rudolph Bandas was professor at the St. Paul Seminary in St. Paul, Minnesota, and also the pastor of the Church of St. Agnes. A respected scholar, Msgr. Bandas was a longtime seminary educator and was the author of many religion texts for use in high schools. When the Council was called, Archbishop William Brady called upon his services in Rome. While there, he was a participant in the commission for seminaries and priestly training as well as on the commission for bishops. As a result of his service, he was taken away from his parish during most of the sessions of the Council (1963-1965). Upon his arrival back in the States, he was appalled at the opining and prognostications in the public square, so to speak. In what can be said to be one of the earliest instances of media and elitist sabotage, Msgr. Bandas was asked to appear for a discussion of the Council on television shortly after his return and he was made to look as a grouchy old man out of touch with the "new direction" of the Church. He was said to have a "Roman mentality," which, in the minds of the media and the more popular of his fellow *periti*, meant "authoritarian," "mean," "doctrinaire," and "unloving."

Not one to be deterred by theological lightweights – be they in the media or prelates who never met a camera they didn't like – Bandas, as a consummate teacher, continued to articulate what the Council actually said. In a St. Agnes church bulletin of 1967, he ran down a long list of items that the Council supposedly promulgated. Largely, these issues were ones that impacted the devotional and liturgical life of Catholics. If the Eucharist was the "source and summit" of the Christian life, as *Sacrosanctum concilium* stated, how could the traditional expression of worship of this most august sacrament (e.g., adoration of the Blessed Sacrament, genuflections, kneeling for Holy Communion, etc.) be legitimately discouraged? Other issues beyond the liturgical were included in this list.

Stop for a moment and consider: what would our churches be like today if most pastors did in their parishes what Msgr. Bandas did in his? How would the implementation of Vatican II have been different if *periti* like Bandas had been listened to; if the assumption, unfortunately made by many bishops themselves, that the *periti* were the true experts of the Council's interpretation had not been so cavalierly made? I daresay, the theological aberrations seen after the Council would not have come into being, or they would exist on the fringes. If the Conciliar documents were read and understood by the clear meaning of their words and if those words were looked upon and understood as the latest Magisterial statement in the light of two thousand years of tradition, we might have a much different story to tell.

As truth is the most powerful thing in the world and as it has been consistently taught throughout these many years by the Supreme *Magisterium* of the Roman Pontiffs, there has been a slow but real corrective to the tendentious misinterpretation of the Council. As Pope Benedict XVI articulated well, there was the true Council and the "Council of the Media" which was foisted upon the faithful.[4] Thanks to the fidelity and intellectual acumen of many clergy and lay people over the years, the truth has indeed not been obscured. Yet, the truth has not completely broken through the darkness.

The Second Vatican Council was not the final word on the Church, nor was it negligible. It is but the latest expression of the solemn *Magisterium* of the Church acting in the form of an ecumenical council. Those who misinterpret the Council – whether of the tradition-denying and relativist-tending *National Catholic Reporter* types, or the tradition-minded yet obedience-challenged Society of St. Pius X types – both assume things the Council did not say.

In the final analysis, the response we must give as baptized members of the Church is the same response of St. Peter, the first Pope, to Christ: "Lord, to whom shall we go?" Though phrased as a question, it is an act of faith. It is this virtue of faith that we must cultivate in the one true Church that Christ has established, for faith in the Church is faith in Christ Himself. This faith expresses itself in a radical loyalty to the Church's supreme authority – specifically to the Roman Pontiff. In him do we have the rock amidst the turbulent waters of the age. In him, does the Most Holy Trinity repose its special graces for the governance of the Church. Yet, indeed we know that our faith is not in the man who occupies the office of the Supreme Pontiff, it is in Christ Himself.

We are on the winning side! Truth will ultimately triumph for Truth is a person, Our Lord Jesus Christ. We labor here on earth, our job as the laity to fight the culture of death, the dictatorship of relativism, and the "fruit of the spirit of the world that negotiates everything."[5] Pope Francis has articulated well this spirit of the world in his homily of November 18, 2013. He calls it a "spirit of adolescent progressivism"; one in which "any move forward and any choice is better than remaining within the routine of fidelity." The people who think thus "negotiate loyalty to God who is always faithful." The pope then indicts this way of thought: "This is called apostasy...And this is the fruit of the devil, the prince of this world, who leads us forward with a spirit of worldliness."[6]

It is this worldliness, this spirit of the devil, that Pope St. John XXIII wished to combat with the calling of the Second Vatican Council.

ENDNOTES

1. Russell Shaw, "Vatican II and the Culture of Dissent, *Crisis* Magazine, February/March 2006.

2 Xavier Rynne, "Letter from Vatican City," *The New Yorker*, November 2, 1968, p. 131.

3. Charles E. Rice, *Authority and Rebellion: The Case for Orthodoxy in the Catholic Church*. Garden City, NY: Doubleday & Co., Inc. (1971), p. 56-57.

4. Cf. Benedict XVI, Address, "Vatican II – As I Saw It," February 14, 2013 (http://en.radiovaticana.va/storico/2013/02/14/pope_benedicts_last_great_master_class:_vatican_ii,_as_i_saw_i/en1-665030)

5. Pope Francis, Homily, November 18, 2013 (http://en.radiovaticana.va/news/2013/11/18/pope:_lord_save_us_from_the_subtle_conspiracies_of_worldliness/en1-747663)

6. *Ibid.*

JOHN M. DEJAK, an attorney and Catholic educator, was the founding Headmaster of two private high schools in the St. Paul-Minneapolis area: Chesterton Academy and Holy Spirit Academy. Prior to that he practiced law and served on active duty as an officer in the U.S. Army's 10th Mountain Division. He has taught Latin, Greek, literature, government, and theology in schools in Chicago, Cleveland, the Twin Cities, and Ann Arbor. He has served as a researcher for the Cause of Canonization of Fr. Walter J. Ciszek, S.J. and, along with Fr. Marc Lindeijer, S.J., edited *With God in America: The Spiritual Legacy of an Unlikely Jesuit* (Loyola Press, 2016). His articles have appeared in *Chronicles*, *The Bellarmine Forum* magazine, *Gilbert* magazine, *The Distributist Review* and the *St. Austin Review*. He and his wife, Ann, and their eight children live in Saline, Michigan.

Authority and Vatian II
By Ellen Rice

St. Augustine famously remarked, "Love God and then do what you want," since the Great Commandment leads to all others. In the same way, one could fairly say on most Catholic issues, "Read Ralph McInerny, then read what you want," since McInerny's astute understanding of Church teaching provides an average reader with the principles to discerningly read anything else according to the mind of the Church.

Therefore, when examining a book such as Fr. John W. O'Malley's engaging history of Vatican II, *What Happened at Vatican II?* (Harvard University Press, 2008), the advice to give is to read McInerny's distillation of the issues that complicated our understanding of the Council, assimilate it, and then enjoy O'Malley's book. In *What Went Wrong With Vatican II* (Sophia Press, 1998), McInerny correctly identified the "problem" of Vatican II not as the tempting dichotomy of old Church vs. new Church, but of a struggle about the nature of authority that had little or nothing to do with the essential principles presented in the Council documents, or the authority thereof.

In his introduction, McInerny lays out the fundamental premise of his treatise, that

> Whatever problems may have been posed by the documents of Vatican II, contradiction of earlier councils cannot be one of them. It is the Pope who calls an ecumenical council... and he promulgates the documents expressing the judgment of the bishops.... To accept one council is to accept them all; to reject one council is to reject them all: we cannot have pick-and-choose conciliarism (McInerny, p. 14- 15).

So, McInerny's argument is: the Council is valid because of the principle of papal authority. It's very simple and answers one of the major criticisms of the Council by certain conservative groups who challenged its legitimacy.

The next point is that the crisis of Vatican II has been about the understanding of authority, and his book traces the ways in which this came about. He points out that something was seriously flawed:

Massive defections of priests and religious may not have been the aim of the Council, but they came about in great numbers. The impudent attitude of prominent theologians toward the *Magisterium* and their dismissal of the Holy Father... may not have been intended by Vatican II, but their dissent is an all too familiar feature in the Church today. Displays of weakness by pastors and bishops may not have been intended...

but few priests and bishops defend with vigor the Church's teaching. How such a crisis came about is explained by a spiritual problem that McInerny says was presaged at the Fatima apparitions, the ignored calls to prayer and penance, and Jacinta's haunting vision of a Pope kneeling with his face in his hands, crying, as people outside the house threw stones, cursed him and used foul language.

McInerny next proceeds to outline the forgotten teachings of Vatican II amidst the emphasis on collegiality, the voice of the laity, ecumenism and other issues that grabbed the limelight. The Council itself affirms that the Pope is "the supreme pastor and teacher of all the faithful," the successor of St. Peter, the Vicar of Christ on earth. He is head of the college of bishops. He can himself, independent of the bishops, exercise the supreme *Magisterium*. The Council's exact words are:

The college or body of bishops has for all that no authority unless united with the Roman Pontiff, Peter's successor, as its head, whose primatial authority, let it be added, over all, whether pastors or faithful, remains in its integrity. For the Roman Pontiff, by reason of his office as the Vicar of Christ, namely, and as pastor of the entire Church, has full, supreme and universal power over the whole Church, a power which he can always exercise unhindered (p. 35).

After examining the Council's teachings and proving their continuity with Church teaching, which is expected because the Pope called the Council, McInerny describes the dramatic events of 1968, "The Year the Church Fell Apart." The great issue that complicated the understanding of authority was the issue of birth control, the fact that the papacy had called a Birth Control Commission to study the issue, and that priests and laity had jumped the gun in expecting that a 1900-year-old teaching of the Church could be wiped away by *fiat*. The commission and the lapse of logic involved in the idea that a Council called by Papal authority could nullify papal authority, or for that matter a commission to study a teaching taught magisterially for 1900 years and affirmed strongly in 1930, does mystify the observer and the reader. Why study something that cannot change? It does not matter, if one believes that infallibility is not a human matter of *fiat* governance, but of guidance by the Holy Spirit.

Nonetheless, the genie was let out of the bottle, with the unofficial emergence of an evolutionary logic. Theologians reacted to the encyclical *Humanae vitae* with rebellion, anger and even disgust, acting as if a horse about to fly over a hurdle and win the race to the future, had balked at the last minute. In the chapter, "Whose Church Is It, Anyway?" McInerny describes how *America*, the Jesuit weekly,

> claimed that the most serious question raised by the new encyclical was not artificial contraception, but the exercise of teaching authority in the Church (p. 79).

McInerny's next chapter, "Theologians Whipsaw the Laity," describes the novel teachings on conscience, that each Catholic must form his or her own conscience on whether to use birth control. McInerny's argument about the need for a *Magisterium* is reminiscent of St. Thomas's Question 1 of the *Summa*, "*Is Philosophy Enough?*" St. Thomas said philosophy was not enough because the small number of only the intelligent could arrive at the truth, after a long search, and with an admixture of much error. Therefore God gave us revelation so we could know more about Himself with certainty and that truth about Him would be available to all. Makes sense, it is consistent with the nature of an all-loving, non-elitist God who would be born in a stable and die on a cross. Similarly, McInerny has no problem saying that the crux of the matter is "It is unreasonable to demand that each and every Catholic settle this disagreement for himself. In order to do so, he would have to become a professional philosopher and a professional theologian" (p.87).

The liberal/conservative dialectic sharpened over the next 30-35 years until the Vatican responded with the publication of the *Ratzinger Report*, in which the future Pope Benedict explained in cogent terms that the Council was fine, but the implementation and understanding of it was poor. Additionally, the 1985 Synod reaffirmed the Council and called for the publication of the *Catechism of the Catholic Church*, which when published would eliminate doubt about what the Church actually taught.

What is needed to heal a Church scarred by a power struggle, by misunderstandings of authority and doctrine and indeed of our very calling as Catholics? McInerny concludes:

> What is needed today is not a refutation of the bad arguments of the dissenters, but a change of heart. *Lumen gentium*, Vatican II's *Dogmatic Constitution on the Church*, culminates in a chapter on the Blessed Virgin Mary as Mother of the Church. John XXIII ended his opening address to the council with a prayer to Mary. John Paul II's *Veritatis splendor*, like so many other writings of the Holy Father, culminates in a prayer to Mary. At the beginning of these pages, I suggested that it will be by following Mary's wishes as expressed to the children at Fatima that the promise of Vatican II will be fulfilled. She advised prayer and fasting. Prayer and fasting will drive out the demon of dissent and fill the Church once more with the great hope and optimism of Vatican II (p. 158).
>
> Indeed, we serve a Savior "who, though He was in the form of God, did not count equality with God a thing to be grasped, but emptied Himself, taking the form of a servant being born in the likeness of men. And being found in human form He humbled himself and became obedient unto death, even death on a cross" (*Philippians* 2:6-8, *RSV* Catholic edition).

As time and distance grow between the present and the crisis period of Vatican II, it becomes undeniable that many modern ills in the Church were neither caused nor ameliorated by the Council per se. Such a glaring example is the absolute evil of clergy sex abuse, which has found its way into both conservative groups such as the Society of St. John and the Legionaries of Christ, and liberal strongholds such as the Archdiocese of Los Angeles. Deep problems concerning the use and abuse of power exist in the Church, and these attitudes also surfaced in the day to day struggles during the Council meetings, the flight from religious life, the problem of dissent, the general problem of the will to power.

O'Malley's narrative, *What Happened at Vatican II?* definitely presents a history of the Council where the will to power explains dynamics and subcurrents. Once safe in the assurance that doctrine and continuity are preserved, it is certainly advisable to read about the havoc caused by power, the factionalism that arose, and the unChristlike politicking that often went on – on all sides. The story he tells is in so many ways the story of sin, the story of an adversary doing his best to ruin or blunt the teaching of truth. Infallible teachings inspired by the Holy Spirit are beyond the reach of the devil, but the next best thing for Screwtape to do is to stir up rancor, division, confusion.

O'Malley's intent in writing *What Happened at Vatican II?* is threefold:

> ... to "provide the essential story line from the moment Pope John XXIII announced the Council on January 25, 1959, until it concluded on December 8, 1965;...set the issues that emerge in that narrative into their contexts, large and small, historical and theological; third, thereby provide some keys for grasping what the council hoped to accomplish. That is the space on the shelves that I hope to fill with this book" (p.1).

While McInerny presented the theological and philosophical view, O'Malley's view is from the sidelines, and therefore shows the human grappling and power dynamics involved in shaping the conciliar teachings. O'Malley writes a gripping and informative narrative that details events, controversies and personalities in such a way that a Catholic born in the post-conciliar period can grasp the events that took place. Especially helpful is a "who's who" index in the back of the book which offers short biographies of all the Council Fathers and characters mentioned in the history.

Titles such as "The First Period: The Lines are Drawn"; "The Second Period: A Majority Prevailing"; and "The Third Period: Triumphs and Tribulations" show that as O'Malley has evaluated the historical facts, he sees a power struggle in play, based on positions relative to the papacy and tradition. One characteristic expression of O'Malley's perspective is when he writes that the bishops "had flexed their muscles in the rejection of the schema *On the Sources of Revelation*, which showed they could do more than be a rubber stamp... They knew the Council had taken an unexpected turn" (p. 160). Another, on page 246, describing the "grim" face of Pope Paul VI after the approval of *Lumen gentium* and the *Decree on Ecumenism*: "No one doubted that the week had seriously damaged the relationship between the Pope and the assembly. Could the loss of trust be repaired?"

McInerny's work regards the Council as the work of the Holy Spirit proceeding under the authority of the Pope; O'Malley's chapter on the

Third Session and Pope Paul VI's intervention in what was called "the black week" shows that the Pope could and did intervene, attending and directing a working session to correct the intent of the Council Fathers on such matters as collegiality and ecumenism. If anyone thought the Council was a revolution, a perspective O'Malley presents the progressive majority took, they were caught by surprise and dismayed by the Pope's intervention. One flaw in O'Malley's narrative in this case is that the substance of the amendments and the exact reasons for the intervention are not clearly spelled out. Without having the content of the proposed schema and of the changes, one is a little stupefied why the Pope intervened in the process. McInerny would certainly prompt us to think about why the Holy Spirit led the Pope to do something incredibly unpopular and undemocratic; where did God think the meeting was going off the rails?

O'Malley's storytelling is mainly concerned with explaining changes in Catholic experience, attitudes and perspective. He describes the pro- and anti-Catholic thinkers of the nineteenth century, from Newman to Marx, that the Council addressed implicitly or explicitly. He explains the phenomenon of Modernism that threatened to demythologize every doctrine once taught as true. Then there were the political realities of Communism, Nazism, the reactionary Catholicism of Franco and the *via media* of the Christian Democrats. A Council to maneuver the Barque of Peter through the choppy waters of the modern world had to address these upheavals in attitude and practice that seemed to threaten faith itself.

The chapter, "The Council Opens," contains a fascinating section (pages 108-126) on Personalities and Alignments. Members of the minority group led by Cardinal Ottoviani are profiled, and the roles of Cardinal Bea and Archbishop Suenens, leaders of the majority, are very helpful. The descriptions of the minority's relationship to the Curia, and Suenens' relationship to Pope John XXIII are invaluable for the novice reader who did not live through that time.

The chapters on the sessions themselves are important and informative, but confusing at times. With the passage of time, it becomes difficult to see how the use of the vernacular in the Mass, the rejection of modernism, the introduction of the language of the "people of God," and changes that now shape our daily experiences of parish life, could be controversial. Now that the dust has settled, the thought that the Church could hang in the balance seems foreign to us. Or rather, if one believes in the charism of infallibility and the promise that the Church will never teach error, the fright one might feel when reading about controversies about the inerrancy of Revelation simply disappears. Like football fans watching reruns of last week's win, we know the story ends well.

Unlike McInerny, O'Malley does not include an introduction outlining the theology of councils and papal infallibility, and indeed this reviewer considers it fairly viewpoint-agnostic. But the method itself is a statement on the power of process and procedure. Because O'Malley's narrative is concerned with personalities, power struggles and a worm's eye view of procedural changes, it certainly bears enough ambiguity to be used or championed by liberal propagandists who mistakenly believe that a Council could occasion a rupture between an old Church and a new Church.

O'Malley's book is a good history, it is recommended reading for understanding the Council, but only as part of a corpus that includes McInerny, Magisterial documents such as the *Catechism*, and the *Ratzinger Report*. It is a simple narrative describing power dynamics, and discussing various Council Fathers putting forth bad ideas or blocking good ones, tells the story of sin, not the story of Christ's promise "to be with us always." The actual outcome, the substance of the ideas, and the reasons why God allowed certain changes to prevail and not others, is a higher narrative – the "why" that completes our understanding of the "how." The story of ecclesial power, which is the story of folly and fallibility, is only complete when the true story of divine guidance and infallibility, accompanies it. Nonetheless, the rancor caused by the will to power is an essential reality to confront – with penance, prayer, most of all with awareness, since the terrible sins which make headlines and ruin lives even today stem from the same root, the *non serviam* and the desire to use the Church for one's own purposes. Truly, a story to be continued.

ELLEN RICE holds B.A. degrees from the University of Notre Dame in Art History and Philosophy, and an M.B.A in Management from Indiana University, where she has taught Business Communications. She was editor of *Catholic Dossier* for 4 years, was director of Marketing and Development at St. Augustine's Press in South Bend, Indiana, as well as a publication consultant for several high profile clients. Rice is the author of several articles and books, including two history texts as part of the Catholic Schools Textbook Project and the *John Paul II LifeGuide: Words to Live By*, published by St. Augustine's Press.

Vatican II and the Priesthood:
Surprised and Sorrowed

By Dr. William H. Marshner

Cast your mind back to 1971. It is time for another Synod of Bishops. The Second Vatican Council closed just six years ago, amid great euphoria, and now selected bishops are back in Rome for a third post-conciliar synod on a topic proposed by the Pope. The first was on preservation of the Catholic Faith, the second on the episcopal conferences – all things which needed clarification as the supposed interpretations of Vatican II moved on in time and practice.

You recall that the big documents of the Council did not all come out at once. *Sacrosanctum concilium*, the *Constitution on the Sacred Liturgy* came first, all by itself, at the end of 1963. A year later, at the end of '64, came *Lumen gentium*, the *Dogmatic Constitution on the Church*, along with decrees on Ecumenism and one on the Eastern Churches. Everything else came out in the last few months (October – November) of '65, including the decrees on priestly formation and priestly ministry.

So now, in the fall of 1971, the *Constitution on the Liturgy* is already eight years old. Signs of its implementation have had time to appear, as have pockets of disquiet. So if Paul VI had called a synod on liturgy, bringing bishops to Rome to look over the shoulders of Msgr. Bugnini, who was charged with the implementation of same, it would hardly have been surprising.[1] It would have made sense.

But the synod was on the priesthood. The decrees on the priesthood were only six years old. Their effects were almost invisible. In '64 and '65, they both sailed through the Council's debate and amendment process without a ripple of fuss. Why? Because neither said anything very controversial. The one on the priesthood itself, *Presbyterorum ordinis*, was straight patristic theology together with firm insistence on the traditional discipline of celibacy. The one on priestly formation, *Optatam totius*, affirmed the existing (and highly successful) seminary system; it lost a few votes only because it called for other philosophy to be taught along with Thomism.

Why, then, did Paul VI give his 1971 synod the topic of ministerial priesthood? What had gone wrong? The opening lines of the synod's final report, *Ultimis temporibus*, provide no clue.

> In recent times, especially since the close of the Second Vatican Council, the Church is experiencing a profound movement of renewal....The Holy Spirit is present to illumine, strengthen and perfect our mission. Every true renewal brings the Church undoubted benefits of great value. We all know that through the recent Council priests have been fired with new zeal and that they have contributed much to fostering this renewal by their daily solicitude...
>
> We should all scrutinize the signs of the times in this age of renewal and interpret them in the light of the Gospel....Thus by testing everything and holding fast to what is good, the present crisis can give occasion for an increase of faith.[2]

What crisis?

The lines you have just read are soon to become a trope of post-Conciliar church statements, and "trope," alas, is a recurrent theme. In bare form it says:

The renewal is going wonderfully, uh, and there is a crisis.

What it means is not just that there is a "disconnect" between expectation and outcome. Any old sigh of disappointment would mean that much. No, the trope means that the expectation cannot be abandoned; it has to be justified, having been attributed to the Holy Spirit. The Holy Spirit can hardly be failing. There has to be renewal going on, underneath the appearances of demolition.

Estrangement

A few paragraphs further on, the synod's report tells us what the dismal appearances are. The very first one listed, however, is a shocker. It is this:

> Some priests feel themselves estranged from the movements which permeate society and unable to solve the problems which touch men deeply.

You were expecting maybe that the first thing listed would be desertions from the ministry, or a looming vocations crisis? I don't blame you; I would have expected the same. But we would both be wrong, because we would be forgetting what year it is. In 1971, abandoned vocations are barely visible to anyone yet, except the lads in the seminaries and maybe the bishops in Holland. The collapsing numbers of active priests, religious, and seminarians were *end* results of whatever was building behind the "crisis" in '71, not the start of it.

No, the '71 synod has it about right. The first and deepest dismal sign is priests feeling "estranged from the movements which permeate society." This takes a little explaining.

For about 180 years (1780-1960), priests were happy to feel estranged from the movements permeating society. These were movements of atheism, revolution, liberalism, materialism, anti-clericalism, secularism, and license – all proclaimed as "progress" towards a better world. The Church denounced every one of these "isms" repeatedly, not only for what they said, but for the ruin they were making of the European civilization inspired by the Church. Do you remember what Blessed Pius IX did at the end of his Syllabus of Errors? He anathematized the very idea that he, the Holy See, should "reconcile himself" to "progress, liberalism, and modern civilization."

And tutored by the fighting words from Rome (which lasted through the reign of Pius XII), our priests and bishops felt affirmed in their sacred ministry. For even when they disagreed with some of Rome's fights (like the Italian clergy who wanted a unified Italy), they were proud of their sacred role, not only because of the superiority of the supernatural over the natural (much emphasized in 1870 at Vatican I), but also because the collar set them apart from the destructive delusions of their secularist and socialist contemporaries; their access to the altar and the pulpit gave them the profoundly evangelical task of setting the people free in Christ – free from the superstitions of the age. The fresh air, in a word, was the breath of the Holy Spirit; it blew from the Church and upon the world. The Christian attitude of detachment from the world, even *contemptus mundi*, was reinforced and made easier.

But then, under the radar, in academic backrooms of the 1930s and '40s, there came a shift. These backrooms included the French Dominican *studium*, Le Saulchoir at Etoilles near Paris, where people like Yves Congar were busy with the *Nouvelle Theologie* movement. Yes, new theology with a touch of Protestant thought thrown in for good measure. One of the students at the *studium* was Fr. Edward Schillebeeckx, a rising star of the Dominican order.

At the same time *Nouvelle Theologie* was brewing, certain intellectuals said that the ugly "isms" of the century past were not the true spirits of the modern world. Modern society in itself was better than society had ever been, because it was based on evangelical values (like brotherhood, equality, justice). Hence one should see this society as the intended outcome of divine providence, working around and even through the bloody revolutions. So the Church would be well advised to change her tune and embrace the age.

Embracing the Age

When these *nouvelle* ideas came out of the backrooms, their message was first the "New Christendom" of Jacques Maritain (very big in the 1940s and early '50s both in Europe and eventually at Princeton where he was a visiting scholar); and then the "distinction of planes" of Yves Congar (big in the later '50s and early '60s). Meanwhile the Dominican, Schillebeeckx, had begun teaching, first at the Catholic University of Louvain and then, in 1958 at the Catholic University of Nijmegen, Netherlands, where he introduced *Nouvelle Theologie*, to Dutch theologians already with a tenuous hold on the old time religion.[3]

It is truly regrettable that dioceses in the US in those days felt their brighter seminarians needed exposure to the masters of Europe to enhance their intellectual horizons. Whether these prelates or seminary rectors knew of the questionable theological trends in these places cannot be determined. The Catholic University at Louvain was one outstanding choice for the continuing education for these young men, many of whom would eventually become seminary instructors.

Into this simmering pot of dissent came the Second Vatican Council and *aggiornamento,* a word meaning a spirit of change and open-mindedness.

Go through the enormously influential *Gaudium et spes*, the *Constitution on the Church in the Modern World*. It speaks again and again, with unfailing optimism, about the "men of our day" working to "perfect God's creation" and "build a more human society," and it directs the people of God, again and again, clergy and laity, to "cooperate" with all "men of good will" to bring the world's hopeful projects to fruition.

Of course, *Gaudium et spes* did point to some dangers, especially in projects for totalitarian *dirigisme* or population control. The cooperation of lay and clerical Catholics with the world's progressive hopes had to be consistent with the norms of Catholic morality. But there were no sharp warnings, nor even any suggestions, that moral disagreements would be a serious problem. To be fair, the sharp turn of the world's progressive forces to feminism, abortion rights, and gay rights was still in the future. In 1965, a substantial moral consensus between the Church and the liberal democracies was taken for granted. The cautious pastoral strategies of every Pope from Gregory XVI to Pius XII seemed (as the press would trumpet) obsolete.

The Council did not *teach* that the old fights about the "isms" had been wrong, or mostly wrong. No. But its naively optimistic counsels of dialogue, cooperation, reform, and renewal were certainly read that way. That is especially true because for the most part, the "isms" were not the prime issues any longer. So the Council's words about dialogue and reform, etc., were merely applied across the board on mostly everything.

What was never public were the behind-the-scenes work of people like Schillebeeckx of Nijmegen. He had ghost-written the *Dutch Pastoral Letter* about the Council in 1961, a letter which brought him before the Holy Office to defend his ideas. He continued to write after that – anonymously – on various conciliar constitutions up for debate by the Council Fathers, including *Dei verbum* and *Lumen gentium*. In *Lumen gentium*, he suggested a move away from papal authority as defined by Vatican I, and more toward episcopal colleges.[4] While not a *peritus* or official expert, his words influenced many – enough so that even Fr. John O'Malley, S.J., in *What Happened at Vatican II*, noted a power struggle was taking place in the debates on these very documents – and direct papal intervention in the working sessions.[5]

Now imagine that you are a priest or seminarian here in this latter half of the '60s. The Council has closed, leaving you inspired with a new zeal but also with a changed set of signals. Your seminary professor who studied in Europe, has a new take on the faith. In 1966, the Dutch theologians put together a *Catechism*, a reworking of Catholic doctrine (later to be labeled heretical and banned, but not yet). A new journal was at hand, *Concilium*, run by theological greats such as Rahner, Congar, Küng, and Schillebeeckx.[6] Add to that the idea that cooperation with the world's hopes is now mandatory; *contemptus mundi* is unthinkable, and even detachment from the world seems...uncooperative. Maybe even divisive. In matters pertaining to the natural order, like economics, politics, and social justice, it suddenly seems as if the fresh air is blowing from the world and into the Church. (Hadn't John XXIII said as much?) So solving the natural "problems which touch men deeply" is a worthy ambition for any priest and fully authorized; so it is mandatory to be in step with these social "movements which permeate society."

Yet the long tradition of the Church, restated in *Presbyterorum ordinis* and *Lumen gentium*, says that a priest belongs to and makes present in the world another order, above the world and its putative progress. How you can be both "above" something and "in" it?

The Pinch of the Collar

The very concept of the priesthood began to change. The image of the good pastor tending the needs of his flock, visiting homes, bringing the sacraments to the sick, spending hours in the confessional for the greater glory of God is beginning to fade.

Here is where the clerical collar is beginning to pinch. A priest who yearns to struggle for peace, racial equality, economic equality, and all the rest, will no longer see the Church's restraints on his action for what they really are – salutary reminders of his higher calling – but as the unwelcome chains of his office in an all-too-recently reactionary institution – an institution which had fought vainly for 180 years against God's providential plan for human progress!

There you have it. Thanks to the change of signals, many "priests feel themselves estranged from the movements which permeate society and unable to solve the problems which touch men deeply." It won't be long before they feel themselves estranged from the hierarchy and the *Magisterium*, thanks to their own backroom discussions with their enlightened instructors.

Back to the 1971 exhortation. Let us move on to the second dismal appearance noted by the bishops' synod:

> Often too the problems and troubles of priests derive from their having, in their pastoral and missionary care, to use methods which are now perhaps obsolete to meet the modern mentality.

Well sure, if the "modern mentality" is what divine providence has been working to produce in history, it has to be the gold standard for liturgical and catechetical reform. Is scholastic thought opaque to people today, then out with it. Is Latin indigestible? Out with it. Is Palestrina (not to mention Gregorian chant) boring to the kids who want to sing "Kum-ba-ya"? Out with it.

Maybe the catechism publishers can come up with more pictures. Not old saint pictures – pretty, kid-friendly pictures.

Here is the third dismal symptom:

> Serious problems and several questions then arise....Is it possible to exhort the laity as if from outside? Is the Church sufficiently present to certain groups without the active presence of the priest? If the situation characteristic of a priest consists in segregation from secular life, is not the situation of the layman better? What is to be thought of the celibacy of Latin-rite priests in present-day circumstances and [what is to be thought of] the personal spiritual life of the priest immersed in the world?

Here's a mantra we've heard a million times: you can't tell us what to do unless you're one of us. It must be part of the modern mentality. Only a black man can criticize blacks. Only a woman can speak to or about women. As soon as a priest buys into this, he loses his authority to preach to lay people. Here is another mantra, a little more Leninist: you can't be with us unless you join us totally. As soon as a priest accepts it, he can no longer serve a social movement as its coach or advisor. He must be a member. If his collar prevents him, the lay status must be more "with it." How can he "get with it" as long as he is "segregated" off by celibacy, and as long as his spirituality is the old stuff of "detachment from the world" in order to turn more completely toward God? For if God is the hidden but true designer of the modern world and its mentality, why can he not meet God "in the world" without detaching from anything?

These questions soon found novel and sympathetic answers in the (covertly) Hegelian theology of Karl Rahner, in the "political theology" of J. B. Metz, and in the more and more radical thought of Edward Schillebeeckx.

Being Overcome by the World

Here comes the synod's fourth symptom, covering much of the same ground:

Many priests, experiencing within themselves the questionings that have arisen from the secularization of the world, feel the need to sanctify worldly activities by exercising them directly and bring the leaven of the Gospel into the midst of events. Similarly the desire is developing of cooperating with the joint efforts of men to build up a more just and fraternal society. In a world in which almost all problems have political aspects, participation in politics and even in revolutionary activity is by some considered indispensable.

Of course. It all follows logically from the switch of signals. From engaged and "with it" worker priests, one soon comes to striking priests, marching priests, picketing priests, taxicab-driving priests, campaigning priests, gun-toting guerrilla priests, and congressman priests.

Skipping the fifth symptom (a matter of doubts about a "sacramental and cultic system"), we come to the sixth and last:

Happily the recent Council recalled the traditional and fruitful teaching on the common priesthood of the faithful (cf. *LG* 10). That, however, gives rise, as by a swing of the pendulum, to certain questions which seem to obscure the position of the priestly ministry in the Church and which deeply trouble the minds of some priests and faithful. Many activities which in the past were reserved to priests – for instance, catechetical work, administrative activity in the communities, and even liturgical activities – are today frequently carried out by lay people, while on the other hand many priests, for reasons already mentioned, are trying to involve themselves in the condition of life of lay persons. Hence a number of questions are being asked: Does the priestly ministry have any specific nature? Is this ministry necessary? Is the priesthood incapable of being lost? What does being a priest mean today? Would it not be enough to have for the service of the Christian communities *presidents* designated for the preservation of the common good, without sacramental ordination, and exercising their office for a fixed period?

Every one of these "questions," of course, is really a theological proposal for how to re-think everything. (The modern mentality seems to have a special Catholic chat-room, in which nothing is ever denied, only re-thought.) Feeling a bit segregated from lay life? Easy to fix: the only real ordination is the one we all get at baptism. Isn't a priest's ordination something different? Sure, but only juridically: the bishop delegates him to preside at a local affair (in the Catholic chat-room there are no more parishes, only communities). But doesn't this delegation, or whatever you call it, give him an indelible sacramental character? No, that's an outdated, medieval theory. But doesn't he bring Christ onto the altar? No, the words of consecration do that, and any Christian can say them. But if a layperson says them, nothing happens, right? Right, until the layperson is delegated and recognized by the community. Community recognition is what makes the "real Presence" real? Well, the community's faith does; all the sacraments are "sacraments of faith."

Every one of these theological proposals can be found in the post-conciliar works of Edward Schillebeeckx, and they were widely read at first in Holland and then all over the world. Did he really think he could justify such proposals? Yes. The '71 synod goes on to explain how.

> Still more serious questions are posed, some of them as a result of exegetical and historical research, which show a crisis of confidence in the Church: Is the present-day Church too far removed from its origins to proclaim the ancient Gospel credibly to modern man? Is it still possible to reach the reality of Christ after so many critical investigations? Are the essential structures of the early Church well enough known to us that they can and must be considered an invariable scheme for every age, including our own?

Schillebeeckx answers this last question with a resounding no. The New Testament texts on ministry are few and confusing. To reach this conclusion, he follows the Protestant biblical critics who set aside as late, unreliable, and "secondary" the entire apostolic tradition from Ignatius of Antioch down to Trent and Vatican II. Subtract the "secondary" and apostolic tradition and what do you have? Precious little else on which to sustain a young man's call to the altar.

Now you have my whole story, from the switching of signals down to the dissent from Vatican II's own theology of the ministerial priesthood. The dismal symptoms of crisis follow step by step. This is why Paul VI and his synod were surprised and sorrowed. By now the Dutch church is a mess, hardly recognizable as Catholic. The dissent in favor of married clergy had already alarmed the Pope that he felt compelled yet in 1967 to write an encyclical on priestly celibacy, *Sacerdotalis caelibatus*. The procession out the door is about to begin.

Fifty years later, we are still sorrowing, particularly at the tremendous wound the Church suffered in the post-Vatican II years. But we do not give up hope because purgatory carries with it the promise of salvation.

The Besieged Faithful

Many of the seminaries lapped up the new and "relevant" ideas and taught them to future priests. Ordinations proceeded on schedule and soon men and women in the pews began hearing strange things from the pulpit. For you can only teach/preach what you know and many young priests parroted the hang-ups of their instructors.

"Why are you wasting time saying Hail Marys over and over again. Make up your own prayers." "Benediction? I won't do that, I don't believe in it."

"Adoration? We are to pray in community, not individually."

And in confession:

"Please tell me about your problems." "Sins, Father." "Problems." "Sins." Was it necessary to argue over this? Apparently so.

"Father, I was angry with my husband." "Go on Birth control." Over a spat about money?

"Don't come in here with a laundry list of sins."

No wonder General Absolution was such an easy fix, so the priest could go out and do other things important to him.

"Original Sin is the evil around us. If your baby is in danger of death, I'll baptize him as a favor but I don't believe it is necessary."

One abrasive priest bragged about his exploits in his Sunday homily, denigrating the rule in Rome for priests to wear cassocks: "We Americans wore jeans under our cassocks." He went on to say, "We would sneak out of the residence on Friday nights to get pizza."

The collars came off when the civilian clothes went on, about the same time priests dropped "Father" and urged parishioners to "Just call me Bob." As the statues went on sale at flea markets, so did reverence for priests. Questions arose about the validity of some Masses, particularly when long loaves of French bread were brought up in the Offertory procession, "consecrated," and used for communion.

Scandalized laity went elsewhere if they could, sometimes driving hours to attend Mass offered by a reverent priest. Some joined Eastern Rite Catholic congregations where holiness and sanity still reigned. Yet others quit going to Mass altogether.

Some seminarians left, because this kind of priesthood was not what they were called to and they were hard-pressed to find an untainted seminary – remember this was before the internet in which Google does all the searching for you. Some young men left because priesthood was not the life for them and others should have gone sooner than later because after 5 or 10 years of ministry they bailed out, challenging Church teaching as they went out the door.

Another factor in the exodus of young men from the seminaries was sexual abuse, which has only come to light in recent years. More than one young candidate was molested in the very early days of his seminary life. One priest acknowledged this affront in a newspaper interview in a Midwestern diocese, and said he understood from the molestation that this was how Fr. X handled his sexuality and assumed that was the example to follow. The molested priest was later accused of pedophilia.

A few young men stuck it out. One seminarian in the same Midwestern diocese said it was very hard to sit in class listening to the antithesis of Church teaching being taught as gospel. He called it a "schizophrenic" existence. He knew he was called to serve and forced himself to play the game so he could be ordained. He later went on to author solid orthodox books and gained a national reputation. For others, the struggle continued, even into the late 1990s, decades after Vatican II swept conservatives out the door. Seminarians who challenged the prevailing mentality were deemed "unsuitable" for ordination and dismissed: such an action a sure bar to admittance to another institution in the country.

In the turmoil after the Council, several groups formed who operated in a very conservative manner, most notably, the Society of St. Pius X, which was founded in 1969 by Archbishop Marcel Lefebvre. While starting out with temporary Church approval, early on the Archbishop was suspended for ordaining priests for the society without the permission of the local Ordinary. In spite of this, he continued ordaining priests for the Society and they worked in many dioceses, offering the Mass as it was before Vatican II's changes. In this way they attracted many of the laity who were upset by the changes after the Council. In 1988, Lefebvre ordained four men as bishops for the Society, which was viewed as an act of schism by the Roman Catholic Church. The Society was off on their own way, with their own congregations and churches. To this date, they have not reunited with Rome, acceptance of the Second Vatican Council being one of the reasons for the breach.[7]

Within a few weeks of the schismatic episcopal ordinations, 12 priests and several seminarians from the Society of St. Pius X chose a different path. With the stated desire to live as a religious society in the Church and under the Roman Pontiff, they formed the Priestly Fraternity of St. Peter, under the leadership of Fr. Joseph Bisig. The FSSP, now almost 30 years old, is a clerical society of apostolic life. Members do not take vows, but live priestly celibacy and obedience to diocesan authority. The FSSP consists of priests and seminarians who pursue the goal of Christian perfection according to their special charism to offer Mass and other sacraments according to the Roman Rite before the reforms of Vatican II. They serve in dioceses around the world.[8]

What of the faithful when all of this was going on? They prayed for deliverance. Pockets of faithful people started Eucharistic adoration in their parishes, if not before the exposed Blessed Sacrament, then before the tabernacle, wherever it was hidden. Prayer groups, charismatic groups, sprang up. They prayed for the Church. In addition, Bishops don't rule forever. The change of Ordinary could mean great things for a seminary program, particularly if there was a significant personnel change. And by now the home school movement had taken hold and young men, greatly inspired by the faith taught to them by their parents, began to enter the seminaries. Older men, some with successful careers, who had put off the decision in their early years, now began exploring seminary life. Things began to change. A few examples stand out in this regard.

In the early 1990s, in the St. Paul and Minneapolis Archdiocese, there was an influx of young men to the seminary who had been active in prayer groups, charismatic renewal, and lay brotherhoods. The Companions of Christ grew out of such a group. In 1992, with the help of then auxiliary Bishop Robert Carlson, the Companions were established as a public association answering a radical call to holiness. They are committed to the evangelical vows of poverty, chastity and obedience, and they live in community, with 2 or 3 priests together. Different areas of the country are considering introducing this priestly fraternity into their ranks. The Denver archdiocese is one area where the Companions thrive.[9]

Similar to the circumstances with women religious in recent years, new religious orders for men began to arise. The Priestly Fraternity of the Missionaries of St. Charles Borromeo, was established as a Society of Apostolic Life in 1989 to follow Pope John Paul II's exhortation to "Go into all the world and bring the truth, the beauty, and the peace which are found in Christ the Redeemer." The new community, an offshoot of the Communion and Liberation movement, seeks to educate Catholics in their faith and be faithful to the rule of their order through prayer. There are more than 25 missions of the Fraternity around the world.[10]

In 1998, Fr. C. Frank Phillips founded the Canons Regular of St. John Cantius, who serve in parishes, offer the liturgy of the Roman Church in both Ordinary and Extraordinary Forms, and preserve and foster the devotional, musical, catechetical and artistic tradition of the Church. They follow the rule of St. Augustine. Their mission is to praise God through liturgy and restore the sacred in the world, and help themselves and others achieve personal sanctification. A stop at the parish of St. John Cantius in Chicago will convince any visitor that they are doing an outstanding job in achieving their goals.[11]

Dare I say the renewal called for by Vatican II is finally coming to pass? The visible signs are like buds of leaves in spring. A woman from an East Coast diocese said "Our 40 years – no, more than 40 years – of wandering the desert is over. The new priests coming out of the seminary are marvelous. And they are holy." Prayer, adoration, she said, for so many long years has paid off.

Even the liberals recognize the change.

A certain diocese offered a "Ministry Day Retreat" for all the lay people involved in service to the church community – you know, the pastoral ministers, welcome ministers, healing ministers, youth ministers, childcare ministers, liturgical ministers, funeral ministers, *ad infinitum*. A typical feel-good day with breakfast, lunch, speakers, breakout sessions, ending with a Q and A, all for twenty bucks.

Toward the end of the afternoon, the facilitator was asked, "What about these new priests. I'm so afraid they're going to take our ministries away."

Fearful voices could be heard in chorus: "Yes!" "Right!"

"What are we going to do?"

Couple that with a comment by a parish business administrator. He said he was a Vatican II Catholic, loved the post-Vatican II era when everyone was questioning everything, even the priests were questioning things.

"I hate these new priests coming out of the seminary now," he said. "They do what the Bishop tells them."

Amen to that!

ENDNOTES

1. Archbishop Annibale Bugnini was secretary and *factotum* to the *Concilium ad exsequendam* (Council on Implementing the Liturgy after the mind of Vatican II), which Paul VI set up in order to circumvent the regular curial congregation responsible for liturgical matters. This had been the Sacred Congregation for Rites (SCR), a bastion of liturgical conservatism. With the SCR out of the loop, Bugnini had a free hand to revise the Mass as he saw fit, often going far beyond what the Council had said (so as to impose total vernacularization) or even contradicting it (so as to dismantle choirs in favor of congregational singing). So Bugnini was the archetect of the *Novus Ordo*. The excess of his radicalism had been so great that even Paul VI finally fired him in 1976 and sent him off to be nuncio to Iran.

2. The text of *Ultimis temporibus* is found in *Vatican Council II, vol. 2, More Post Conciliar Documents*, by Austin Flannery, O.P., (Daughters of St. Paul, 1982). The text is the product of the Pope's second "ordinary synod," but in a timeline, it was the third Synod, with one called in 1969 being termed the first "Extraordinary" Synod. Such synods were called for by a motu proprio of 1965. The text of *UT* is not attributed to anyone. Once written, it was approved by Paul VI. Hereafter in the text, the document quotes are from *Ultimis Temporibus*.

3. http://en. wikipedia.org/wiki/Edwards_Schillebeeckx.

4. *ibid.*

5. Ellen Rice, "Authority and Vatican II," *Bellarmine Forum* magazine, vol. III, n.1, The Wanderer Forum Foundation, Inc./Bellarmine Forum, Hudson, WI, 2013.

6. http://en. wikipedia.org/wiki/Edward_Schillebeeckx.

7. http://en.wikipedia.org/wiki/Marcel_Lefebvre

8. www.fsp.org/en

9. http://www.companionsofchrist.org/faq/html

10. http://english.clonline.org/whatiscl/default.asp?id=473; Fr. Ettore Ferrario, "From Our Pastor," Church of St. Peter bulletin, July 2, 2017.

11. http://www.canons-regular.org/go/about/charism/

DR. WILLIAM H. MARSHNER became Resident Scholar at Christendom College in Front Royal, Virginia, after his retirement from teaching theology there for 38 years. He holds a B.A. in Greek from Gettysburg College, and S.T.L. and S.T.D. from the Lateran University (John Paul II Institute) in Rome. In 1967, Marshner was received into the Catholic Church and spent his early career as an editor for *Triumph* magazine and as Washington D.C. editor for *The Wanderer* newspaper. Author of books, monographs and numerous articles on Mariology, logic, theology, and philosophy, as well as translations of scholarly documents, Marshner is a popular speaker in the Washington area and in the past addressed several National Wanderer Forums. He is a member of the National Association of Scholars, the Fellowship of Catholic Scholars, the American Philosophical Association, the Mariological Society of America and the Equestrian Order of the Holy Sepulchre.

Religious Life After Vatican II: Forsaking All Others or Forsaking Christ?

By Laurene Conner

(Editor's Note: This article contains the substance of a Wanderer Forum Foundation *Forum* special edition, "A Crumbling Edifice: Consciousness Raising and the Erosion of Religious Life," published in 1989. Very few copies of this edition are available, and the salient points, summarized here, give a picture of the precarious state of Religious Life, particularly women's religious life, after Vatican II. WFF Secretary Laurene Conner did a masterful job of pulling the information together for that special edition 28 years ago. Editing and extra material has been provided by Cindy Paslawski, current secretary of the Wanderer Forum Foundation dba the Bellarmine Forum.)

Prelude

Flash backward in time. Mid-sixties. US participation in Vietnam was ramping up under Lyndon Johnson, the Beatles changed everything from music to hairstyles and clothing. Change, unrest was in the air that year of 1967.

I attended a Catholic girls' school taught by the Benedictines in a large Midwestern city. The black habited Sisters were demanding, the courses rigorous. They put a lot of time and effort into the college bound, but it wasn't a feminist sort of grooming, that hydra was simmering in the societal pot and not yet boiling over. I recall doing a current events report on a *Time* article that stated the Church had approved contraception and the principal, Sister Claire, who was teaching the class, grabbed my arm and shoved me aside and said that was not true, where did I come up with that? And she turned to tell the class that report was in error.

One of the younger Sisters was a real martinet. The rules were the rules were the *rules*. No talking in the halls or you were sent back to the downstairs lunchroom and told to walk ladylike up the stairs to class in SILENCE. Sister X watched and waited like Cerberus.

Three years after graduating, I returned to the school to gather information for a college course. Since the instructor to be interviewed was not yet available, I was invited into the faculty lounge. A nice-looking woman, about 30, clad in a powder blue turtle neck and pleated skirt was reading in there, looked up and greeted me. She kept talking to me as if she knew me. It wasn't until I was summoned for the interview, that she was called by name. She was Sister X!

What happened to the *rules*? Where was her habit? Some of the other Sisters who were teaching in the school were wearing a modified habit of sorts, at least they had legs and hair now and a little veil. Not Sister X. She looked like she came out of a JC Penney catalog. Fashionable. I'd heard the religious were supposed to modernize, but did that mean being unrecognizable as a nun?

It was about a year later, the diocesan paper had a picture of liturgical dance on the front page. The leotard-with-small-skirt-clad figure was photographed doing some interpretation of the Offertory. It was Sister X.

What happened to the *rules*? Where was it written in our liturgy one could whirl around bringing up the gifts? David may have danced and sung before the Lord, but somehow Sister X didn't do it for me.

This was the beginning of the wave. A few years later, a Sister from the same monastery gave a talk at a local Catholics United for the Faith meeting. She wore the traditional Benedictine habit and talked about standing up for what you believe. She later told me of her grief that her order had gone overboard, that she actually felt persecuted because she wanted to remain faithful to her calling, including the habit she promised to wear as a sign of her consecration.

Call it a Vatican II awakening. All of this was after the Council, all of this was how some religious orders interpreted the Council's words. But was this *really* what Vatican II wanted? And if not, what happened? Laurene Conner's incisive research gives a clue.   –CP

Guarding a Divine Inheritance

As with the priesthood, within a few years of the closing of the Second Vatican Council, the state of religious life for women seemed in turmoil, enough so that Pope Paul VI felt he had to issue a *Evangelica testificatio*, the *Apostolic Exhortation on the Renewal of Religious Life* in 1971. In it he noted "the anxiety, uncertainty, instability shown by some...the boldness of certain arbitrary transformations, an exaggerated distrust of the past... and a mentality excessively preoccupied with hastily conforming to the profound changes which disturb our times." These "have succeeded in leading some to consider as outmoded the specific forms of religious life...even...to cast doubt on the very principles of religious life" (n.2).

He called for "necessary discernment" between outmoded "exterior elements" and the "essentials which must be safeguarded" (n.5-6). He reminded religious "the supreme rule of religious life and its ultimate norm is that of following Christ according to the teaching of the Gospel." He said it was this that "has given rise in the Church to the demand for a life that is chaste, poor, and obedient" (n.12). Paul VI described the "essential commitments" as "consecrated chastity, consecrated poverty, consecrated obedience." Under consecrated poverty, he explicitly upheld the significance of the religious habit: "...we cannot pass over in silence the fittingness that the dress of religious men and women should be as the Council wishes, a sign of their consecration and that it should be in some way different from the forms that are clearly secular."

The implication in his writing was that in the few short years since the Council, things had gone off track. *Lumen gentium*, the *Dogmatic Constitution on the Church*, didn't suggest overthrowing the vows and convents. *Perfectae caritatis*, the *Decree on the Adaptation and Renewal of Religious Life* didn't call for being so up-to-date that nuns should seem to be an arm of the National Organization of Women. In fact, just the opposite.

The Lure of the World

Religious life was first mentioned in the Council documents in *Lumen gentium*, the *Dogmatic Constitution on the Church*, promulgated in 1964:

> The teaching and example of Christ provided the foundation for the evangelical counsels of chaste dedication to God, of poverty, and of obedience. The Apostles and Fathers of the Church commend them as an ideal of life and so do her doctors and pastors. They therefore constitute a gift of God which the Church has received from the Lord and which by His grace she always safeguards (n. 43).

In *Perfectae caritatis* (*Decree on the Adaptation and Renewal of Religious Life*) promulgated in 1965, the Council stated:

Before all else religious life is ordered to the following of Christ by its members and to their becoming united with God by the profession of evangelical counsels. For this reason it must be seriously and carefully considered that even the best contrived adaptations to the needs of our time will be of no avail unless they are animated by a spiritual renewal which must always be assigned primary importance even in the active ministry (2e).

These words of the Council are very plain, very traditional and, well, very Catholic. They concern the things of God, not of the world. And that was the problem, for being in the world but not of it was becoming most difficult, especially for those serious about living the faith, and especially those in religious life.

Go back to 1965. Change was in the air in both society and the Church, if the news accounts were to be believed. Bishops and their staffs of *periti* (experts) were freshly back from Rome. People wanted to know what had gone on. And there was nothing stopping the *periti* from telling them. These experts, many of them priests, had been invited to the Council to advise and counsel the Bishops, and they managed to meet with others of their kind to discuss what they thought the Council Fathers should have said. The *periti* ran wild on the talk circuit, writing articles and books and conducting seminars with personal opinions of what went on in Rome and the Council of the Media, to which Pope Benedict referred, lapped it up and served it to the public. If it was controversial, there was a publisher and soon God was dead, no He was alive but didn't care, and speculation on doctrines like the virgin birth and papal infallibility made good sales.

Couple that with the late sixties' move for the Equal Rights Amendment and the screaming women protesters who claimed to be oppressed by men; the new psychology which stressed self-fulfillment over duty; sexual freedom as a right; revolt (student strikes and violent political demonstrations) for the sake of revolt. New ideas, not all of them valid or of value permeated places of education. And then, Pope Paul VI reconfirmed the centuries-long tradition of the Catholic Church against artificial means of birth control in *Humanae vitae*. New fodder for the seminars and books with the theme that the Church was out of touch with the real world.

For Sisters in religious life, one of the first holes in the armor of their consecrated life, was the idea there was a need for more college education and advanced degrees, and that secular universities could accomplish that goal. The idea predated the Council, but gained in popularity as time went on. At the same time, secular universities were being overtaken by radical theories which sounded so logical that Sisters, like any other naive student in those days, bought into the message. Those gifted with the ability to teach, repeated what they learned, expanded on it, became experts, and gave seminars as corrupting as any occasion of sin in the world. Books like *I Leap Over the Wall* (first published in 1941 and conveniently republished after Vatican II) and abandonment of vows seemed a vision of the future. Veils came off, feminism abounded, Sisters got politically active. Religious life was rethought and retooled and wounded. In the process, between 1966 and 1976, 50,000 women would leave religious life (*The Battle for the American Church,* Msgr. George A. Kelly, Image Books (Doubleday), New York, 1979, p. 256).

Repairing The Wounds

Pope John Paul II's visible concern about the state of religious life can be traced to his visit to the United States in 1979 when Sister Theresa Kane, RSM, former president of the Leadership Conference of Women Religious (LCWR) addressed him as the representative of the women religious. She appeared in secular garb and petitioned for the ordination of women, a stance the LCWR holds even today.

(Formed in 1956, the Leadership Conference of Catholic Women represents leaders of religious women and provides resources for living religious life. Their members were no more immune to the societal slide than any other group at the time and ordinary members of religious orders were fed the radical points of view of LCWR officials as gospel. LCWR is now made up of 1350 leaders of the nation's women religious, representing 48,500 members (https://lcwr.org).)

Thus in 1983, Pope John Paul II initiated a series of extraordinary measures that reflected his concern over the deteriorating condition of religious life in the United States. He began the work of calling the Sisters back to their vocation. He appointed a special commission of three bishops to "facilitate the pastoral work" of all the bishops "in helping the religious...to live their ecclesial vocation to the full." Each bishop was sent a document, "Essential Elements," which were guidelines prepared by the Sacred Congregation for Religious and Secular Institutes. The essential elements of religious life were listed as public vows, a stable community life, personal and community prayer, public witness, specific relation to the Church. Without these essential elements, the document said, "religious life loses its identity" (n.4). The vows, in particular, embody the three ways of pledging oneself to Christ in areas which cover the whole of life: possessions (poverty), affections (chastity), autonomy (obedience). The revision of the Code of Canon Law, which was promulgated in 1983, also gave emphasis to the evangelical counsels as "valuable aid and a sure guide...for faithfully and generously living [the] magnificent vocation in the Church."

During the *ad limina* visits of the US bishops that year, Pope John Paul reiterated his words about the impairment of consecrated life. He asked the bishops "to speak to the religious about their ecclesial identity and to explain to the whole People of God how the religious are who they are only because the Church is what she is in her sacramental reality." He asked the bishops to "emphasize the special feminine role of women religious....Personifying the Church as Spouse of Christ, they are called to live for Christ, faithfully, exclusively, and permanently, in the consciousness of being able to make visible the spousal aspect of the Church's love for Christ....The greatest offense to their dignity and person comes from those who try to *situate their life or mission outside its ecclesial context*. Religious are betrayed by anyone who would attempt to have them embrace teaching against the *Magisterium* of the Church...."

Four years later, the commission's results brought no surprises. James Cardinal Hickey wrote:

Within the same religious institute divergent views have arisen on many seminal issues which previously bound members closely together [including] the centrality of living in community, the value of various religious practices and the authority of the ordinary *Magisterium*.

He identified "two basic orientations with respect to religious life: the first stresses mission and ministry; the second stresses consecration and community."

The focus on mission seems characteristic of the majority of Religious institutes of men and women in the United States. Since the Council, these institutes have stressed the importance of being in the midst of the world in order to address its needs. Consequently, the exterior structures of Religious life are deemphasized with a view toward immersion in ministry.

He continued, mentioning some religious live alone in apartments or small communities.

> Some "engage in works not specifically related to the Church. Some institutes have turned from teaching and health care to social justice issues." This "emphasis on justice issues and concern for social needs has profoundly affected the way religious view themselves and their ministries. Some religious imbued with liberation theology are engaged in political activism. The feminist critique strongly influences the way some religious men and women understand, experience, and evaluate their calling."

He then outlined the other approach to religious life:

> The second approach focuses on consecration through the vows as a value in itself and as a basis for community apostolate. This view represents a smaller percentage of institutes sometimes described as "traditional" or "conservative." Some, not all of these institutes, "draw a steady stream of candidates." These religious stress the transcendent nature of the consecrated religious life even as they serve human needs here and now.

Pope John Paul responded to the commission's results:

> The study of the Pontifical Commission and your own letters point out an apparent tension between consecration and mission. The centrality of the evangelical counsels must continue to be emphasized. Consecrated life of its very nature is linked to the profession and living of consecrated chastity, poverty, and obedience. Religious are not merely clerical or lay persons dedicated to good works....Religious must truly bring Christ to others. Identification with Jesus brings with it death to self. You and I must be concerned that we call religious to that dying. Tendencies to excessive self-fulfillment and autonomy in living, working, and decision making are not reflections of Jesus who came to do the will of the Father.

For What End?

The response? One nun wrote, "Some religious were weary of hearing the emphasis the Holy Father places on the vows. While most religious are in accord with the Vatican II interpretation of the vows," when they hear the Pope's "challenge to make the vows more central they wonder for what end?"

But it was Vatican II's interpretation of the vows that Pope John Paul was supporting!

The Leadership Conference of Women Religious held that

We need to raise the question of whether or not the traditional vowed commitment, arising as it did in a male ambiance, might be related to specifically masculine energies and designed to address areas of concern experienced specifically by males. Would the experience of a community of women lead them to design something similar? Are the vows really compatible with feminine consciousness?...Recent experiences... suggest that the Church hierarchy, at times shows more willingness to maintain their institutional power base than to attend to the groaning Spirit within our lives. Taken together, these experiences intimate that much is at stake when women religious begin to alter their place within the Church (*Claiming our Truth, Reflections on Identity by United States Women Religious,* edited by Nadine Foley, OP, president of LCWR in 1988).

So what is it, consecration or mission? According to a chapter written by a St. Joseph Sister in *Claiming our Truth* in 1988, it is "mission as consecration." There was a "shift in consciousness" women religious experienced when they rejected the "dichotomy between consecration and mission." This occurred over "the past twenty years as we have begun to interpret our consecration with a heightened sense of mission....[M]ission is the governing principle because we perceive that our consecration does not set us apart from the world.....The emphasis given to the word *as* is to draw attention to the claim that consecration by the women Religious is not just *for* the mission of Jesus. We do not enter a religious community in order to perform apostolic works for the Church....Not flight from the world, but apostolic involvement in society is viewed as constitutive of religious life."

It is not surprising then to read the admission that "many of us have participated in the women's movement" as a result of "dialogue with modern culture." Even less surprising is the mention by name of the "National Organization for Women, the largest organization active in the work of lobbying for women's rights." The quest for women's rights spilled into the church with the LCWR Religious focusing on what is described as "dualisms in ecclesiastical legislation about our lives as women and in magisterial teachings about human sexuality" with dissention not only on *Humanae vitae* but also the "patterns of Church life."

Feminism is obvious, particularly in a subsequent chapter.

Naming ourselves *women*...strikes at the root of the patriarchal delineations of women...Calling ourselves *women* says we participate in the global women's liberation movements shaped by and in turn shaping U.S. women's efforts....Consciously adopting the designation *women* in a Church that largely encourages traditional supportive roles for women commits us and other members of the Church to liberating the Church, as well as society from sexism.

Meetings and seminars bolstered feminist ideals. At the 1983 annual LCWR meeting, ex-priest Daniel Maguire talked on "Transforming Consciousness." Maguire, a pro-abortion professor at [Catholic] Marquette University, spoke of "the terrible hatred of women in the Church. We must realize that the Church has an indentured hatred of women." He called obedience "a dubious evangelical virtue."

With religious in general, not just their superiors, gadding about and attending seminars given by people like Maguire or ex-priest Matthew Fox with his New Age creationism, or Hans Küng on empowerment or infallibility, it was inevitable that confusion reigned within the souls of women who were told to be angry, to fight for their rights, particularly the right to ordination, and be Church, that is, Women-Church, liberated from patriarchy.

What happened is LCWR-leaning women religious lost their vision, the sense of the transcendent nature of religious life. In casting about for something to be *mission*, since consecrated service for the Church wasn't good enough, Sisters became involved in different popular causes such as the peace movement, attacking corporate power by attending stockholder meetings, liberation theology, social justice lobbying particularly through NETWORK, and even today, immigration issues.

Bleak Future

Was the outlook bleak? For some religious orders, yes. Pope Benedict XVI initiated an apostolic visitation of the nation's women's religious orders, a process that took three years. Recommendations were made to renew several of these orders.

In addition, an investigation of LCWR was launched by Pope Benedict which clearly revealed those who would not serve then still do not serve today. An investigation of the manuals and practices of the Leadership Conference of Women Religious by the Congregation for the Doctrine of the Faith found serious faults. The CDF said "the work of any conference of major superiors of women religious can and should be a fruitful means of addressing the contemporary situation and supporting religious life in its most 'radical' sense – that is, in the *faith* in which it is *rooted*."

Instead, the CDF found that "while there has been a great deal of work on the part of LCWR promoting issues of social justice in harmony with the Church's social doctrine, it is silent on the right to life from conception to natural death, a question that is part of the lively public debate about abortion and euthanasia in the United Sates. Further, issues of crucial importance to the life of Church and society, such as the Church's biblical view of family life and human sexuality, are not part of the LCWR agenda in a way that promotes Church teaching. Moreover, occasional public statements by the LCWR that disagree with or challenge positions taken by the bishops, who are the Church's authentic teachers of faith and morals are not compatible with its purpose."

Speakers at LCWR conferences were found to protest Church teaching on homosexuality and support women's ordination and radical feminist themes "incompatible with the Catholic faith" ("For US Nuns, A Vatican Shake-Up," http://whispersintheloggia.blogspot.com/2012/04).

Deliver Us, O Lord

Amidst the turmoil of the Sisterhood, even as far back as the late sixties, loyal Sisters, suffering in silence and many times ostracized, tried to remain faithful to their vows and apostolic consecration. They prayed to be led out of the desert.

According to an article in the *National Catholic Register*, a group split off from the LCWR in 1970-71, partly over feminist issues. Calling itself the *Consortium Perfectae Caritatis*, it was made up of women religious who were committed to spiritual renewal, authentic updating based on the founder's charisms of each order (http://www.catholic.org/national/national_story.php?id=20774). As contentious and angry as LCWR speakers were, those of the Consortium spoke on holiness and fidelity and peace. In 1974, Fr. John Hardon, SJ, established the Institute on Religious Life, promoting and supporting the growth, development, and renewal of the consecrated life as a gift to the Church and evangelical witness to the world. Fidelity to the Magisterium is its hallmark and since its inception it has inspired countless religious with its annual conference (http://religiouslife.com).

The Council of Major Superiors of Women was formed in 1992 as an alternative to the radical LCWR. One of the requirements of the CMSW is that members wear a defined habit ("For US Nuns, A Vatican Shake-Up," http://whispersintheloggia.blogspot.com/2012/04).

While radical Sisters were demanding the hierarchy "attend to the groaning Spirit within our lives," many faithful Sisters felt the Spirit calling them to new foundations, new religious orders. The Sisters of Life and the Sisters of Mary, Mother of the Eucharist are two such orders.

John Joseph Cardinal O'Connor of New York was never silent on life issues. With an article in the diocesan paper entitled, "Help Wanted: Sisters of Life," he asked women of higher education to consider joining a new religious community in the Church, dedicated to the promotion of pro-life causes, working for an end to abortion and euthanasia. On June 1, 1991, eight women joined the new order and worked for 13 years as a public association of lay faithful until March 25, 2004 when they were formally established as a religious institute. The Sisters share common prayer, and their daily work includes aid and support to pregnant women, giving retreats for post-abortive women, and directing the New York Archdiocesan Family Life/Respect Life Office. They serve over 700 women a year in crisis pregnancies and also provide housing for some of them (http://en.wikipedia.org/wiki/Sisters_of_Life).

While the hurricane of change roared through the ranks of nuns, the Dominican Sisters of St. Cecelia remained ever faithful, habited, and a sign of contradiction. The words of Pope John Paul II's apostolic exhortation *Vita consecrata* (1996) called for renewal of religious life. Inspired by his words, Mother Mary Assumpta Long, former superior of the Dominicans of St. Cecilia and three other Sisters of the community set off to "undertake a new initiative." In February of 1997, Cardinal O'Connor established the new foundation as a "Public Association of Christ's Faithful." After their canonical establishment, the new Dominican Sisters of Mary, Mother of the Eucharist accepted the invitation of the Bishop of Lansing to teach in the diocese (http://en.wikipedia.org/wiki/Sister_of_Mary,_Mother _of_the_Eucharist).

In the movie, *Field of Dreams*, one quote stands out: "If you build it, they will come." And truly, they came after the founding of this new order. Four women grew to eight and then twelve more women came. The order now has over 128 members, the average age is 28 and many young women attend the summer retreats to discern vocations. The sisters now teach in several states.

According to the *Catholic Spirit* newspaper (August 10, 2017), the Handmaids of the Heart of Jesus have accepted Archbishop Bernard Hebda's invitation to come to open a convent in the Archdiocese of St. Paul and Minneapolis. The order was founded in 2007 in New Ulm, Minnesota. The sisters wish "to serve...the archdiocese in whatever way the Lord desires," according to Mother Mary Clare. In New Ulm, they have worked at the Cathedral, in campus ministry, and in diocesan offices. There are 16 members now, with 7 new postulants arriving soon.

God's good time brought the increase and the re-flowering of religious life for women in the United States. While many Sisters have taken one well-traveled, vocal and protesting visible road for their mission, others have chosen "the one less traveled by, and that has made all the difference" (Robert Frost, "The Road Not Taken," http://www.poemhunter.com/poem/the-road-not-taken/).

LAURENE CONNER was one of the co-founders of the Wanderer Forum Foundation with her husband, the late Stillwell J. Conner and Alphonse J. Matt Sr., in 1965. She served as Secretary/Treasurer of the Foundation, managing the annual National Forums, selecting topics and speakers to fit the yearly themes for the event. She also managed the correspondence which led to the realization that there was a need for published documentation for Catholics about some of the experimentation in the wake of the Second Vatican Council. She served as co-editor and research director for *Forum Focus* magazine since its origin in 1985, until her retirement in 2003. Some of the topics covered included the original Campaign for Human Development, the left-leaning bent of the bureaucracy of the U.S. Catholic Conference at the time, secularism, liturgical innovation, and a variety of lay movements. One issue of the magazine, "Unholy Alliance," concerned liberation theology, Jesuits, Communists, and subversive activities in Latin America. Mrs. Conner and Frank Morriss collaborated on this extensive study which included translated news articles by a Latin journalist about the reality of what was going on behind the scenes of the open turmoil. This issue is still available from the Foundation and in recent years had been sent to young Jesuits in El Salvador by a priest who had helped in the research. He reported the piece had a profound and positive influence on their thinking. Mrs. Conner wrote many articles and reported on many Church conferences for *The Wanderer* newspaper. Mrs. Conner passed from this life July 2, 2007.

Prelude to a Persecution
By Ellen Rice

At a time when the Catholic Church in America is under persecution, notably through immoral government rules, it is helpful to reflect on the forces that weakened the Church in this country in the immediate post-Conciliar era. Msgr. George A. Kelly, who was during his lifetime a prolific author, a member of the Papal Birth Control Commission appointed by Pope John XXIII, and the founder of the Fellowship of Catholic Scholars, authored *The Battle for the American Church* (Image Books, 1979), a classic volume on this topic, at the beginning of Pope John Paul II's pontificate. For the John Paul II, Benedict XVI, and Francis generations, Kelly's book is essential historical reading to understand the crises that weakened the Church, how it has recovered, and what issues remain unresolved.

In Kelly's Introduction, "Who's in Charge?" he frames the issue as a crisis of doctrine and of the Church's influence over its people.

A guerrilla-type warfare is going on inside the Church and its outcome is clearly doubtful. The Pope and Roman Curia are fending off...attacks of their own theologians, who...demand more radical accommodation with Protestant and secular thought. *The issues at stake are the correctness of Catholic doctrine and the survival of the Catholic Church as a significant influence in the life of her own communicants* (vii), (emphasis added).

The weakening of doctrine and Catholic identity explains why the thinking of modern Catholics on abortion, contraception, end-of-life issues, and same-sex marriage are indistinguishable from their secular peers.

Kelly's history is divided into two parts, "Of Modernism and Modernization" and "The Battle for the American Church." He concludes with a lengthy epilogue, "Whither Goes the Future of the Catholic Church?"

Part One, "Of Modernism and Modernization," explains the

ecclesiastical and theoretical roots of the post-Conciliar crisis. "Vatican II: Aftershocks of an Ecclesiastical Earthquake" is a shocking title to younger generations of Catholics who have seen the integration of the Council into the life of the Church under the papacies of John Paul II, Benedict XVI, and Francis. It was not always so.

Disillusionment

The question asked by leading figures of the day, from Hans Küng to Malachi Martin and Archbishop Lefebvre was: Could the Council fail? "What happened to cause disillusion over such a wide area of Catholic thought, when the early hopes everywhere were so high?" (p. 5) Kelly asked. This chapter explores the universal feelings of let-down, among progressives and conservatives, after the Council.

In the following chapter, "Reading and Misreading the Council Documents," Kelly suggests that Pope John XXIII's multiple goals in convoking the Council were overwhelming, leading proponents of individual goals to believe the Council had failed. "What were the objectives sought by the pope in convoking Vatican II?" (p. 23) The stated purposes (p.24), in Pope John's statements from the announcement until his address at the opening session were several, including: growth of the Catholic Faith, diffusion of revealed truth, outreach to separated brethren and all men of good will, doctrinal clarity, concern for the temporal order, vindication of the Church's liberty, to name a few.

Of course, taking a long view, we are able to see progress in achieving these goals; it was not so visible then.

Msgr. Kelly suggests that the "sources of unanticipated difficulty" with John XXIII's goals were:

1. Objectives that were "too numerous and frequently conflicting" such as growth in the Catholic faith vs. appeals to non-Catholics;

2. attempting more than one council could possibly accomplish;

3. seeking to dismantle ancient structures before adequate substitutes were developed;

4. reaching out to non-Catholics without making provision for solidifying the ongoing commitment of faithful Catholics; and

5. adopting broad conciliar policies without evaluation of their possible dysfunctional aspects.

Kelly describes the struggle going on in the Church as a "battle of ideas." In the chapter, "Of Modernism and Modernization: Alfred Loisy and Hans Küng," he writes, "The expected prize is control of the lives of the faithful accomplished through control of Church machinery itself.... Whose ideas?...The Catholic way of life is built around the claims of Christ and His Church to reveal and represent the mind and will of God about what human beings should do in this life in order to be happy with Him forever....The battle of ideas is as old as the Church" (pp. 37-38).

But in the 20th century, the battle outside the Church made this battle of ideas different from preceding crises "because Church authorities themselves in the Council decided to experiment with applying some of these 'alien' ideas to Catholic thought structures...to fight the battle of Christ in terms that modern man understands and accepts." Scientific rationality, relativism, pluralism, religious experience, psychology, evolution of individuals and societies, immanence, dialectical progress are some of the ideas identified by Kelly as part of the experimentation.

The bulk of the chapter is spent tracing the roots of modernism with Alfred Loisy, and its expression by radical contemporary spokesman Hans Küng.

> A common thread of understanding runs through the thinking of Hans Küng, as it did in earlier days for Alfred Loisy: Christianity is a human invention, the "revelation" on which it is based really no revelation at all....Even Christ the Son of God is the creature of His followers. It was they who made Him equal to God as surely as they made the Church (p. 53).

Kelly posits that many of the controversies in the American Church stem from modernism – "ongoing revelation, process theology, existential morality, and experiential catechesis have their beginning with this acceptance" (p. 54). Traces of these problems remain, in catechetical method if nothing else, and Kelly's reminder that our faith is in the supernatural revelation of the Son of God in the Incarnation and in the Church rather than the reductive propositions of the Enlightenment is essential in seeking personal renewal in our daily lives.

Part Two: The Battle for the American Church outlines the specific arenas in which the battle was fought and the strength of institutions was undermined by confusion and ill-thought-out reform.

Kelly begins the chapter on "The Catholic Campus" by detailing a renaissance of Catholic scholarship in the 20th century, including in the United States. Nonetheless, a "post-Vatican II rush to gain scholarly respectability" led Catholic universities to declare their independence from the Church in Rome, as if faith was holding back reason.

Independence Day for the American Catholic revolution in Catholic higher education was July 23, 1967, when twenty-six Catholic educators representing ten institutions signed the 'Land O'Lakes Document,' declaring independence of Church authority to be a desirable quality in those Catholic universities and colleges that intended to compete on equal footing with their secular counterparts. Catholic presence...was to be maintained through... the Christian witness of faculty and a campus ministry... (p. 62-63).

The battles in Catholic colleges thereafter, with the reluctant adoption of *Ex corde ecclesiae*, the battle over the *mandatum* (a requirement that those teaching about Catholic Faith in colleges adhere completely to that Faith), the issue of non-Catholic faculty hiring, and so forth, reflect the weakening of Catholic identity on college campuses that began during this era.

No Control

In the chapter, "Theologians," Msgr. Kelly states,

[T]he revolt of the theologians against the bishops and Pope (which began in Germany and France)...now firmly in the hands of American theologians, is real and more dangerous than the other[s]....If the new Catholic university wishes to be liberated from 'juridical control,' the Catholic theologians want no 'juridical control' either....Control by theologians over Catholic meaning and function is to come through Church democracy (p. 102).

The roots of a long battle over doctrinal orthodoxy stem from the debate between dissenting theologians and bishops and the papacy during these times. "A tide once with bishops and Pope is now running against them. Bishops have been talked out of using certain scholars or using certain texts because they are 'too orthodox'" (p. 125).

This battle was fought in the lives of the faithful on several fronts. The first, detailed in the "Birth Control" chapter, is legendary. "Fr. Andrew Greeley...announced with ferocious certainty that the deterioration in American Catholicism [was] due to the encyclical *Humanae vitae*..."(p. 129). Msgr. Kelly examines the "Greeley hypothesis," reaching the conclusion that the problem was of course not the encyclical, but its undermining even at the Vatican level, beginning with the Vatican press secretary's two undercutting remarks to the press that "the encyclical was *not an infallible pronouncement*" (p.164).

"That public acceptance of the encyclical did not follow should surprise no one. Charles Curran and fifty-one Washington priests gained notoriety over their rejection." And all over the United States priests and theologians followed suit (p. 165). American Bishops, Cardinal O'Boyle excepted, shied from boldly enforcing *Humanae vitae* at a diocesan-wide level. Kelly details the rebellion against Paul VI in Holland, France, Sweden and Canada, and the "right to dissent" that the theologians claimed, under the auspices of the "spirit of Vatican II." At the time Kelly wrote, "a major management problem remain[ed]... [t]he dissonance between doctrine and practice. The issue is no longer contraception but the ability of the Church to make its doctrine live in the lives of the faithful" (p. 198).

A little-known landmark in post-conciliar history is the Cana Conference of Chicago. In a chapter called, "Family: Siege of Chicago," Kelly chronicles a shocking population control conference held under Catholic auspices.

> On September 5, 1963, the University of Notre Dame and the Cana Conference of Chicago co-sponsored what would become three lengthy meetings over eighteen months on the moral and theological considerations of the population problem. The *Ford Foundation* provided the money, which was to be used to promote other regionals of this kind (p. 201).

The meetings, held to "formulate a Catholic position" on the population issue, resulted in a 1965 statement by 37 American Catholic scholars to suggest "a change in the Church's traditional position on birth control." This document was first brought to Rome by Notre Dame President Fr. Theodore M. Hesburgh and once more by Joseph Cardinal Ritter.

(Note: This was done even though the matter was already under study by chosen experts *before* the beginning of the Council.)

The battle for the American Church definitely involved children, and in the next chapter, "The Battle for the American Child (or Psychology vs. Parents), Kelly details the trauma of the use of children as pawns in the ideological war.

"[I]t was the parents who held an attentive ear to what Pope and bishops were saying. They had reason to be concerned about the things their children were hearing in the classroom. In early post-Vatican II years, no novel theological concept escaped experimentation in the classroom" (p. 237).

Msgr. Kelly enumerates three characteristics of post-conciliar catechesis:

1. "Search and inquiry" replaced "transmission of knowledge";

2. "Stress on the authority and tradition of the Church was diminished"; and

3. "Subjective interpretations became more important than objective reality or the good of the Church." In many schools, children were even being taught that missing Sunday Mass was no longer a mortal sin.

The Bad Old Days

Those of the John Paul II generation have no idea what transpired in the "bad old days" without a history book like Kelly's. The section, "The Textbooks Tell the Story," includes a moronic excerpt from a catechism of the day:

"I sit at my desk, head cupped in my hands, staring into space. What do I see? I see me. I see myself as doing my own thing, the master of my own destiny. I see the child who loves home and parents, who rebels against rules and yet wants them. I see challenge and security all mixed up in me. I sit staring into space. What do I see? I see others...."

Kelly also describes the saturation of religious education by developmental and experiential psychology. This situation, unfortunately, persists in textbooks, despite the doctrinal corrections implemented by the US Catholic Conference of Bishops after the publication of the *Catechism of the Catholic Church*. With a preponderance of textbooks still modeled after educational psychology methods, it is appropriate for authors, parents, and directors of religious education to peruse texts carefully.

"What happened to the nuns?" a young Catholic might ask, baffled by the joyful surprise that accompanies the announcement of young people entering religious life in recent times. The chapter "Embattled Nuns" explains. Kelly presents the growing disrespect towards traditional Sisters alongside the puzzling fact of the massive post-Conciliar walkout.

"We are still too close to the scene to evaluate why fifty thousand nuns left the convent between 1966 and 1976, or why so few are interested in entering now" (p. 256).

Instead, Kelly presents several case studies, the most important of which is the "Milwaukee Case" of the School Sisters of St. Francis. When Sr. Francis Borgia Rothluebber was elected mother general in 1966, she launched a "community-wide experiment in communal living." Democratic adoption of secular garb, a directive releasing nuns from taking vows, optional community Mass attendance, and "naked hate," as one Sister described it, were among the changes that ensued. There were several areas of concern, including overt secularization; lay lifestyle; exodus from the Catholic schools; disobedience to the Holy See; community disregard for religious obedience; temporary membership; and neglect of the elderly, (most shockingly in the sale of buildings for retired sisters and placement of them in nursing homes). In order to avoid censure, the Sisters threatened to abandon the Catholic schools completely. Kelly tells the story of an era of flagrant rebellion that today's young Catholics can scarcely imagine.

Finally, Kelly looks at the decline of the priesthood itself. In "Embattled Priests, or the Disorder of Melchisedech." He reminisces,

> The Catholic priesthood once was one of America's most respected institutions. Hats were doffed at the coming of priests. Ladies rose in their presence. Doors were opened to their influence....Esteem did not come to priests because the Roman pontiff called them "consecrated and sanctified." They earned it by hard work (p. 305).

Kelly begins by briefly describing the ascendancy of the priesthood as an American social institution, and then turns to the problems that arose when "protective barriers," such as the canonical statutes to sleep in the rectory every night, wear clerical garb, attend retreats and clergy conferences, plus lay approval of the priestly lifestyle, were lifted by the "spirit of Vatican II."

Kelly sees "low morale" in his era as one problem: "A grand design that would rally priests around their bishops seems to be missing" (p. 313). Departing priests and nuns, such as war protestors/folk heroes Fr. Philip Berrigan and Sr. Liz McAlister (secretly married for four years before departing religious life), crushed the morale of clergy. Kelly also alluded to the problem of disturbed priests in the ranks who should not have been allowed to remain. The remainder of Kelly's chapter focuses on structural problems and a crisis of meaning. As we know after the release of the Boston child sex abuse files, deeper problems of hidden evil lurked in the American clergy in various dioceses by this time, evil far more satanic than secret marriages to nuns. Why did this happen?

Sin is No Big Deal

Perhaps the answer to this most disturbing question is hinted at in the next chapter: "The Defeat of the Bishops." The level of disorganization and division within the US Catholic Conference (later the US Conference of Catholic Bishops) after Vatican II was best exemplified by a wrangle with Rome about the small, but important question of whether children were required to make their First Confession before receiving First Communion. "Family spats over eight-year-olds seem inanity for a Church in turmoil on more serious counts, yet if anger is a measure of seriousness, then this battle between Rome and professional catechists in the United States is not a small skirmish." (p. 388) The right of Rome to impose discipline was at stake, not the question of whether eight-year-olds could commit mortal sin. In a related fight, Rome began to restrict the practice of General Absolution, which was common in many dioceses and with the bishop's blessing. Only in the reign of John Paul II years later was it mostly curtailed (there are still a few rebels around) except in emergency situations. Notice in both examples, Kelly dealt with the minimization of the problem of sin, even in the eyes of some bishops. There was, overall, a loss of the sense of sin on the part of the priests and the laity they led. Is this a key to understanding how iniquity was working in many hidden diocesan child sex rings at that time?

The final chapter of Kelly's book is as dreary as its title, "The Sack of Rome, or Rome Has Spoken, the Case is Still Open." He presents grim case studies: The Lefebvre *de facto* schism over the Council and the Dutch *de facto* schism rejecting traditional doctrine. 1979, the year the book was published, was the post-Conciliar nadir; two popes had died the prior year and the future was precarious. Little did he know that within two years of publication, all eyes worldwide would be fixed on Rome, as Mehmet Ali Acga attempted the assassination of John Paul II in St. Peter's Square.

Fortunately, Msgr. Kelly's epilogue, "Whither Goes the Future of the Catholic Church?" does not leave this history on a hopeless note. We know the story ended well on some fronts, got worse on others, and that we face a persecution of epic worldwide proportions. "All is not lost," Kelly insisted (p. 453). He called for a Second Spring in the Church in America, much as Newman called for a Second Spring in the buried, persecuted English Church.

Since Kelly wrote *The Battle for the American Church*, several dramatic events have intervened toward the development of a Second Spring. First, the pontificate of John Paul II and the publication of the new *Catechism of the Catholic Church* cleared the post-conciliar theological muddy waters. Today there is no doubt what the Church teaches. Discipline in many Catholic colleges has been restored by the publication of and widespread – but not universal – adoption of *Ex corde ecclesiae*. The Mass according to the Roman Missal of 1962 has been restored and Paul VI's Roman Missal of 1970 has received much needed clarifications and added precision to the original vernacular translations. Worship now is more standardized and reverent than it was when Kelly wrote.

Second, the sex scandals within, that began in earnest during the post-conciliar period, have mercifully been exposed – mercifully for the Church, the priesthood, and the victims. Unfortunately, the revelation of these scandals created greater cynicism toward the Church, at a time when New Age ideas and secularism lay in wait to ensnare many.

But the Holy Spirit has not been sitting idly by. Pope Francis is calling the Church to a worldwide Second Spring, by refocusing on essentials of faith, hope, charity, service, and love of the poor. Second springs usually follow great winters and we are facing an historic persecution of all Christians, not only in the U.S., but in other parts of the world. We must be unified in living the Catholic life, not battling each other over the embers of a phantom Vatican II that was nothing like the true Council. There is no time for a Battle for the American Church, we must go forward together, in kindness and courage, bearing witness to the world of the One Faith, perhaps with our very lives.

ELLEN RICE holds B.A. degrees from the University of Notre Dame in Art History and Philosophy, and an M.B.A in Management from Indiana University, where she taught Business Communications. She was editor of *Catholic Dossier* for 4 years, was director of Marketing and Development at St. Augustine's Press in South Bend, Indiana, as well as a publication consultant for several high profile clients. Rice is the author of several articles and books, including two history texts as part of the Catholic Schools Textbook Project and the *John Paul II LifeGuide: Words to Live By*, published by St. Augustine's Press.

The Church in the Modern World As I Lived It

By Fr. Timothy Sauppé, S.T.L.

Note: In the Fall of 2012, then Pope Benedict XVI, now Pope Emeritus, called for a "Year of Faith." He also asked pastors and faithful Catholics to celebrate the fiftieth anniversary of the Second Vatican Ecumenical Council and the twentieth anniversary of the *Catechism of the Catholic Church*. Since many have undertaken to compile a narrative of the post-Vatican II Church in the Modern World, I too wish to offer my own eyewitness reflections.

"Foundations, Once Destroyed, What Can the Just Do?"
(Psalm 11:3)

His words, after twenty years of priesthood, still haunt me to this day: "You should never be a priest!" Coming from my pastoral studies professor at the Catholic University of America (CUA) in Washington, D.C., I knew exactly what he meant, for he said the words with such depth and conviction. Sitting face to face at the teacher/student review session at the end of the first of two semesters, I knew exactly what he meant: "You should never be a priest" meant that I should not be a priest in the post-Vatican II Church – or at least, *his* post-Vatican II Church.

I knew, because after Vatican II, the pastoral emphasis had shifted. Before Vatican II, pastoral care dealt with one's soul; after, the focus became healing the psyche. Though the Vatican II documents described the priest as being a "pastor of souls," many priests were trained instead to be amateur psychologists. This happened because the Council documents challenged the Church to update using the most modern sciences. While this effort to update was and is praiseworthy, in many pastoral ministry programs, it was done regardless of its effectiveness and regardless of the base philosophical and anthropological assumptions of those who developed these various methods. I was prepared for his assertion that I should not become a priest, because I had read both *Psychological Seduction*[1] by William Kilpatrick and Dr. Paul Vitz's *Psychology as Religion:*

The Cult of Self-Worship.[2] These men warned about the abuse of modern psychology in religious life. They critiqued the base anthropological assumptions of these systems and found that they held to a denial of Original Sin, and thus, the lack of the need for grace and, of course, God. At best, modern psychologists often held agnostic, if not atheistic viewpoints.

I also knew what he meant because CUA (a university under the U.S. Bishops' own authority), allowed Fr. Charles Curran to teach his heretical system of morality, Proportionalism, to men who would become future priests. Proportionalism[3] is a system of moral thought in which one could evaluate all the moral choices and "weigh" the proportion of the good effects over the alternatives of the evil effects. Thus an evil act could be justified morally, if the good effect is proportionally greater than the evil which in turn, would violate the long standing moral principle that one could never do an evil for a good. Fr. Curran taught class after class of seminarians and the CUA Theology Department was full of others who taught Proportionalism as well until Pope John Paul II finally removed Fr. Curran's Pontifical License to teach in 1986. Thus, when I was at CUA, there was plenty of ill will toward anyone who was orthodox[4] on that campus.

When I think about those words and that time, I have to remind myself of what the professor told us on the first day of class. During a round-robin introduction of the small class with each other, he told us that he was a former Lutheran pastor, and he was divorced and remarried. He told us that the other professors in the theology department did not have a problem with him teaching pastoral ministry to Catholic seminarians and priests. Then he asked us if we had a problem with him teaching; and I exclaimed, "Why yes; yes I do!" Of course, I said this to myself. It took me five years of studies to learn to keep silent in the face of heterodoxy. And I tried; I really did try to keep mum in his class, but not enough, for he went on during the review session to threaten to flunk me in the second semester.

In this CUA professor's mind, I was all wrong for the modern Church, and as one of many gatekeepers of the post-Vatican II Church, he had me by the proverbial "short hairs." But then I told him flunking me might happen, for I was under obedience from my religious superiors to take his class. In an instant, smugness went to open mouth bewilderment. I never did take that second semester. In fact, after graduating from the Dominican House of Studies that May of 1989, I left the Discalced Carmelite Friars, the religious order that I had joined in 1982, and became a layman.

While the above incident did contribute to my decision to leave, it was minor compared to having two senior members of the Order dying of AIDS, and after learning that our house prior/superior was saying Dignity Masses.

What became known as AIDS in the mid-to-late 1980s was brand new to us students and we were questioning both the health risks and the homosexual "lifestyle." The house superiors felt we needed a workshop to cover our concerns and so they contacted St. Luke's Institute in Silver Spring, Maryland, an institute with specialists in the treatment of priests, and religious men and women with sexual and mental disorders. On the eve before our Saturday workshop we were told it was canceled; the presenter, Fr. Peterson, could not make it. It was not long after this, that the news came out that the founder of St. Luke's Institute, Fr. Peterson, had AIDS and died in April of 1987.

In 1981, the Vatican had asked for a formal review of all seminaries throughout the world. For the purpose of integrity, national seminaries would be investigated by an outside Episcopal investigator – someone from outside the country being reviewed. This happened everywhere, except in the U.S. The U.S. Bishops protested at being investigated by an outsider. And so, the Vatican named Bishop John Marshall of Burlington, VT., as an Apostolic Visitator, and he and other U.S. bishops became involved in the formal investigation. The official visits would entail talking with us seminarians in private, as well as the seminary staff.

By the time the Marshall Review Board came to our seminary, it was 1987, and it was after the above events in the seminary. We were told that the Bishop interviewer would keep everything private, everything confidential. About a week after his visit, the Order's Provincial flew in to D.C. for a special house meeting. He announced, both to the senior religiously professed members and to the students, that he had been contacted by a particular Bishop Visitator who said our Washington community was in trouble. Our Provincial then put us under obedience not to speak of any of this to anyone; not even to those members of the Order outside of the house in Washington, D.C. If I were to pinpoint the time where I would have made my decision to leave, it would have been at this meeting. Those years were my first up close experience to the

Church in the Modern World.

As a layman, I then continued my studies at the Pope John Paul II Institute for Studies on Marriage and Family.[5] After two years, I obtained a Pontifical License in Sacred Theology in 1991, after which, I came to the Diocese of Peoria, IL and was ordained in Rock Island, IL, in 1992. I taught for three years in one of our Catholic High Schools, and for the next seventeen years, I have been a pastor. While everyone will have a different experience of the joys, hopes, grief, and anxieties of the post-Vatican II modern Church, what I experienced was the unfortunate norm for any seminarian or priest who was orthodox and faithful to the *Magisterium* of the Church. A Discalced Carmelite Brother described to me the era before Vatican II as being like Nazi Germany to him; well, my experience of the post-Conciliar Church, up until then, was like Dresden. As to what should have happened after the Council, let us look at the opening address to the Council, Pope John XXIII, and his intentions.

A Gift of God to the Church and to the Modern World
(Extraordinary Synod, 1985)

Pope John XXIII called for a new Council in 1959 and there was a three-year preparation period. The Second Ecumenical Council opened with great pomp on the Feast Day of the Motherhood of the Blessed Virgin Mary, October 11, 1962.[6] Then over four sessions, the Council would conclude on December 8, 1965. It produced sixteen documents addressing various issues and needs of the then "modern" post World War II, East versus West, Communist versus Capitalist, luxury versus want, First versus Third, world.

In his opening address to the 2500 assembled Bishops, official non-Catholic observers, and invited guests, Pope John XXIII set the tone and stated his desires for the Council. He said, *"Quod Concilii Oecumenici maxime interest, hoc est, ut sacrum christianae doctrinae depositum efficaciore ratione custodiatur atque proponatur."* That is, "The major interest of the Ecumenical Council is this: that the sacred heritage of Christian truth be safeguarded and expounded with greater efficacy."[7] He went on to say,

> And our duty is not just to guard this treasure, as though it were some museum-piece and we the curators, but earnestly and fearlessly to dedicate ourselves to the work that needs to be done in this modern

age of ours, pursuing the path which the Church has followed for almost twenty centuries.

Nor are we here primarily to discuss certain fundamentals of Catholic doctrine, or to restate in greater detail the traditional teaching of the Fathers....

What is needed at the present time is a new enthusiasm, a new joy and serenity of mind in the unreserved acceptance by all of the entire Christian faith, without forfeiting that accuracy and precision in its presentation which characterized the proceedings of the Council of Trent and the First Vatican Council. What is needed, and what everyone imbued with a truly Christian, Catholic and apostolic spirit craves today, is that this doctrine shall be more widely known, more deeply understood, and more penetrating in its effects on men's moral lives. What is needed is that this certain and immutable doctrine, to which the faithful owe obedience, be studied afresh and reformulated in contemporary terms. *For this deposit of faith, or truths which are contained in our time-honored teaching is one thing; the manner in which these truths are set forth (with their meaning preserved intact) is something else.*[8] (emphasis mine)

Here, Pope John faintly intimates what Pope Emeritus Benedict XVI laid out explicitly at the beginning of his papacy in 2005: the need for an interpretation, or hermeneutic, that holds the Church's *Magisterium* in continuity and harmony, before and during the Council. However, as we will see, this is not what has happened following the Council.

As opposed to errors of the day, Pope John wanted to promote the Church as "Christ's Bride [who] prefers the balm of mercy to the arm of severity. Lifting aloft the "torch of truth," Pope John XXIII wanted the world to see the Church as a "loving mother of all mankind; gentle, patient and full of tenderness and sympathy for her separated children." In short, his desire for the Council was unity within the One, Holy, Catholic, and Apostolic Church.

Pope John knew however, that many within his own Curia, were skeptical of the success of the Council and he called them, "prophets of gloom/doom/misfortune":

In the daily exercise of Our pastoral office, it sometimes happens that We hear certain opinions which disturb Us – opinions expressed by people who, though fired with a commendable zeal for religion, are lacking in sufficient prudence and judgment in their evaluation of events. They can see nothing but calamity and disaster in the present state of the world. They say over and over that this modern age of ours, in comparison with past ages, is definitely deteriorating. One would think from their attitude that history, that great teacher of life, had taught them nothing. They seem to imagine that in the days of the earlier councils everything was as it should be so far as doctrine and morality and the Church's rightful liberty were concerned. We feel that We must disagree with these prophets of doom,[9] who are always forecasting worse disasters, as though the end of the world were at hand.

Present indications are that the human family is on the threshold of a new era. We must recognize here the hand of God, who, as the years roll by, is ever directing men's efforts, whether they realize it or not, towards the fulfillment of the inscrutable designs of His providence, wisely arranging everything, even adverse human fortune, for the Church's good.[10]

That was then, and over the next three years and four sessions, the Council Fathers met and deliberated and finally produced the sixteen documents – the last of which is a document on the Church in the Modern World, arguably, the most important document in the years following the Council.

Gaudium et Spes

It is customary to refer to an ecclesial document by choosing a word or two from the opening words or lines, and the opening words of this document are "*Gaudium et spes, luctus et angor*" (Joy and Hope, Griefs and Anxieties). It was proposed to call the document, "*luctus et angor*" but "*Gaudium*"/Joy, and "*Spes*"/Hope sounded better than "griefs and anxieties." Pope Paul VI promulgated *The Church in the Modern World*, on December 7, the day before the closing of the Council, December 8, 1965. As a document, its status is as a Pastoral Constitution as opposed to the only two Dogmatic Constitutions of Council i.e. *Lumen gentium* (*On the Church*), and *Dei verbum* (*On Divine Revelation*). The purpose of *Gaudium et spes* was to speak to all men of good will from the heart of the Council and attempt to address all the various necessities of the modern *polis*/city, thereby showing the world that the Catholic Church not only cares but has solutions to problems in the world.

What followed the Council was perhaps unexpected, but the Pope and the Church did not need to wait long to find out.

The first major crisis that Pope Paul VI had to confront was from the Netherlands. In March of 1966, the Dutch Cardinal Bernard Jan Alfrink gave his imprimatur to a new heterodox, if not heretical, catechism, *De Nieuwe Katchismus*, from the Dutch Bishops.[11] It became widely known as the *Dutch Catechism* and its influence was worldwide. Pope Paul VI responded in July of 1966 by issuing a circular letter to the Presidents of Bishops' Conferences, warning them of the misreading of the Vatican II documents on various topics e.g. false ecumenism, original sin, the priesthood, and evolution. In 1968 he wrote the *Credo of the People of God* to counteract the Dutch influence.

Another of the threats to Catholic doctrine and practice had to do with priestly celibacy, particularly the policy in the Roman Rite of the Catholic Church of ordaining only unmarried men who then would remain unmarried. In response, Pope Paul VI issued an encyclical, *Sacerdotalis caelibatus* on June 24, 1967, upholding the tradition of ordaining only unmarried men. In response to the Pope's encyclical in July of 1967, there was an apparently secret meeting of 76 "progressive" bishops, including eight cardinals at an obscure seminary near Leyden, Holland."[12] Under the *Watertown Daily Times* headline, "Bishops' Anti-Rome Session in Holland Disturbing to Vatican," news correspondent, George Weller, reported that Msgr. Carlo Colombo was sent from the Vatican to help quell the call for a married clergy.

Continuing the Dialogue

One of the great fruits that came out of the Council of Vatican II was a system or way to continue the experience of collegial dialogue into the post-Conciliar years. On September 15, 1965, Pope Paul VI established a post-Vatican II "Synod of Bishops" with his *motu proprio*, *Apostolica sollicitudo*. This Synod of Bishops would meet every few years (every two years at first, then every three years), and would deal with current problems or themes in need of immediate action. The first began September 29, 1967 with the topic of preservation of the Catholic Faith. Since 1967 there have been thirteen Ordinary Synods of Bishops and various Extraordinary and Special ones. (See Appendix II with dates, themes, and the name of any post-Synodal Apostolic Exhortations from the various Popes.)

All these papal documents and meetings are the direct fruit of Vatican II, as are all the various encyclical letters, apostolic constitutions, exhortations, speeches, and homilies of the popes. They have an important place in understanding the role of Vatican II and its sixteen documents. The Synod of Bishops in 2012 carried the theme of the "New Evangelization," and the one 2014 was on the "Family and Evangelization." The Fifteenth Ordinary Synod (2018) has the theme, "Young People, The Faith and Vocational Discernment." As we can see from the list of Synods, the Popes and the Bishops have not been lax in meeting or in writing about what goes on in the modern world. They were not writing for themselves or fellow clerics but rather addressing all of the faithful. Therefore, being a faithful modern churchman or churchwoman, means one has to read and absorb all of these documents as well as come to terms with the key bombshell encyclical of 1968.

Humanae vitae

On May 9, 1960, the first chemical contraceptive pill was introduced to the world when it was approved by the U.S. Food and Drug Administration. Not knowing the moral impact of this technology, Pope John XXIII in 1963, formed a special committee to investigate it and kept the issue "off the table" during the ongoing Council. With the passing of John XXIII, Pope Paul VI re-commissioned the Pontifical Commission of Population, Family, and Birth-rate (aka, the "Birth Control Commission") and expanded its members. In June of 1966, they produced their private report, which was meant only for the Pope. However, someone had leaked the secret report to both the *New York Times* (April 17, 1967) and the *National Catholic Reporter* (April 19, 1967) which described two reports – a majority in favor and a minority against artificial birth control. According to Professor Germain Grisez of Mount St. Mary's in Emmittsburg, Maryland, the public perception of two reports to the Pope was incorrect. Grisez surmises that whoever leaked the Commission's findings did so to give the impression of two "reports," instead of the one written in French, *Rapport Final*, that had two *parts*. For the benefit of researchers and scholars, Professor Grisez has posted to his website various documents from this period.[13]

The so-called "majority report" of the misnamed "Birth Control

Commission" was in favor of allowing couples to use the "Pill"; and conversely, the "minority" theological assessment was against it, as it would lead to an unraveling of the Church's understanding of the Natural Law, and its subsequent moral teachings. For whatever reason, Pope Paul VI did not respond immediately, and in fact, he kept the topic of the Birth Control Commission's report from the agenda for the 1967 first Synod of Bishops.[14] And, while he waited, everyone was reading the public and "Catholic" press about this issue. Some priests and bishops (following the advice from well known theologians), were telling couples to go ahead and use artificial contraception, since the change was coming from the Vatican itself.

Then, on July 25, 1968, Pope Paul VI shocked the Catholic world by following the committee's *theological* advice, issuing his encyclical, *Humanae vitae, On Human Life*, defending Natural Law. Why it took so long to respond is a question for the ages, for delay allowed an expectation of change. Immediately following the release of the encyclical there was protest. In the U.S., Fr. Charles Curran, professor at Catholic University of America, organized public dissent of hundreds of Catholic theologians and priests and nuns via full page newspaper ads dissenting from the new encyclical.

Now, fifty years later, Pope Paul VI can be seen as prophetic, having written about adopting a contraceptive mentality and its consequences:

17. Responsible men can become more deeply convinced of the truth of the doctrine laid down by the Church on this issue if they reflect on the consequences of methods and plans for artificial birth control. Let them first consider how easily this course of action could open wide the way for marital infidelity and a general lowering of moral standards. Not much experience is needed to be fully aware of human weakness and to understand that human beings – and especially the young, who are so exposed to temptation – need incentives to keep the moral law, and it is an evil thing to make it easy for them to break that law. Another effect that gives cause for alarm is that a man who grows accustomed to the use of contraceptive methods may forget the reverence due to a woman, and, disregarding her physical and emotional equilibrium, reduce her to being a mere instrument for the satisfaction of his own desires, no longer considering her as his partner whom he should surround with care and affection.[15]

Why many bishops and priests have not taught *Humanae vitae* even to this day, is another question for the ages. What seems clear is the demographic future of the Catholic Church.[16] When our lay Catholics are using contraception, or aborting their babies, or otherwise having themselves sterilized below replacement level, there is no future. In this demographic "winter," the Culture of Death mentality takes hold, and just hoping for a forthcoming new springtime for the Church will not do, because nature never forgives.

What also seems clear is that when you compare the papal statements, decrees, encyclicals, and the various post-synodal apostolic exhortations with their historical era, it is evident that much of the tenures of Pope Paul VI and the other Popes as well were taken up with a type of "rear guard action"; that is, the post-Vatican II Popes were and are responding to the various heretical fires spreading throughout the post-Conciliar Church down to our day.

"Simon, Satan has asked to sift you..." (Luke 22:31)

If one were to ask for just one source that would describe the post-Vatican II Church in the modern world, unarguably it would have occurred during a homily of Pope Paul VI on the Feast of Sts. Peter and Paul, June 29, 1972. The Vatican's website has a commentary of the homily in Italian, and it is a report with selective quotes since there is no direct record of this homily. Here, the Pope is reported to have lamented that "*il Santo Padre afferma di avere la sensazione che 'da qualche fessur sia entrato il fumo di Satana nel tempio di Dio'*"; that is, "through some fissure, 'the smoke of Satan has entered the temple of God.'" And he was reported to have said of the post-Vatican II period, that there was "*C'è il dubbio, l'incertezza, la problematica, l'inquietudine, l'insoddisfazione, il confronto*" – that is, "doubt, uncertainty, questioning, dissatisfaction, confrontation." Pope Paul VI then is quoted as saying, "We thought that after the Council a day of sunshine would have dawned for the history of the Church. What dawned, instead, was a day of clouds and storms, of darkness, of searching and uncertainties."[17] Here, of course, Pope Paul VI had Pope John XXIII's words from the opening of the Council in mind: "For with the opening of this Council a new day is dawning on the Church, bathing her in radiant splendor. It is yet the dawn, but the sun in its rising has already set our hearts aglow. All around is the fragrance of holiness and joy."[18]

What was Pope Paul VI referring to in this homily? It was all of the above problems, combined with the fact that within ten years of the end of the Council, tens of thousands of priests, sisters, and nuns would leave their vocations at the Church door; the laity, the People of God, would join the secular world in massive numbers, aborting and contracepting and sterilizing themselves to a demographic death; Mass attendance would plummet; and the once famous Catholic universities would rally round the flag of academic freedom[19] and end up becoming wards of the state – beholden to government grants while in return granting honorary degrees to pro-abortion Catholic and non-Catholic politicians. The reversal was stunning.

"Go out to all the nations, and teach them..." (Matt. 28:19)

How did this all happen? The short answer is Satan, as Pope Paul VI suggests; but the efficient cause was the infidelity among bishops, priests, sisters, and laity. Many books describe the post-Vatican II Church: Michael Rose's book, *Goodbye, Good Men* chronicles the causes of the unfortunate decline of the seminaries; Ann Carey's study of the decline of women religious in her updated work, *Sisters in Crisis: Revisited*; Anne Roche Muggeridge's *The Desolate City: Revolution in the Catholic Church;* and Dietrich Von Hildebrand's *The Devastated Vineyard.* Msgr. George Kelly's books, *The Battle for the American Church* and *The Battle for the American Church Revisited* are useful as well. The best overall work of note is Ralph Wiltgen's 1967 must read, *The Rhine Flows Into the Tiber*.

What all these books have in common is that they tell of a progressive wind which blew through the sails of the barque of Peter. They tell of the role of the Great Fishermen, the Popes, with their various hands on the tiller – trying to get us back on course. What they also have in common, is the last document of Vatican II, *Gaudium et spes,* which, rightly or wrongly, became the touchstone and controlling document of the post-Vatican II period: a period of profound rupture with the previous magisterial teachings. As we saw in his opening address to the Council, Pope John XXIII was not hoping for rupture, but for unity.

Gaudium et spes says many wonderful sentiments about the Church engaging the modern world and uses Sacred Scripture to bolster its case, however, it is section 22 which became the *cause célèbre* of the progressive Catholics, for it reads, in part:

All this holds true not only for Christians, but for all men of good will *in whose hearts grace works in an unseen way*. For, since Christ died for all men (cf. *Rom.* 8:32), and since the ultimate vocation of man is in fact one, and divine, we ought to believe that the Holy Spirit in a manner known only to God offers to every man the possibility of being associated with this paschal mystery.[20] (Emphasis mine.)

This portion of section 22 was interpreted by many in keeping with the then popular theologian, Fr. Karl Rahner, S.J.'s notion of the "anonymous Christian."

Prior to Vatican II, the scholastic notion of "grace" was multifaceted, starting with actual grace of the moment; but the only real necessary grace was that which came through the sacraments. Starting with Baptism's redemptive/salvific grace, *sine qua non*, there is no salvation – "It is Baptism which saves you now" (I *Peter* 3:21). This is what impelled the missionaries of old, this is why saints have had their fingers gnawed off: for spreading salvation via the sacraments. However, when section 22 is reread via Rahner's "anonymous Christianity," missionary efforts are not really needed for salvation, for God's grace touches everyone, whether they know it or not. This was and is a profound change in missionary emphasis, and this sentence in section 22, unintentionally devastated the various missionary orders following the Council. What is most needed for the Church in the modern world today is a correct interpretation of *Gaudium et spes* n. 22, emphasizing in particular the divine gift of "grace": when, where, how, and why it works for the Christian believer and the non-believer.

The Extraordinary Synod of 1985

As mentioned above, the Synod of Bishops was created to help the Pope in dealing with various issues of the day. In addition to any ordinarily scheduled synod, the Pope could call an extraordinary meeting, which he did in 1985, to discuss the twentieth anniversary of Vatican II. Of all the post-Conciliar synods, this one is most important for those trying to understand, love, and appreciate the Second Vatican Council. I say this, for it was called specifically to discuss the post-Vatican period, and present a corrective interpretation to the teachings of the Second Vatican Council.

This Extraordinary Synod produced two documents, "Message to the People of God," and "The Final Report" neither of which are on the

Vatican official website. "The Final Report" can be found online on the *New York Times* webpage.[21] The source that I have for both is from the Daughters of St. Paul, *The Extraordinary Synod, 1985*.[22] It seems that these documents are little known.

The "Message to the People of God" is divided into four short sections. In section I, the Synod Fathers note that their purpose is to evaluate Vatican II's implementation. They desire to promote the Second Vatican Council as "a gift from God to the Church and to the World."[23] They mention that they will "not fix upon the errors, confusions and defects which, because of sin and human weakness, have been the occasion of suffering in the midst of the People of God."[24] However, the Fathers do mention that there have been "errors, confusions and defects" following the Council. In section II, they recall that the Church "is, in Christ, the 'mystery' of the love of God present in the history of mankind."[25] They point out that the first chapter of *Lumen gentium*, the *Dogmatic Constitution on the Church*, bears the title, "The Mystery of the Church," for a reason, and that the Church should not be equated with anything less. Section III invites a deeper reading of the documents of the Council:

> It is also a question of putting them [the documents] more deeply into practice: in communion with Christ present in the Church (*Lumen gentium*), in listening to the Word of God (*Dei verbum*), in the holy liturgy (*Sacrosanctum concilium*), in the service of mankind, especially of the poor (*Gaudium et spes*).[26]

In Section IV, the final section, the Synod reminds us that, "The Council, in effect, had been convoked in order to promote the renewal of the Church with a view to evangelizing a radically changed world."[27] The Synod Fathers pledge to work with the laity and work in solidarity with every nation, to build a "civilization of love"[28] and they looked forward to the coming Synod of Bishops in 1987 on the laity.

The real import of the 1985 Extraordinary Synod is found in the "Final Report" which acts as a type of lens to the whole of Vatican II. The document is divided into two main sections:

I. Celebration, Verification, Promotion of the Second Vatican Council, and

II. Particular Themes viz.

  a) Church as Mystery,

  b) Sources of Life for the Church,

c) The Church as Communion, and

d) The Mission of the Church in the World. Each of these sections is combined with subsections and suggestions.

In the first section of the final report, the 1985 Synod Fathers thanked God for the spiritual benefits arising out of the Extraordinary Synod. While acknowledging that the Second Vatican Council, as a whole, has been well received,

> Nonetheless, although great fruits have been obtained from the Council, we have at the same time recognized, with great sincerity, deficiencies and difficulties in the acceptance of the Council. In truth, there certainly have also been shadows in the post-Conciliar period; in part due to an incomplete understanding and application of the Council, in part due to other causes. However, in no way can it be affirmed that everything which took place after the Council was caused by the Council.[29]

The title in section 4 of the first part is "External and internal causes of the difficulties." A part of the external difficulties is the lack of both personnel and material goods to build up the Church; and, of course, materialism on the part of the general culture is a great problem because it is greatly influenced by the "prince of this world," and the "mystery of iniquity." For the internal causes, however,

> On the one hand, there have been disappointments because we have been too hesitant in the application of the true doctrine of the Council. On the other hand, because of a partial reading of the Council, a unilateral presentation of the Church as a purely institutional structure devoid of her mystery has been made....Have we not perhaps favored this opinion...by speaking too much of the renewal of the Church's external structures and too little of God and of Christ? From time to time there has been a lack of discernment of spirits, with the failure to correctly distinguish between a legitimate openness of the Council to the world and the acceptance of a secularized world's mentality and order of values.[30]

The Synod Fathers then propose a four-fold effort to a deeper reception of the Council. Any theological interpretation to one document must be seen in light of the whole canon of sixteen documents. And then this important and telling part,

> It is not licit to separate the pastoral character from the doctrinal

vigor of the documents. In the same way, it is not legitimate to separate the spirit and the letter of the Council. Moreover, the Council must be understood in continuity with the great tradition of the Church, and at the same time we must receive light from the Council's own doctrine for today's Church and the people of our time. The Church is one and the same throughout all the councils.[31]

The Fathers recommend a permanent course in the formation of priests and for adult catechesis to help solidify this important connection between the spirit and the letter of Vatican II and its connections to the wider *Magisterium* of the teaching Church. This is what Pope Benedict XVI emphasized in his Christmas address on December 22, 2005.

In the second of two sections, the Synod moves toward particular themes. First is the "Mystery of Church," and here they encounter secularism as the main enemy of the sacred and they call for a "return to the sacred."[32] "The Church makes herself more credible if she speaks less of herself and ever more preaches Christ crucified and witnesses with her own life."[33]

The Church remains holy, and yet, is in need of purification because of sinners. The Church must promote a universal call to holiness and "must preserve and energetically promote the sense of penance, prayer, adoration, sacrifice, self-giving, charity, and justice."[34] "Popular devotion, rightly understood and practiced, is very useful in nourishing the holiness of the people. It therefore merits greater attention on the part of pastors."[35] They go on to suggest a spirituality of the laity founded on the Sacrament of Baptism and to promote marital spirituality which is necessary "for the transmission of the Faith to future generations."[36]

Under the next section, "Sources of Life for the Church," the Synod Fathers call for a greater emphasis on the *Dogmatic Constitution, Dei verbum, On Divine Revelation*, which they note has been too neglected. Here they state that the post-Conciliar period focused too much on the exegesis of the meaning of Sacred Scripture (asked for by the Council) to the detriment of the "living tradition of the Church."[37] They also greatly recommend the apostolic exhortation by Pope Paul VI, *Evangelii nuntiandi*. They continue with a call for universal evangelization starting with the self and continuing through the laity, priests, and bishops.

While praising the work of theologians following the Council, the Synod Fathers state, "On the other hand, we regret that the theological discussions of our day have sometimes occasioned confusion among the faithful."[38] They suggest a "compendium of all Catholic doctrine" be forthcoming. This request manifested itself in 1993 via the new *Catechism of the Catholic Church* and on May 24, 1990, the Congregation for the Doctrine of the Faith issued a document for theologians, entitled *Instructions on the Ecclesial Vocation of the Theologian, Donum veritatis.*[39]

In perhaps the most under-analyzed theme, the Sacred Liturgy, the Synod Fathers simply noted, "Even if there have been some difficulties, [the Mass] has generally been received joyfully and fruitfully by the faithful."[40] They went on,

> The active participation so happily increased after the Council does not consist only in external activity, but above all in interior and spiritual participation, in living and fruitful participation in the paschal mystery of Jesus Christ (cf. *Sacrosanctum concilium*, n.11). It is evident that the liturgy must favor the sense of the sacred and make it shine forth. It must be permeated by the spirit of reverence, adoration and the glory of God.[41]

In the section, "Church as Communion," the Synod reemphasizes the meaning of communion starting from the Word of God and the Sacraments of the Church, particularly the Eucharist. They note the need for both unity and pluriformity centered on and under and with Peter and his successors, which is not an obstacle "but anticipation and prophetic sign of a fuller unity."[42] They call for ever increasing collegiality amongst the Bishops with each other and with the Bishop of Rome, the Pope. Further, the Synod Fathers call for greater cooperation with the laity, collabortion with women[43] and continuing ecumenical dialogue.[44]

In the last section, they deal with the "Mission of the Church" to go out into the World and the document, *Gaudium et spes.* They note that missionary effort is both important and necessary but that the times are different (e.g. worse off than in 1965).

The Synod deals with a key word and concept arising from the Council of Vatican II, i.e. *aggiornamento*, meaning change/updating. Here the Synod says:

> An easy accommodation that could lead to the secularization of the Church is to be excluded. Also excluded is an immobile closing in upon itself of the community of the faithful. Affirmed instead is a missionary openness for the integral salvation of the world[45]... The Council also affirmed that God does not deny the possibility of salvation to anyone of good will" (*Lumen gentium*, n. 16).[46]

The Synod Fathers conclude this section by restating the four themes that must be put into practice:

a) The theology of the Cross and the Paschal Mystery in the preaching, the sacraments and the life of the Church of our day;

b) The theory and practice of inculturation, as well as the dialogue with non-Christian religions and with non-believers;

c) The preferential option for the poor i.e. both the materially and spiritually poor and especially the unborn;[47]

d) The social doctrine of the Church as it relates to human promotion in ever new situations.[48]

They conclude the "Final Report" with a call to renew their thanks to the Trinity for the "greatest grace of this century, that is, the Second Vatican Council." They call its documents "the Magna Charta for the future," and pray for a new Pentecost for the Church.[49]

In short, the twenty years between the closing of the Second Vatican Council and the Extraordinary Synod could have gone better. There were some notable corrections. For example, when the Extraordinary Synod Fathers stressed that the Church is "Mystery," they were trying to correct the uneven emphasis that the Church is first and foremost, "the People of God." Following the Second Vatican Council, the democratizing forces of the progressive theologians promoted this notion over all others. When the Bishops called for a "return to the sacred," they were addressing all the illicit and irreverent Masses that occurred following the Council. Here, they could have at least quoted or otherwise acknowledged what Pope John Paul II did in his 1980 letter to Bishops. Here is his apology to the universal Church for illicit and or illegal Masses.

As I bring these considerations [on the mystery and worship of the Eucharist] to an end, I would like to ask forgiveness – in my own name and in the name of all of you, venerable and dear brothers in the episcopate – for everything which, for whatever reason, through whatever human weakness, impatience or negligence, and also through the at times partial, one-sided and erroneous application of the directives of the Second Vatican Council, may have caused scandal and disturbance concerning the interpretation of the doctrine and the veneration due to this great sacrament. And I pray the Lord Jesus that in the future we may avoid in our manner of dealing with this sacred mystery [The Mass] anything which could weaken or disorient in any way the sense of reverence and love that exists in our faithful people.[50]

The "Final Report" of this Extraordinary Synod of 1985, is meant as a corrective and guidance for the future. In fact, I would argue that it is the seventeenth document of Vatican II; the key document through which we are to study the other sixteen.[51]

Christmas Address to the Roman Curia (December 22, 2005)

On April 19, 2005, Joseph Cardinal Ratzinger, a man who lived through this period and who was intimately knowledgeable about the causes behind the troubles following Vatican II, became Pope. He was Pope John Paul II's right hand man as he sat at the desk as Prefect of the Congregation for the Doctrine of the Faith since 1981. As Prefect, he oversaw all the doctrinal troubles from around the world and attempted to deal with them. Pope Benedict XVI, at the start of his tenure as Bishop of Rome, gave a Christmas address to the Roman Curia on December 22, 2005. Because he saw firsthand things go awry following the Council, he knew both the problem and the solution. In this address, he posits that the post-Vatican II era of conflict arose because of a dominant spirit of the times, i.e., the spirit of rupture stemming from a "hermeneutic of discontinuity"; and the solution would be holding to the Church's "Analogy of Faith," or "hermeneutic of continuity."

Like Pope Paul VI's "Smoke of Satan" homily of June 29, 1972, Pope Benedict's candid appraisal in his address is refreshing while at the same time stunning for its honesty:

> No one can deny that in vast areas of the Church the implementation of the Council has been somewhat difficult, even without wishing to apply to what occurred in these years the description of St. Basil... [for] he compares [the Church's] situation [after the Council of Nicea] to a naval battle in the darkness of the storm, saying among other things: "The raucous shouting of those who through disagreement rise up against one another, the incomprehensible chatter, the confused din of uninterrupted clamouring, has now filled almost the whole of the Church, falsifying through excess or failure the right doctrine of the faith...". We do not want to apply precisely this dramatic description to the situation of the post-conciliar period, yet something from all that occurred is nevertheless reflected in it.

The question arises: Why has the implementation of the Council, in large parts of the Church, thus far been so difficult?[52]

Mysterium Iniquitatis/Mystery of Evil

Clergy sex abuse scandals have occurred around the world and across denominational lines; they have occurred in the secular world as well, and in percentages much greater than amongst the clergy, albeit, when clergy commit this heinous crime against the innocence of minors, it is reprehensible. To their credit, the Linacre Institute has done a wonderful service for the Church in their study of the U.S. Bishops' *John Jay Report* on the clergy abuse called *After Asceticism: Sex, Prayer, and Deviant Priests*.[53] They posit that much of the abuse occurred after a jettisoning of practical asceticism on the part of priests and religious after Vatican II. Those time-tested religious and spiritual practices of fasting, abstaining, and other voluntary penitential means as well as prayers, e.g., vesting prayers for priests before Mass,[54] that the saints used to control their concupiscent appetites, were all abandoned in favor of therapeutic psychologies.

Regarding the cause of all this, I cannot understand why the U.S. Bishops were so determined to identify the sex abuse problem as pedophilia (the sexual sodomizing of small children) when, according to the U.S. Bishops' own study (*The John Jay Report*[55]), 85.4% of the victims were boys 11 to 14 and 85.2% were aged from 15 to 17 (cf. Table 3.5.4).[56] (Other statistics are contained within this footnote.) In short, the U.S. Bishops seemed to have gone out of their way to call this evil phenomenon by a name other than what it truly is. One does not need to ask the sexual orientation of the individual clergy sodomites – the problem is priests and deacons committing sodomy on mostly (85.3%) teenage boys. This same-sex attraction is called homosexuality. Perhaps Father Alfred Kunz[57] and Fr. Enrique Rueda,[58] could have enlightened us on the matter had they lived long enough.

Personal Conclusion

As a seminarian and then as a priest, one could say that my experiences of the post-Vatican II period were *sui generis*, i.e. unique to me. However, when you have the above experiences and statements of Popes Paul VI, John Paul II, and Benedict XVI, one has to admit something has gone wrong with the implementation of the Second Vatican Council. Like

Pope Paul VI, one cannot help but wonder if what has happened has been done on purpose.

Having lived through this post-Conciliar period of deconstructionism, I compare the rush to both liturgical and doctrinal banality to the experience of being at the Roma Termini train station. While waiting in a ticket line, a Gypsy mother and young child came begging to me for money. I knew she had a type of Munchausen syndrome for the child was obviously either intentionally sickened, or made to look sick for the purpose of gaining attention for herself. While the other passengers in line warned me not to give her any money, I did so, believing it is better to err on the side of charity.

It seems to me, that following the Council, this is what has happened to the Church. That is, many churchmen and women had experienced Munchausen syndrome on a massive scale. In order to curry favor from our separated brethren – the Protestants, non-Christians, and the secular world, some in the Church disfigured the Bride of Christ on purpose to make her more acceptable, and themselves by association, to various denominations of Christians and the world.

Another impression is that Vatican II had been a gambit with the secular world. Many believed that we could dialogue in good faith with secularists who are controlled by the "prince of this world." But Satan has called our bluff, resulting in so many ruined churches, vocations, marriages, universities, and a culture of death mentality that has resulted in so many Catholic Christians aborting, contracepting, and sterilizing themselves like the pagans do. In short, the call to holiness of the Council was not heeded; it was largely unheard/ignored.

Despite all this, overall, Vatican Council II is the Council of our time, but only if we follow the teachings of the 1985 Extraordinary Synod Fathers and Pope Benedict XVI's hermeneutic of continuity. That is, we need to *read* the sixteen documents as a whole and this must include the footnotes that link the Council with the other Magisterial teachings of the Church. We must use the hermeneutic of continuity in all that we propose for the faithful. Yes, we are to hold to the image of the Church as being the "People of God," but more so, to the Church as the "Mystical Body of Christ." We are to "return to the sacred" within our liturgies. "A return to the sacred," is also needed for the sake of priestly identity. The clergy abuse scandal, as terrible as it is for the victims, is also an attack on the sacral nature of the priest being *in persona Christi*, in the place of

Christ – an attack truly of demonic origin.

Viewed as such, I would propose any clergy committing these crimes against both nature and the nature of the priesthood should be automatically excommunicated and that any reconciliation be reserved to the Archbishop Primate of the area, if not the Pope himself. Conversely, anyone who falsely accuses a clergy member of these crimes should also incur automatic excommunication and any reconciliation be based on a public recantation and period of sorrow for, again, attacking not so much the man, but who he is representing, that is, Christ Jesus our Lord.

To combat the evils of the culture of death, the Church community should be obliged to do penance, which would foster a proper asceticism. At the very least, a return to Friday abstinence from meat and a longer fast before Holy Communion would greatly help in this and in fostering the reverence for the presence of the Lord. Another way to foster reverence would be a return to the traditional orientation for the Mass called *ad orientem,* that is, everyone would be facing the same direction, *towards* the altar of sacrifice, something Pope Benedict preferred.[59] When both priest and the people of God are facing *ad orientem*, or liturgical East, it removes the priest as the center of action and the focus of attention is on the Blessed Sacrament. I say this purely for evangelical reasons. He is the Lord.

What sustained me through the seminary and is getting me through my priesthood is the fact, that the Church in the modern world is the same Church to which Christ covenanted Himself from the Cross, i.e. the Church is the Bride of Christ. She may look battered, and She may look weary, but She belongs to Jesus. As a priest, I am a special friend to Jesus the Bridegroom, and it is my task to present His Bride to the modern world as Christ would have her look: beautiful, without spot or wrinkle.

Of course, not everything following the Council has been negative. There have been the joys of World Youth Days and the hopes of so many marriages and perhaps a resurgence of vocations to the priesthood and religious life. But it all comes down to and starts with me, trying to be holy through His grace, and the gifts of the Holy Spirit. When G.K. Chesterton was asked what was wrong with the world, he responded, "I am."[60] I second his answer, for I too am a sinner, trying to be a priest of Jesus Christ in the modern world.

The seminary formation team told us seminarians, that the first hundred years following a Church Council were always the hardest. Fifty years have passed. Please Lord, let the next fifty years be easier for the Church in the modern world! Our Lady, undoer of knots: Pray for us!

ENDNOTES

1. William Kilpatrick, *Psychological Seduction: The Failure of Modern Psychology,* Nashville, Tenn: Thomas Nelson Inc., 1983.

2. Dr. Paul Vitz, *Psychology as Religion: The Cult of Self-Worship,* Grand Rapids, Mich: Wm. B. Eerdmans Publishing Co., 1995.

3. http://en.wikipedia.org/wiki/Proportionalism. accessed on October 15, 2013,

4. July 25 was the date on which the encyclical, *Humanae vitae,* was promulgated in 1968. Fr. Curran was the most active dissenter against this document; so it was appropriate to have his License to teach theology removed on July 25, 1986.

5. Thanks to a $10,000 grant from the Knights of Columbus, I was able to attend.

6. After Vatican II, this feast was switched to January 1.

7. "*Allocutio Ioannis PP. XXIII In Sollemni SS. Concilii Inauguratione,* http://www.vatican.va/_holy_ father_/john_xxiii_/speeches/1962/documents/hf_j-xxiii_spe_19621011_opening-council_ lt.html, in Latin, website accessed on October 10, 2013. Translated speech in English at Catholichurch.org, http://www.catholicculture.org/culture/library/view.cfm?RecNum=3233, accessed on October 10, 2013.

8. "Opening Address to the Council" by Pope John XXIII," Catholicculture.org, http://www. catholicculture.org/culture/library/view.cfm?RecNum=3233, accessed on October 10, 2013.

9. *Ibid.*, on the Vatican Website for Pope John XXIII under speeches, October 11, 1962, this opening speech to the Council is available in Italian, Latin, Portuguese, and Spanish. The Italian translation is "*profeti di sventura*" In the Latin, "*qui deteriora semper praenuntiant,*" "who always predict [the] worst." (I used Google translate webpage.) Accessed on October 10, 2013.

10. *Ibid.*

11. *A New Catechism,* trans. by Kevin Smyth, New York: The Seabury Press, 1969.

12. "Bishops' Anti-Rome Session in Holland Disturbing to Vatican," by George Weller in the *Watertown Daily Times,* July 14, 1967. http://fultonhistory.com/Newspapers%20Disk3 / Watertown%20Times/Watertown%20Ny%20Daily%20Times%20Grayscale%20July%201967. pdf/Watertown%20Ny%20Daily%20Times%20Grayscale%20July%201967%20-%200241.pdf. Fultonhistory.com accessed on October 10, 2013

13. Professor Grisez was a personal friend to a commission member, Fr. Ford, S.J. and was able to obtain a number of documents related to this special papal commission. See: http://www.twotlj. org/BCCommission.html

14. Bernard Häring, "The Encyclical Crisis," in *The Debate on Birth Control,* edited by Andrew Bauer, (New York: Hawthorn Books, Inc., 1969) 49.

15. "Encyclical Letter, *Humanae vitae,*" by Pope Paul VI. www.vatican.va accessed on October 10, 2013 http://www.vatican.va/holy_father/paul_vi/ encyclicals/documents/hf_p-vi_enc_25071968 _humanae-vitae_en.html.

16. According to the U.S. Census Bureau as of 2010 and national average of children per household is 1.91; 2.1 is needed just to maintain a stable population, cf. http://www.census.gov/hhes/families/ files/cps2012/tabAVG3.xls.

17. "Omella Di Paolo VI" by Pope Paul VI (June 29, 1972) www.vatican.va Accessed on October 10, 2013, http://www.vatican.va/holy_father/paul_vi/homilies/1972/documents/hf_p-vi_ hom_19720629_it.html.

18. "Opening Address to the Council" by Pope John XXIII," Catholicculture.org, accessed on October 10, 2013, http://www.catholicculture.org/culture/library/view.cfm?RecNum=3233

19. Martin R. Tripole, *Church In Crisis: The Enlightenment and Its Impact upon Today's Church* (Ave Maria, FL: Sapientia Press, 2012) 231. In the US, this de-Catholicization of certain major Catholic universities was done by agreement among the various university presidents following the infamous, 1967 "Land O'Lakes Statement." Land O'Lakes is a small town in northern Wisconsin

where the Jesuits have a retreat center and where Fr. Theodore Hesburgh CSC, of Notre Dame and 25 other Catholic university presidents and leaders came to together July 20-23, 1967 to discuss the restructuring of their respective Catholic universities. The statement purposed a total reorientation that would give them both institutional autonomy and "religious freedom" (sic) from the local Bishop and the Pope, and "academic freedom in the face of authority of whatever kind, lay or clerical, external to the academic community itself." Over two decades later, Pope John Paul II issued his *Apostolic Constitution on Catholic Universities, Ex corde ecclesiae* (From the Heart of the Church), but by then it was too late; and even now, two decades after John Paul's constitution, too many Catholic universities have yet to implement it and too many bishops are loathe to properly intervene.

20. Pastoral Constitution, *Gaudium et spes*, promulgated by Pope Paul VI, December 7, 1965, www.vatican.va, accessed on October 10, 2013, http://www.vatican.va/archive/hist_councils/ii_vatican_council/documents/vat-ii_const_19651207_gaudium-et-spes_en.html.

21. "Text of Final Report Adopted by Synod of Bishops in Rome," *New York Times*, December 8, 1985, accessed on October 10, 2013, http://www.nytimes.com/1985 /12/08/world/text-of-final-report-adopted-by-synod-of-bishops-in-rome.html.

22. At the time of this writing, a new copy on Amazon.com goes for $236.28, while two used ones sell for $29.60.http://www.amazon.com/The-Extraordinary-Synod-1985/dp/0819823163

23. *The Extraordinary Synod, 1985* (Boston: The Daughters of St. Paul) 30.

24. *Ibid.*, 30.

25. *Ibid.*, 31.

26. *Ibid.*, 32.

27. *Ibid.*, 34.

28. *Ibid.*, 35.

29. *Ibid.*, 39.

30. *Ibid.*, 40-41.

31. *Ibid.*, 41-42.

32. *Ibid.*, 44.

33. *Ibid.*, 45.

34. *Ibid.*, 47.

35. *Ibid.*, 48.

36. *Ibid.*, 49.

37. *Ibid.*, 49.

38. *Ibid.*, 51.

39. *Donum Veritatis*, "On the Ecclesial Vocation of the Theologian," Congregation For the Doctrine of the Faith, May 24, 1990, Vatican.va accessed on October 15, 2013, http://www.vatican.va/roman_curia/congregations /cfaith/documents/rc _con_cfaith_doc_19900524_theologian-vocation_en.html.

40. *Ibid.*, 54.

41. *Ibid.*, 52.

42. *Ibid.*, 54.

43. *Ibid.*, 58.

44. *Ibid.*, 60.

45. *Ibid.*, 63.

46. *Ibid.*, 64.

47. *Ibid.*, 65-66.

48. *Ibid.*, 67.

49. *Ibid.*, 68.

50. Pope John Paul II, *Dominicae cenae*, Letter to All Bishops, on the Mystery and Worship of the Eucharist (February 24, 1980), 12.

51. Unfortunately, the seventeenth document for far too many Catholic theologians is the 1520 work of then Augustinian Friar and declared heretic, Martin Luther's, *The Babylonian Captivity of the*

Church. Here he calls for the sharing of the chalice, the vernacular, and facing the people during Mass; all the while calling the Catholic Church the whore of Babylon.

52. "Address of His Holiness Benedict XVI to the Roman Curia," by Pope Benedict XVI, (December 22, 2005). www.vatican.va accessed on October 10, 2013, http://www.vatican.va/holy_father/benedict_xvi/speeches/2005/december/documents/hf_ben_xvi_spe_20051222_roman-curia_en.html.

53. The Linacre Institute, *After Asceticism: Sex, Prayer and Deviant Priests* (Bloomington, IN: AuthorHouse, 2006).

54. Vesting Prayers are those prayers that accompany the priest while he prepares himself for the Holy Sacrifice of the Mass. Here the Church highly encourages the priest to pray while he readies himself for Mass, reflecting on the need for spiritual combat with the devil and his own concupiscent impulses, e.g. "Give virtue, O Lord, to my hands that every stain may be wiped away, that I may be enabled to serve You without defilement of mind or body" (*St. Andrew's Daily Missal,* 1962).

55. United States Conference of Catholic Bishops, *The Nature and Scope of Sexual Abuse of Minors by Catholic Priests and Deacons in the United States 1950–2000*: A research Study Conducted by the John Jay College of Criminal Justice (Washington D.C.: USCCB Publishing, 2004).

56. Ibid. Table 3.5.4, Alleged Victims of sexual Abuse incidents, Grouped by Gender and Age.

According to Table 4.3.2, which breaks down the individual ages of the victims, when you combine the teens (13 to 17) together, the teenaged male and female victims represented 65.5% of the cases, while the truly young babies (1 to 5) comes to only 1.8% of the victims, and if you include ages 6 and 7, it is up to 6.1% Further, when looked at by the decades, the past five (cf. Table 3.5.5) shows an increasing percentage of the victims (male and female) were aged from 11 to 17: 1950s (72.3%), 1960s (77.3%), 1970s (83.1%), 1980s (86.6%), and the 1990s (90.3%).

57. Fr. Alfred Kunz, canon lawyer, was helping victims of priest abusers when he was viciously murdered, perhaps satanically, at his rectory on March 4, 1998. Cf. http://en.wikipedia.org/wiki/Murder_of_Alfred_Kunz

58. Fr. Enrique Rueda is noted for his 1982 book, *The Homosexual Network.* After publishing this book, he was suspended from public ministry by Bishop Clark of Rochester, NY. He apparently died on December 14, 2009, and a short unofficial biography can be read here by Thomas Ryan, "*Tu Es Sacerdos in Aeternum,*" accessed October 15, 2013, http://remantnewspaper.com/Archives/2010-ryan-rueda-rip.htm.

59. *The Roman Missal: Third Latin Typical Edition 2008* (Italy: Magnificat, 2011) 45. General Instruction of the Roman Missal, number 124 reads in part, "Then, facing the people and extending his hands, the Priest greets the people, using one of the formulas indicated." The norm is facing with the people, toward the Lord, in a common direction, usually East. The exception to this norm is allowed for after Vatican II is to have the altar in the center so that the ministers may move around it to face the people, "which is desirable wherever possible." #299.

60. According to the Chesterton Society, this quote may or may not be true since there is no documentary evidence found in his reply to the *Times* of London or any other newspaper. Accessed October 11, 2013, cf. http://www.chesterton.org.

FR. TIMOTHY SAUPPÉ entered religious life in 1982 and left before solemn vows in 1989. He holds a License in Sacred Theology (S.T.L.) from the Pope John Paul II Institute for Studies on Marriage and Family Life, 1991 and was ordained in 1992 for the Diocese of Peoria, Illinois. He serves as pastor of St. Mary's in Westville and St. Isaac Jogues in Georgetown, Illinois. He has written several articles for the Bellarmine Forum website and is a doctoral candidate with the International Marian Research Institute, IMRI, Dayton Ohio.

The Biggest Hurdle to My Conversion: The Second Vatican Council

By Matt Yonke

I come to the Second Vatican Council with an odd set of influences. As a child growing up Protestant in Wheaton, Illinois, an Evangelical bastion where I was raised a non-denominational pastor's son, Catholicism was an odd and distant thing. All my impressions were caricatures, including the notion that there had been a council where the Catholic Church became more modernized.

According to the voices I was hearing, the Catholic Church had given in to syncretism and the notion that God was identical to the Allah of the Muslims, they had given up on Christ as the exclusive path to God, they had placed their Traditions over the Scriptures. With no actual Catholics in my life outside one neighborhood friend (with whom I could tell my parents were wary of me spending too much time), I had no way to cross-check the claims I heard about Catholicism, so I believed them.

Many years later, a good friend of mine became Catholic and, to make a long story short, in trying to talk him out of becoming Catholic, I ended up talking myself into it. But one of the biggest hurdles I had to overcome before I could believe that the Catholic Church was truly the Church Christ founded was this notion that the Church had been corrupted and liberalized by the Second Vatican Council.

It's somewhat ironic that my fears of a liberalized Church were stoked by the more traditionally minded Catholics who surrounded me at that time, whom I love dearly and without whom I would not be Catholic. They believed the Church had erred grievously at the Council, and thought up plenty of ways to work around it and minimize its teaching authority. They claimed that the Council was pastoral, not dogmatic, for example, so any portions of the Council documents or interpretations of same with which they disagreed could be summarily discarded.

And they were technically correct. No new earthshaking dogmas like the Immaculate Conception or Papal Infallibility were defined at Vatican II. But the bishops did deliver a new ethos to the faithful that they hoped would equip them to do the work of Christ in the rapidly changing late 20th century. And because of the nature of the Council, many of my friends and I at the time felt we could simply shelve it because it did not demand assent in the same way Trent or Nicaea did, perhaps an example of that very ethos at work.

Since they did not deeply engage with the Council and attempt to learn from it, my traditional Catholic friends blamed the Council for everything from guitar Masses to empty pews and confessionals to the general decline of public morality in the culture. And I could see why they thought so from quotes from the Council I'd read in apologetics articles I'd read which referred to the Protestants, whom I had so recently left and sacrificed greatly to do so, as "separated brethren" in *Unitatis redintegratio,* rather than heretics, as was done to the Arians and the Monophysites.

Nostra aetate said "God holds the Jews most dear for the sake of their Fathers ..." which seemed to me and my friends to directly contradict St. Paul who said that "[the Jews] were broken off because of their unbelief, but you stand fast through faith. So do not become proud, but fear. For if God did not spare the natural branches, neither will he spare you" (*Romans* 11:21). It didn't sound to me like the Lord had much of a soft spot for the people who still hold to the Old Covenant!

Perhaps most troubling were *Nostra aetate's* comments about Muslims. "The Church regards with esteem also the Muslems. They adore the one God, living and subsisting in Himself, merciful and all-powerful, the Creator of heaven and earth, who has spoken to men; they take pains to submit wholeheartedly to even His inscrutable decrees, just as Abraham, with whom the faith of Islam takes pleasure in linking itself, submitted to God." I couldn't believe what I was reading at the time, but I was heartened by my friends' assurance that it was merely a pastoral Council and could be safely ignored.

The Council seemed part and parcel with the freewheeling spirit of the '60s and it seemed to have led to the modern Catholic Church and its eschewal of all the reverence, gravitas, and stability that had drawn me to Catholicism in the first place.

Luckily, by a series of happy accidents, I entered the Church in a Romanian Catholic parish that serves the Divine Liturgy of St. John Chrysostom and has preserved the liturgical and aesthetic traditions of the Church, so I didn't have to worry about guitars or glad-handing priests walking the aisles at the sign of peace, and I was able to forget about Vatican II for a time and focus on learning how to live and pray as a Catholic.

If necessity or travel steered us to a Roman Rite Mass, I would roll my eyes at a banal hymn or an extraordinary minister giving me a sidelong glance for requesting to receive Holy Communion on the tongue. I'd just chalk it up to the "Spirit of Vatican II" I'd heard so much about.

One day, I was at a thrift store looking for good books to rescue from among the sea of John Grisham novels when I came across a tattered blue paperback. It was the complete writings of the Second Vatican Council. It wasn't what I was looking for, but I wasn't about to leave it behind either, so I picked it up and started reading.

What I found was incredibly surprising. As a musician and student of the liturgy, I went straight for *Sacrosanctum concilium*, the *Constitution on the Sacred Liturgy*, from whence I presumed the glut of bad liturgy in the Roman Church had flowed, and found that nothing could be further from the truth.

Sacrosanctum concilium is clear and firm in its priorities and principles, chief among them that the Liturgy is not a plaything to be tinkered with by anyone with a creative idea. Latin and Gregorian Chant are given pride of place, along with a strong concern for reverence.

If a person knew nothing of the heady years of post-conciliar liturgical abuse and was asked how the Catholic Liturgy would change after the implementation of *Sacrosanctum concilium*, I don't imagine they would think it would cause very much change at all. A bit of newer religious art from local cultures, perhaps, maybe some use of the vernacular language (only with approval from the Apostolic See), small changes and certainly nothing would be accomplished quickly.

But, of course, history tells a different story. Changes and experiments to the liturgy were swift and drastic. Given an inch, pastors and liturgists took a mile. We've all seen the outlying cases of polka masses, clown masses, liturgical dance run amok, it wasn't a pretty scene.

Doctrinal innovation was a similar case. The writings of the Council were intelligent, thoughtful, Scriptural and traditional. There was development, to be sure, but it was consistent with the Tradition. The

Church had to address the concerns of a world that had changed radically since the Council of Trent all those hundreds of years ago. Muslims were no longer directly threatening to take over our civilization. Jews were being persecuted by Christians, if deeply misled Christians, in new and deeply disturbing ways. Protestants were no longer Catholics who had rejected the Church, but people who had lived for hundreds of years in an authentic, if schismatic, Christian tradition. Pluralism had taken hold of the West and the Church simply could not govern as she had in the glory days of Christendom. The clericalism that eventually allowed the American sexual abuse crisis to occur had to be addressed.

In short, the Church needed to re-image herself to be who she needed to be for the world in the coming new millennium. I'm reminded of Walter Miller's *A Canticle for Lebowitz*, in which Miller, a convert of only a few years after the horrors he witnessed serving in the Second World War, imagined the Church progressing through several millennia in the microcosm of a small desert abbey. Through war, strife, apocalyptic disasters, moral crises, and the development of new technology, Miller envisions how the Church would need to change while remaining true to Her essence.

So too, at Vatican II, the Church realized the need to recognize the specific needs of the world in the present day, and the documents themselves are a treasure trove of wisdom. Recognizing the commonalities of all monotheists in the face of a looming revolution in public morality, the Church saw the need to strengthen our bonds with Muslims, Jews, and Protestants who all share a belief in the One God who created all things in *Nostra aetate*, the *Declaration on the Relation of the Church to Non-Christian Religions*. Seeing the change in power dynamics between the Church and civil governments, she saw the need to affirm the right to freedom of religion rather than face the prospect of losing any voice at all in the public square in *Dignitatis humanae*, the *Declaration on Religious Freedom*. She addressed the clericalism of the modern age by emphasizing the role of the laity to not just go to church, but to BE the Church in *Lumen gentium*, the *Dogmatic Constitution on the Church*.

But these solid lessons did not trickle down immediately, at least not with the clarity one would have hoped. Just like the innovation in the liturgy, doctrinal innovation was inaccurate, rapid and rampant, and the ramifications still can be felt down to today in homilies that reduce miracles to sharing or weather conditions, and the general shabby state of liturgical and artistic expression.

Again, speaking as a former Protestant, I was perhaps most heartened by reading the Council's document on Holy Scripture, *Dei verbum*, the *Dogmatic Constitution on Divine Revelation*. As a Protestant, I valued the Scriptures above all. They were the only word of God and the only source of ultimate truth. Whatever misguided notions I may have had about the exclusive authority of Scripture, I am forever grateful to my parents for giving it a true pride of place in our home, my education, and our spiritual life. *Dei verbum* confirmed for me that the Catholic Church believed that the Scriptures were every bit as important as my parents taught me, just through a different lens – a lens that understood the place of tradition and the living authority of the Church.

After reading the documents and reviewing the history of the Council, which had its factions and troubles, as most councils do, I was encouraged. It's been said it takes a hundred years for a council of the Church to be fully absorbed and implemented. If that's the case, we're more than halfway there.

Today, the fruits of the Council can be seen growing out of the morass of the early festival of novelty and innovation. The Church is vibrant, growing, and firmly orthodox in many parts of the world. Interests in traditional religious orders and rites far outpace interest in their innovative alternatives among young Catholics. Whatever one might think of Pope Francis' foibles, he has certainly imbibed the Council's message of communicating the love of Christ to the world in a way that it can receive, and the world is listening.

As a Byzantine Catholic, we sometimes refer to ourselves as Orthodox Christians in union with Rome, because, as St. John Paul II implored us, we hold to our own liturgical and doctrinal traditions along with all we shared with the Latin Church in the first millennium. As I survey the Church entering the third millennium, there's an interesting contrast between the Catholic and Orthodox Churches.

The Orthodox Church succeeded in preserving the liturgical and aesthetic tradition of the Church, which is critical to her mission, in nearly unchanged form through two thousand years. The Latin Church, where the liturgy has suffered, but not died, has learned to adapt to the world in ways that the Orthodox have not, and in a way that has made her better able to communicate the truth of Christ to the modern and post-modern world.

The inability of the Orthodox Church to call a Council at all is critical here. Even when they attempt to hold a Council without Rome, which reasonable Orthodox acknowledge that they can't, there's no mechanism to decide who will preside in the absence of the Roman Pontiff, so they are stuck frozen where they have been for centuries. They have been unable to even address issues vitally pertinent to the modern world like the morality of contraception, which has only recently become easily available, effective, and socially acceptable. The Catholic Church is the only Apostolic Church who can address these issues with real authority.

In the end, it was the question of authority that brought me into the Catholic Church. I could not square the idea that laymen could grant to one another the authority to rule Christ's Church. According to the Scripture, there is only one source for the authority to rule the Church, and that is receiving that authority from one who already has it by the laying on of hands. Martin Luther did not have the authority to ordain a priest, and neither do any of his successors or imitators. The authority of the Church lies first of all with the Pope as Peter's successor first and the bishops in union with him who hold the Apostolic Succession.

And so, after reading the actual words of the men who hold that authority, I came to embrace the Second Vatican Council, and continue to learn from it. It has affected my opinions on a multitude of subjects profoundly.

I'm far more optimistic about the future of the Roman Liturgy than I was as a new convert. The Council provides a road map for true liturgical reform that has yet to be faithfully implemented, but that certainly does not mean that it won't be. Generations of the faithful who have more critical distance from the immediate post-conciliar era will have the opportunity to look at the guidelines the Council laid out for the liturgy and follow them faithfully, as some parishes like St. John Cantius in Chicago near me have in serving the *Novus Ordo* in Latin with English readings, or even simply saying the Mass in the vernacular but with true pride of place given to Latin and Gregorian chant as the Council instructed.

I've seen interreligious dialog flourish in a way they simply hadn't prior to the Council, especially in America. I've been privileged to write for the website CalledToCommunion.com where former Reformed Protestants like myself write to our former co-religionists about the Catholic faith, and the site has yielded many conversions. Muslim conversions have surged in recent decades. One can't help but wonder if that isn't due in part to the Church treating Muslims as people who are sincerely seeking the one true God rather than a militant army seeking the destruction of the West, which has its roots in historical fact and current concerns, to be sure, but doesn't describe most Muslims in practice. I've been pleased to have Rabbis speak eloquently for our shared concern for the unborn at pro-life events I've organized – something that would not have been possible in the decades before the Church began to speak of the Jewish people as our elder brothers in the faith. And perhaps most importantly, the possibility of reunion with the Eastern Churches has become a much more real possibility with the Catholic Church's recognition of the status of the Eastern bodies as true Churches, closer by an order of magnitude to the one, holy, Catholic and apostolic Church than the Protestant ecclesial communities.

But perhaps the most important thing I've learned from Vatican II is that the Church is a living, breathing body that exists in the world and must change with it. She cannot ossify in one mode of being anymore than humanity as a whole does, and, perhaps more importantly, she never has. This is why the Church has dozens of rites as it is. She must respond to the world as it changes and bring her unchanging truth in a manner the world can accept. As Aquinas said, "*Quidquid recipitur, ad modum recipientis recipitur,*" that is *a thing received can only be received according to the mode of the receiver.* The Church must constantly shape her presentation of the Gospel to the mode of the world to which She is speaking. That is what the Council attempted to do, and I believe the fruit of that attempt is being seen more and more all the time as the Church processes the message of the Council.

To be sure, there are still great misinterpretations of the Council's message, which can be seen in the overextension of mercy to the unrepentant on the part of some teachers of the faith. Controversy particularly over sexual issues – the plight of the divorced and remarried, how the Church should best address the spiritual needs of people struggling with same-sex attraction, constant pleas for a re-thinking of *Humanae vitae* or the question of female priests – show that there is still work to be done, but that is our part in the fight. We as the faithful of this time must learn how to bring the Gospel message to the 21st century, and it is a trying task.

But as we face that work, I am grateful to be a part of a Church that can adapt, learn and grow in the face of new challenges and ever varying societal conditions. What seemed such a disruptive and untraditional event in the life of the Church at the beginning of my journey into the Church has transformed into a deep source of wisdom and inspiration. I suppose that's what time can do, and I hope that's what time will do with the wisdom of the Second Vatican Council for the Church as a whole and for all of us.

MATT YONKE is the Assistant Communications Director for the Pro-Life Action League, a Chicago-based non-profit pro-life grassroots activism organization. He studied classical liberal arts at New St. Andrews College in Moscow, Idaho and lives in Aurora, Illinois with his wife Erin and their six children. He is a cantor at St. George Byzantine Catholic Church and writes poetry and music as well as theological and cultural commentary.

Making Sense of *Gaudium et Spes*
By Michael J. Adkins

Introduction

Addressing Pope John Paul II, the Archbishop of Chicago, the late Francis Cardinal George, lamented the following during an *ad limina* visit to Rome in 2004:

> The Church's mission is threatened internally by divisions which paralyze her ability to act forcefully and decisively. On the left, the Church's teachings on sexual morality and the nature of ordained priesthood and of the Church herself are publicly opposed, as are the bishops who preach and defend these teachings. On the right, the Church's teachings might be accepted, but bishops who do not govern exactly and to the last detail in the way expected are publicly opposed. The Church is an arena of ideological warfare rather than a way of discipleship shepherded by bishops.[1]

Implicit in these remarks are two things: first, that the bishops themselves are divided on Church teaching, pastoral approaches, and governance; and second, that confusion is the hallmark of the post-conciliar period. The remarks of Cardinal George are now over a decade old, those remarks could have been spoken yesterday. It seems that many are tempted to ask, is all of this mess the result of the Second Vatican Council?

Certainly, one of the most controversial documents of the Council is the *Pastoral Constitution on the Church in the Modern World, Gaudium et spes* (referenced as "*GS*" hereafter). When considering the letter and "spirit" of both the Council and *GS*, it seems to me that there are four types of Catholics: 1) the progressive liberal; 2) the conservative reactionary; 3) the confused (orthodox or otherwise); and 4) the smallest group by far: the orthodox Catholic. In addition, it seems to me that very few of the aforementioned Catholics seem to have actually read *GS* or the other fifteen documents of the Council. Save an orthodox understanding, it is hard to imagine how any one ideological camp can claim to possess a victory or to have suffered defeat via the text of *GS*. This essay will provide principles toward an orthodox and appropriately critical reading of *GS* and the Council in general. First, I will provide a brief summary of *GS*'s core content. Second, I will review problems of interpretation, including but not limited to "the spirit" of the 1960s and '70s, the revolt of various camps within the Church, the "Council of the media," and examples of problematic language, for which *GS* is famous. Finally, I will propose several guidelines on how to accept, read and understand the document as an authentic teaching of the living *Magisterium*, and how those principles are universally helpful for understanding the Council.

I. What Is GS?

Gaudium et spes was the final of the four constitutions promulgated by Pope Paul VI and the Council Fathers on December 7, 1965.[2] The title of the document is our first key to greater understanding: it is a "pastoral" constitution, rather than a "dogmatic" one. A "dogmatic" constitution considers matters such as divine revelation, and thus its teaching is binding on the faithful. On the other hand, a "pastoral" constitution expresses the prudential judgment of the hierarchy in union with the Bishop of Rome on how the Church is to relate to the surrounding world, reading the "signs of the times"; in other words, its teaching and approach are not binding but debatable, and may even, in part, be superseded within a period of time. Yet, further clarification is needed as there are both doctrinal and pastoral principles throughout the document: "therefore, [*GS*] has contingent and permanent elements."[3] By its very nature, *GS* is yoked to the authoritative teaching of the dogmatic constitutions which define revelation and the nature of the Church.[4] To put it another way, in grammatical terms *Lumen gentium* provides the "Who" we are as a Church; *Dei verbum* provides the "What and Why" we believe; and *GS* is the "How" we spread the message.[5] In this analogy, notice that *GS* is neither the subject nor the direct object. In this way, *GS* does not contradict the words of *Lumen gentium*, for example, neither does it nor can it propose a contrary teaching – despite what many commentators may insist; *GS* is extremely important to the purposes of Vatican II, but it is fundamentally grounded in *Lumen gentium* and *Dei verbum*.

Although *GS* does not contain binding teaching, that does not mean that Catholics can simply ignore it. On the contrary, *GS* proposes a new approach to addressing the modern world and, in many ways, this approach has caught on successfully and disastrously – all Catholics of good will need to pay attention to this fact. For example, the following remark magnificently summarizes both the great success and manifest failures of implementing *GS*:

> As a young priest in the early 1970s, I was privileged to witness the influence of *Gaudium et spes* on the re-make of Catholic Charities in the United States. No longer was the work of charity to be summed up in emergency assistance and family counseling. The diocesan charity agencies also were called upon by the historical Cadre Report[6] to expand their activities by including advocacy for just social policies and legislation and convening of people at national, diocesan, and parish levels with the ultimate goal of humanizing and transforming the social order.

This same pastoral constitution also helped to re-form the global solidarity efforts of the Church. Thus Catholic Relief Services and sister Caritas organizations in other parts of the world moved beyond an almost exclusive reliance on emergency relief to a development-oriented interaction with people in developing countries. They began to treat those benefiting from their generosity as partners rather than as recipients. Within their home countries, they expended energy and funds to change the social policies and laws that often led to the further marginalization and victimization of the poor and vulnerable in developing countries. They promoted efforts to increase civic participation and reconciliation in areas affected by oppression and conflict. They worked to make accessible medications, treatment, and livelihoods for those affected by illnesses such as HIV and AIDS, tuberculosis, and malaria, all of which can constitute a swift and sure death sentence in low-income countries.

> It is my firm belief that *Gaudium et spes* served as the principal source of inspiration for the Catholic bishops of our country when they made their prophetic decision to establish the Catholic Campaign for Human Development.[7]

The remarks above, posted on the USCCB website for the fortieth anniversary of the Council, will more than suffice. *GS* has been used as the primary tool by which progressives have defended turning the Church into what Pope Francis has excoriated as "a pitiful NGO"[8] devoid of the saving and demanding message of Jesus Christ; doctrine and dogma suffered a back-seat role in the age of the leftivist diktat. At the same time, one can understand how the many practical suggestions posited in the second half of *GS* provided an important framework for expanding and organizing necessary social justice outreaches as well as relief services. Yet what did the document actually say? The best thing for any serious Catholic to do is read the entire text of *GS* and the other fifteen documents (more on that later). Admitting that this will hardly be exhaustive, the following paragraphs briefly summarize the content of *GS*.

The Preface

There is a strong Christocentric orientation to *GS*, particularly the Preface. As the opening remarks state, the Council Fathers not only wish to speak to the sons of the Church, but they also wish to address "all who invoke the name of Christ" and "the whole of humanity."[9] After highlighting the astounding changes and advances man experienced in preceding centuries,[10] it is noted that with these changes and advances new and grave problems have arisen such as a questioning of accepted values and moral norms, the denial of God or of religion, and the subjugation of virtually all areas of study by utilitarian, atheistic and materialistic philosophies; of this, man himself is the cause and the victim.[11] The Council proposes Jesus Christ as the answer.[12] Subsequently, *GS* is divided into two parts: the first on the dignity of man and the Church's role in the modern world; the second on contemporary problems that promise to jeopardize the Church's lofty goals and ultimately human flourishing.

Part I

The first chapter of Part I provides an overview of the Church's philosophy of the human person. The Council Fathers note that man is aided by the Natural Law, which "holds him to obedience," and by the wisdom wrought by faith and the Holy Spirit. A significant amount of text is dedicated to great concern over the growing atheism of the age and other "poisonous doctrines," the medicine being "a proper presentation of the Church's teaching as well as in the integral life of the Church and her members."[13]

The second chapter speaks of the community of man and universal human rights. The Gospel has and continues to arouse in man's heart the "irresistible requirements of his dignity" and "this Council lays stress on reverence for man; everyone must consider his every neighbor without exception as another self."[14] This radical call to solidarity and self gift motivated by the Gospel, points out "the growing awareness of the exalted dignity proper to the human person" and the basic rights of man. This section, once again grounded in Church teaching, emphasizes the human community employing expressions that are near and dear to the left. That said, strong language is used against "abortion, euthanasia or willful self-destruction...," tempering and redirecting the overemphasis on what are often today called "Gospel values." Nevertheless, this chapter expresses hope and optimism for mankind after a half-century of unprecedented violence and disregard for human life.

Chapter three underlines the dignity of labor and aims to bridge the perceived chasm between the Church and modern scientific and technological progress. Chapter four restates *Lumen gentium*'s eschatological role of the Church as a "visible association and a spiritual community" serving "as a leaven and as a kind of soul for human society as it is to be renewed in Christ and transformed into God's family."[15] The Church wishes to reveal more deeply that her work is not simply limited to bringing salvation to believers, but to proclaim "the rights of man."[16] The Council Fathers exhort all Christians to reject any division between the "faith which they profess and their daily lives" for it "jeopardizes [their] eternal salvation," and this false division is "to be counted among the more serious errors of our age."[17] Laymen are encouraged to "take on [their] own distinctive role" in the service of the world, and the Council Fathers aim to curb laxity on the part of the laity. "Let the layman not imagine that his pastors are always such experts, that to every problem which arises, however complicated, they can readily give him a concrete solution, or even that such is their mission."[18]

Part II

The second part of *GS*, massive in scope and size, aims to apply Church teaching and the exhortations of part one to a number of modern issues that "go to the roots of the human race": "marriage and the family, human progress, life in its economic, social and political dimensions, the bonds between the family of nations, and peace."[19] This part of the document reads almost as a set of instructions for individuals to read within each circumstance: for priests ministering in foreign nations, doctors advising families, politicians in peace talks, religious serving the poor, educators developing university programs, and Christian laity initiating a non-profit service organization in the developing world.

II. Problems of Interpretation

Fr. James Schall, S.J., reflecting on the importance of liberal studies, concisely summarized St. Thomas Aquinas' three-point introduction to students of the *Summa*:

> The three reasons for the difficulty of learning are: 1) the baffling multiplicity of useless questions and arguments; 2) the things we want to know are not treated according to the order of the discipline but only according to what is required for explaining some book or dispute; and 3) the frequent repetition of these questions causes confusion and boredom in the minds of students.[20]

I open with this quote because in many ways this can be applied to *GS* and the Council: have not the multiplicity of questions and disputes within the Church driven the faithful to confusion, boredom and even apathy? Indeed, there are many reasons why it has been difficult for Catholics to understand and properly apply *GS* and the conciliar documents. Part of the problem is due to the fact that so many individuals and groups within and around the Church claim to "know" the true meaning of the Council, or claim to possess the proper interpretive keys. This myriad of commentary has, in effect, confused the message of the Council to such an extent that neither progressives nor reactionaries properly speak about the Council's spirit and letter; these opposing camps ignore one to the detriment of the other.[21] In fact, the Council's intent has been hijacked to such a degree that often Catholics cannot agree upon the content of the two dogmatic constitutions, let alone *GS*.

Liberals vs. Conservatives

For instance, progressives tend to enshrine a "spirit of the Council" almost as a superdogma: a hermeneutical lens that focuses exclusively on the social justice aspects of the "letter" while ignoring the rich dogmatic and doctrinal context within which it resides. The "spirit of the Council" view also proclaims to have ushered in a new era, one in which the Church no longer needs the preceding centuries of

Christendom or her moral teachings. Even worse, the "spirit" language is used to speak of reforms that, allegedly, the Council Fathers intended to enact, but the Church simply was not ready for such greatness. On the other hand, conservatives tend to ignore the call to mission, social justice and solidarity, citing that the document is merely "pastoral" and therefore can be ignored. Often this is in reaction to the fact that progressives controlled the implementation of the Council for the first forty years; to ignore the pastoral stuff is to undercut the leftist position. The conservative approach also has another negative aspect: the true, doctrinal development and renewal of Vatican II is ignored,[22] rendering the Council merely a dead letter or a crisis that can be fixed only by conservative reactionaries. The "hermeneutic of continuity" has been frequently referenced by some conservatives to imply that "continuity" equates "no change at all," yet even Benedict XVI himself also calls it "a hermeneutic of reform" where true doctrinal development has occurred in continuity.[23] In fact, neither the liberal nor conservative approach captures the real essence of the Council, let alone *GS*, and therefore the Council and its teachings are lost in the perennial battle between the political left and the political right.

Historical Context: The Age of Aquarius

Another stumbling block for interpretation of *GS* is the cultural and historical context of the 1960s and '70s, the era of upheaval in which the Council was convoked, closed and initially implemented. It is no surprise that the age is both enshrined by some and anathematized by others for the revolutionary spirit that swept the culture. It was the age of political and social revolutions – throwing off the yoke of so-called structures of oppression and ushering in drug use, free love and social justice movements. It was an age of anti-authoritarianism, where hierarchies of power were viewed with suspicion and disgust. Higher education was among the first cultural institutions to embrace the radical secularism and atheism of the age, denying God's existence in even the most fundamental fields of study. Just as a break was consummated by the cultural revolution, the Council and its documents are often spoken of as if they had erased the past, even though the most frequently cited sources in the totality of the documents' endnotes are Pope Pius XII and Sacred Scripture. If the same Council were to have been held a decade prior during Pius' pontificate, would it be claimed by various camps in the

Church as a standard (or antithesis) of their cause? That said, the context of the age was part of the need for the Council, and yet even among the hierarchy some wore rose colored glasses in an era of incremental decline. Reflecting on those halcyon days as a young theological expert, Pope Benedict said:

> [W]e went to the Council not only with joy, but with enthusiasm. The expectation was incredible. We hoped that everything would be renewed, that *a new Pentecost really would come*, a new era of the Church, because the Church was not robust enough at that time: the Sunday practice was still good, even vocations to the priesthood and religious life were already somewhat fewer, but still sufficient. But nevertheless, *there was the feeling that the Church was going on, but getting smaller, that somehow it seemed like a reality of the past and not the bearer of the future.* And now, we hoped that this relationship would be renewed, changed, that the Church would once again be source of strength for today and tomorrow. [24] [emphasis added]

The seeds of discontinuity, rupture and neglect were already present in the Church and ready to be unleashed; the evangelical hope of the Council became the justification (or scapegoat) of radicalism.

False Teachers and the Council of the Media

One key ingredient of widespread confusion came from media's control over the Council's message. The media had unprecedented access to the Council and took advantage of the opportunity to sell the Council as a break with the past. The media knighted her darling theological experts on the left, whose ideologies were sold as the true intent of the Council. These individuals used their prominence to promote their own personal program of reforms and heresies as the "spirit of the Council" was manufactured and sold in opposition to the letter.[25] Those darlings of the media's "virtual Council" included Hans Küng, Karl Rahner, S.J., Edward Schillebeeckx, O.P., Gustavo Gutierrez (of liberation theology fame) and their successors in spreading the "spirit of Vatican II" errors: Richard McBrien, Thomas Reese, S.J., Sr. Joan Chittister and Theodore Hesburgh, C.S.C. Pope Emeritus Benedict XVI spoke about this in one of his final addresses as the Roman Pontiff, stating:

> [T]here was the Council of the Fathers – the true Council – but there

was also the Council of the media. It was almost a Council in and of itself, and the world perceived the Council through them, through the media. So the immediately efficiently Council that got through to the people, was that of the media, not that of the Fathers.... The Council of journalists did not, naturally, take place within the world of faith but within the categories of the media of today, that is outside of the faith, with different hermeneutics. It was a hermeneutic of politics. The media saw the Council as a political struggle, a struggle for power between different currents within the Church. It was obvious that the media would take the side of whatever faction best suited their world.[26]

The Holy Father references how this "Council of the media" ultimately aimed to tear down the hierarchical structure of the Church and replace it with "popular sovereignty."[27] The battle over Vatican II still rages on, but the true Council has begun slowly to emerge, thanks to the strong corpus of teaching out of the pontificates of John Paul II and Benedict XVI.

Poor Implementation & Confusion

Of all the misleading hermeneutics of the Council, reactions due to the confusing implementation of the Council are the ones with which I have the most sympathy. The fact is that the Council has not been properly understood and in many ways it has been, at best, poorly implemented. The statistics following the Council are devastating: the numbers of men and women who left the priesthood and religious life; the decline in Catholic schools; the decline in Mass attendance; the decline in understanding the basic tenets of the faith.[28] Something did not register, for the hope of John XXIII and the Council Fathers was that Catholics more profoundly own their faith, plumb the rich depths of the ancient sources for renewal and engage the troubled world around them with the saving message of Christ. Instead, Catholics witnessed virtual apostasy among the priesthood, false teaching in our schools, banal liturgies and dumbed-down catechesis; the only thing that appears to have improved as a direct benefit of GS is a deeper awareness of Catholic missionary work and a focus on service and social justice. Certainly, much of the blame for this phenomenon is to be placed at the feet of false teachers, silent bishops and the progressive media for intending to derail the true Council and substitute it with a counterfeit one.

More Catholic than the Pope

There is an additional faction of Catholics who defy the normal labels of conservative and liberal: it is the radical traditionalist. These Catholics claim to be the sole purveyors of all that is orthodox, but, ironically, they do so by lecturing the Holy Father and the *Magisterium* on what it means to be Catholic. These Catholics are in virtual schism, paradoxically demanding a centralized papacy that is strict and disciplinarian, but only when such measures suit their sensibilities. They speak the language of tradition and revere the popes and times of the past, but they fail to remember that the Council was convoked and run exclusively by pre-conciliar shepherds who said the Holy Sacrifice of the Mass according to the *Missale Romanum* of 1962. They instinctively fail to grasp what it means to think like a Catholic: to view all of reality with the mind and heart of the Church. Ignoring the teaching of Blessed John Henry Newman on the development of doctrine, they cannot comprehend that the orthodox Faith could be formulated in a mode other than the manuals of Cajetan and Suarez. John XXIII said of such men: "They behave as though at the time of former Councils everything was a full triumph for the Christian idea and life and for proper religious liberty."[29] These traditionalist groups, like the conservative camp, will go so far as to deny the importance of the corporal works of mercy because they sound too "social justice" or are, in their opinion, "too vague and unclear."[30] These individuals, happier only when complaining, are more concerned about defending their false ideal of Christendom and the Catholic Church from the likes of Vatican II, Pope Francis and Bishop Robert Barron than they are about spreading the message of Jesus Christ. The truth is that it takes effort and even, at times, an uncomfortable risk to think and live like a Catholic, following the guidance of Holy Mother Church; particularly, it takes effort to evaluate the documents of Vatican II.[31]

Some Language Issues Within the Texts

Throughout Vatican II's sixteen documents, the Council Fathers refer to the Church by many names (old formulae and new formulae), ostensibly to reveal more fully the connection *all* men have to the Church and her mission of salvation.[32] For instance, the Church is called a "Body" and a "People." These two titles, albeit used somewhat interchangeably, appear to indicate the implicit and explicit membership of this "People of God" which appears to be a new emphasis indicating that though some men may not be Catholic, Christian, or even believe in a deity at all, they are, by the interconnected nature of man created by the one and true God, still part of His family, albeit broken. That said, this new use of language to describe the Church looks, itself, as a break with the past, disorienting some readers.

Similarly, it is not uncommon for the language of *GS* to be more impassioned and inspiring through the areas of text that include newer formulations or that propose novelties and elements of prudential judgment. This added element provided another impetus for progressives: that the purpose of the Council is to break from the past, rather than *aggiornomento* (updating) called for by John XXIII. In addition, *GS*'s intent on addressing mankind, focusing on the condition of the human person, at times seems to ignore the need for Christ in the sphere of man. *GS*'s outlook on man could rightly be called naïve following two world wars, genocide, totalitarian regimes, Hiroshima and Nagasaki and the arms race during the contemporary period of the Cold War. An important criticism of the document as a whole, and in particular this chapter, is that there is a conspicuous tendency to overstate man's dignity and accomplishments to the repression of the fact that he is fallen; this may have led Joseph Cardinal Ratzinger to call the language of *GS* at times "downright Pelagian."[33]

> Let the layman not imagine that his pastors are always such experts, that to every problem which arises, however complicated, they can readily give him a concrete solution, or even that such is their mission.[34]

The language used here is, in my opinion, unsettling and somewhat undercuts the role of the hierarchy (particularly the local priest) which is to teach, govern and sanctify. The warning against lackadaisical laity is well noted, but perhaps overstated; the text seems to lend itself too easily to misinterpretation. In other ways, the text overstates the "the accomplishments, culture and progress of the sciences by the work of men throughout the world and in ages past" as profitable tools for evangelization. The novelty of this section leads one to assume that the Council Fathers are referring to other traditions beyond Christendom and the heritage of the Catholic intellectual tradition, but how truly useful are those sources? Has not the best already been appropriated to the Faith? Essentially, one can see that the Council Fathers are encouraging Catholics not to fear truth wherever it is found, but one thinks of the religious syncretism and eclecticism that is so prevalent in our day.

Part II of *GS* is massive in scope and detail leaving this reader wondering: "Why?" So much is said that is left to prudential judgment. There is an adage that Pope Francis recently employed: "When you express too much, you run the risk of being misunderstood."[35] This is, in my opinion, the problem with Part II of *GS*. With this in mind, the document at times sounds like it is guilty of prescribing utopia or that it is naïve to the fallenness of man. Part II of *GS* appears to demand a very different hermeneutical lens than Part I, further complicating the matter of fully understanding the document.

III. Making Sense of the Mess

How to understand *GS* and the Council as a whole? Allow me to revisit my own section on language issues. To begin, all of the aforementioned problems are the result of taking a single quote out of the context of the whole document; once the quote is understood within the proper context of the paragraph in which it resides as well as the overall message of *GS*, its meaning becomes clear. For example, paragraph 36 of *GS* states:

> If by the autonomy of earthly affairs we mean that created things and societies themselves enjoy their own laws and values which must gradually be deciphered, put to use, and regulated by men, then it is entirely right to demand that autonomy. Such is not merely required by modern men, but harmonizes also with the will of the Creator. For by the very circumstances of their having been created, all things are endowed with their own stability, truth, goodness, proper laws, and order.[36]

Alone, this quote could be (and has been) interpreted to mean that there are some realms of human life which are completely autonomous from the Church and even God: essentially a proposal of secular humanism. One can understand Cardinal Ratzinger's blunt reference to the Pelagian tone of some sections of *GS*, including this isolated quotation. Yet, the document is imbued with a strong Christocentrism that redirects misinterpretation and finds its strength in paragraph 22:

> The truth is that only in the mystery of the Incarnate Word does the

mystery of man take on light. For Adam, the first man, was a figure of Him Who was to come, namely Christ the Lord. Christ, the final Adam, by the revelation of the mystery of the Father and His love, fully reveals man to man himself and makes his supreme calling clear. It is not surprising, then, that in Him all the aforementioned truths find their root and attain their crown.[37]

Obviously, stating that mankind can only be fully understood in light of Jesus Christ ought to anchor and orient any subsequent remarks in *GS* about "earthly affairs" to Christ and His Church. By placing *GS* 36 back within the document, the reader can clearly see how *GS* 22 orders and directs any interpretation. Thus, one can properly surmise that *GS* 36 is really stating that there are realms within human life that ought to be governed by the laity rather than the denial of the relationship of those realms from the Church and God. The Church cannot be responsible for all human institutions, and therefore the Church relies on the faithful to go out into the world and be leaven to secular society and institutions. As with this example, most criticisms of *GS* are criticisms of style and approach in the language rather than overall content and message (when taken as a whole). For example, Cardinal Ratzinger did not negate *GS* as an authentic document of the Council, but rather he pointed out the failure of specific sections within *GS* to avoid misinterpretation through more precise language.

So what to do, ignore all of this because it is too hard to contemplate? Not at all. There are certain principles to be followed in reading *GS* or any of the documents of Vatican II.

Principle I: Just Read the Documents!

The half century since the Council has produced innumerable books and articles (including this one) – all of which claim to provide the keys for interpreting the Council. Rather than rely on the so called "experts," I propose that Catholics simply read *GS*, setting aside biases and previous reports about what it allegedly teaches. C.S. Lewis, in an introduction for an English edition of St. Athanasius' *On the Incarnation*, wisely observed a modern phenomenon that can easily be applied to the problem of reading of *GS*:

I have found as a tutor in English Literature that if the average student wants to find out something about Platonism, the very last thing he thinks of doing is to take a translation of Plato off the library shelf and read the *Symposium*. He would rather read some dreary modern book ten times as long, all about 'isms' and influences and only once in twelve pages telling him what Plato actually said.[38]

In the case of *GS* and Vatican II, the media have controlled the translation and transmission of the message. Adrift among the myriad of commentaries, many Catholics have become fearful – or worse, indifferent – to engage the documents themselves, having been given the impression by a vast cadre of quarreling "experts" that the documents are virtually unintelligible. John O'Malley, S.J. argues that it is important to know the various diaries and interviews about the inner workings of the Council, but I cannot disagree more.[39] Knowing which ideological camps crafted which utterances of *GS* will only hinder readers from embracing the documents as a whole. The documents were not promulgated by the allies of Ottavianni or the Jesuit progressives, but the Church. How the documents came together in committee is not important for they were promulgated for the whole Church and signed by Christ's Vicar. Just read the documents!

Principle II: Read the Documents in the Proper Context & Order

There are only a couple other things to remember when reading *GS* and other Vatican II documents. First, one must read *GS* through the eyes of an orthodox Faith. Readers must remember that the Council's documents are promulgated under the inspiration of the Holy Spirit, expressed by the bishops of the world in communion with the Bishop of Rome, and therefore Catholics need not be nervous or fear Vatican II. Christ has protected His Church from the gates of Hell – they will not prevail against her. The Holy Spirit not only protects the Church from error through the hierarchy, but also inspires the Church toward a deeper understanding of Christ's call to discipleship and how to evangelize the world in every given age through that same hierarchy. The core teachings of the Faith, dogma and doctrine, have not and will not be altered. *GS* provides both doctrinal and pastoral principles, many of which rely on the prudential judgment of the hierarchy. Both the level of authority of a conciliar document as well as the element of teaching must be taken in proper order in the hierarchy of goods: Dogma is greater than doctrine and doctrine is greater than a pastoral approach.

Second, *GS* and the other documents are best read in the order in which they were promulgated. This is important because the order of the promulgation reveals the organic development of the Council's teachings in subsequent documents and also situates how they are to be understood.[40] For example, if one were to read only the four constitutions, the reader is advised to read *GS last*, well situated in the dogmatic statements and teachings of the previous documents. Admittedly, this essay is intended to focus on *GS*, but, like Sacred Scripture, one cannot read *GS* or the other conciliar documents in isolation from the Faith or one another; they must be read in continuity with the Faith and as a body of work, as chapters in a book.

Principle III: *Ubi Petrus ibi Ecclesia*

Although one could cite many reasons for ignorance of the Council's teachings, the ultimate rebuttal is the teaching of the subsequent popes. If *GS* were a document that had rolled back traditional Catholic moral teaching, Paul VI would not have issued the encyclical *Humanae vitae*. If *GS* had ushered in an age where the Church no longer needed doctrine and dogma, St. John Paul II would not have promulgated the universal *Catechism of the Catholic Church*. If *GS* had abandoned the Natural Law and Catholic anthropology, Benedict XVI would not have spoken about the "dehellenization" of the west and the need to recover the Natural Law at Regensburg. If *GS* had promoted universalism and syncretism, insisting that no one need be Catholic or Christian, Pope Francis would not have bothered to dialogue with an atheistic journalist and challenge his views.[41] If *GS* had... *but it didn't. GS* could not have done any of these aforementioned things, not only because it is a single document of a Council – a Council legitimately convoked by the pope – but also because it is yoked to the Faith. In *Gaudet mater ecclesia*, John XXIII spoke the following at the opening of the Council:

> The greatest concern of the ecumenical Council is this: that the sacred deposit of Christian doctrine should be guarded and taught more efficaciously.... In order, however, that this doctrine may influence the numerous fields of human activity, with reference to individuals, to families and to social life, it is necessary first of all that the Church should never depart from the sacred patrimony of truth received from the Fathers....The salient point of this Council is not, therefore, a discussion of one article or another of the fundamental doctrine of the Church which has repeatedly been

taught by the Fathers and by ancient and modern theologians, and which is presumed to be well known and familiar to all.[42]

Those who cite John XXIII as a progressive or a man who intended to break from Tradition have not read his writings and addresses. Can any reasonable person state that *GS* or the Council are solely to blame for the Church's current woes? For good Pope John, the Council was about engaging a troubled modern world with the medicine of mercy for the sake of saving souls:

> The substance of the ancient doctrine of the Deposit of Faith is one thing, and the way in which it is presented is another. And it is the latter that must be taken into great consideration with patience if necessary, everything being measured in the forms and proportions of a Magisterium which is predominantly pastoral in character.[43]

Throughout *GS* and the documents of the Council, salvation is highlighted as the most important mission of the Church; everything else is subject to and derived for the purpose of saving souls and drawing men to Christ and His Church. One can debate the choice of language used by the texts of the Council or the merits of the teachings made in prudential judgment (something that *GS* itself insists[44]), but one cannot accuse the documents of heresy and error.

The papacy of St. John Paul II is rich with cues on how to read the Council. From *Missio redemptoris* to *Fides et ratio* to *Dominus Iesus*, John Paul II's pontificate is in many ways the embodiment of the Council's call to *ressourcement*, renewing the rich patrimony of the Church's sources, and underlining the doctrinal and pastoral teaching of Vatican II. John Paul himself was a key author of *GS* and he was instrumental in shaping its Christocentric focus. Perhaps the greatest fruit of Vatican II and *GS* – and its most perfect implementation – was John Paul's visit to Krakow, Poland, in June of 1979, the now famous "Nine Days that Changed the World."[45] For nine days, John Paul spoke about the dignity of the human person, solidarity and the saving message of Christ. Not once did the pope condemn, not once did he utter the word "Communism," but armed with the saving Faith and appealing to man's innate desire for true freedom, John Paul II is largely responsible for dismantling Communism without firing a single shot. The Pope's message was not just to the Poles but also to everyone suffering oppression, and he was able to speak to them from the common basis of the dignity of the human person. Those nine days were a revolution of conscience that ultimately liberated millions of people from Communist oppression. At the final Mass, attended by upwards of three million people, John Paul's homily was interrupted by the chanting of the crowd: "We want God, we want God!" For eleven minutes the oppressed chanted while their oppressors looked on in amazement. To this author, these nine days that changed the world are the premier example of an approach to the modern world fashioned after *GS*. When one considers the impact of John Paul's pilgrimage to Poland, the intramural debates inside the Church about *GS* and Vatican II begin rapidly to pale.

Conclusion

After a fresh re-reading of *GS* and other Vatican II documents, I have renewed hope and renewed perspective. Fifty years later, perhaps the faithful can lay aside the baggage of the post-conciliar period, well armed with the teachings of St. John Paul II and Benedict XVI. Perhaps we can, with Francis, truly live the Council's evangelical call. *GS* reminds us that the Church is alive and dynamic, always seeking to save the lost sheep. There is much to be praised in *GS* and much from which we can learn. Certainly the document is not above criticism with regard to tone, language and its program for human flourishing. Perhaps one day the Church will have learned to be more careful with language in her official documents, but if that is the hardest lesson, then so be it. That said, to quote Newman, "ten thousand difficulties do not make one doubt."[46] Let us set aside the various ideological camps and think like Catholics – those who are unafraid of truth and its demands in our time. Read the documents, learn from them, and help to set the record straight about *GS* and Vatican II. Finally, pray, hope and do not despair: we do not need to worry about saving the Church from *Gaudium et spes* and Vatican II! Pope Benedict's final, public words about the Second Vatican Council before he resigned from office of Bishop of Rome are a fitting reminder:

> It seems to me that 50 years after the Council, we see how this Virtual Council is breaking down, getting lost and the true Council is emerging with all its spiritual strength. And it is our task, in this Year of Faith, starting from this Year of Faith, to work so that the true Council with the power of the Holy Spirit is realized and [the]

Church is really renewed. We hope that the Lord will help us. I, retired in prayer, will always be with you, and together we will move ahead with the Lord in certainty. *The Lord is victorious.*[47] Amen.

ENDNOTES

1. Francis Cardinal George, "Remarks to the Pope: Church's Ability to Evangelize is Diminished," www.zenit.org, June 1, 2004.

2. *GS* followed on the heels of *Dei verbum, the Dogmatic Constitution on Divine Revelation* (Nov. 18, 1965), *Lumen gentium, the Dogmatic Constitution on the Church* (Nov. 21, 1964), and *Sacrosanctum concilium, the Constitution on the Sacred Liturgy* (Dec. 4, 1963).

3. Lamb, Matthew and Levering, Matthew, ed., 147, *Vatican II: Renewal within Tradition*, Oxford University Press, 2008.

4. *Ibid.*

5. These documents, of course, are in line with the Deposit of Faith already handed down through Tradition and protected by the *Magisterium*. Both *LG* and *DV* reaffirmed and organically developed in continuity our understanding of the nature of the Church as well as natural and divine revelation.

6. The "Cadre Report" was a document that helped change the direction of Catholic Charities in 1972. The Cadre Report is described as follows: "The Cadre Report of the National Conference of Catholic Charities in 1972 was a primary catalyst that influenced Catholic Charities mission and expanded its role to reach out to the needy beyond direct assistance. Catholic Charities broadened its focus to include the pursuit of social justice and social awareness of the root causes of poverty. Catholic Charities developed additional objectives and activities including advocacy, social planning, and public policy development while influencing social welfare legislation on behalf of the poor and vulnerable." Quote from Catholic Charities, Diocese of Albany, "History" page: http://www.ccrcda.org/history.htm

7. Rev. Robert J. Vitillo; "40 Years after *Gaudium et spes*," delivered to Catholic Social Ministry Gathering; February 20, 2005: http://www.usccb.org/issues-and-action/human-life-and-dignity/forty-years-after-gaudium-et-spes-rev-robert-j-vitillo.cfm Note: the problems with Catholic Charities and Campaign for Human Development, etc.

8. Catholic News Service, "Pope Francis: Without Faith in Christ, Church Is just 'Pitiful NGO'" http://www.catholicnews.com/data/stories/cns/1301190.htm

9. *Gaudium et spes, The Pastoral Constitution on the Church in the Modern World*, 2, Second Vatican Council, http://www.vatican.va/archive/hist_councils/ii_vatican_council/documents/vat-ii_cons_19651207_gaudium-et-spes_en.html

10. *GS*, 4.

11. *GS*, 7.

12. *GS*, 10.

13. *GS*, 21.

14. *GS*, 27.

15. *GS*, 40.

16. *GS*, 41.

17. *GS*, 43.

18. *GS*, 43.

19. *GS*, 46.

20. James Schall, S.J., "A Student's Guide to Liberal Learning", Intercollegiate Studies Institute (ISI), 2000.

21. John O'Malley, S.J. makes an excellent point about the "spirit" of the Council in his article

entitled "Misdirections." He warns against banishing the expression "the spirit of the Council:" "Sure, the expression is easily manipulated, but we need to recall that the distinction between spirit and letter is venerable in the Christian tradition. We should therefore be loathe to toss it in the dust bin. More important, spirit, rightly understood, indicates themes and orientations that imbue the Council with its identity because they are found not in one document but in all or almost all of them. Thus, the 'spirit of the Council,' while based solidly on the 'letter' of the Council's documents, transcends any specific one of them. It enables us to see the bigger message of the Council and the direction in which it pointed the Church, which was in many regards different from the direction before the council." http://americamagazine.org/issue/article/ misdirections.

22. Religious freedom in *Dignitatis humanae*; collegiality; the universal call to holiness; definitions of the Church as the fullness of the truth in *Lumen gentium*; approaches to natural and divine revelation and Scriptural exegesis in *Dei verbum*, to name a few.

23. Pope Benedict XVI, 2005 Christmas Address to the Roman Curia.

http://www.vatican.va/holy_father/benedict _xvi/speeches/2005/december/documents/ hf_ben_xvi_spe_20051222_roman-curia_en.html

24. Pope Benedict XVI, address to the Clergy of the Diocese of Rome on 2-14-2013; Vatican Radio transcript: http://en.radiovaticana.va/storico/2013/02/14/pope_benedicts_last_great_master_class:_vatican_ii,_as_i_saw_i/en1-665030.

25. The texts of the Council are not documents but "essays" according to Cardinal Garrone.

26. Pope Benedict XVI, address to the Clergy of the Diocese of Rome on 2-14-2013; Vatican Radio transcript: http://en.radiovaticana.va/storico/2013/02/14/pope_benedicts_last_great_master_class: _vatican_ii,_as_i_saw_i/en1-665030.

27. *Ibid.*

28. Patrick Buchanan, "An Index of Catholicism's Decline," WND Commentary; http://www.wnd.com/ 2002/12/16195/

29. Pope John XXIII, *Gaudet mater ecclesia*, The opening address of the Second Vatican Council. http://conciliaria.com/tag/gaudet-mater-ecclesia/

30. Church Militant TV host, Michael Voris, stated this in a public debate with Mark Shea in St. Paul, Minnesota on October 8, 2013.

31. Not unlike Sacred Scripture, GS and other Vatican II documents must be read together and with the proper hermeneutics. Obviously, Scripture is the inspired Word of God and inerrant, unlike the conciliar documents of Vatican II, and so the analogy has some limitations yet it is instructive.

32. Other titles: The Church is called a "Temple", for in her dwells the Holy Spirit; she is called "our mother," implying guide and teacher; she is called "the spotless spouse of the spotless Lamb," meaning the "Bride of Christ" for whom our Lord delivered Himself up that He might sanctify her; she is called "a sheepfold" as she gathers the lost ones for her Master.

33. Tracey Rowland: "The Good, the Bad and *Gaudium et spes*"; *Inside the Vatican*. http://www.catholicworldreport.com/Item/1944/the_good_the_bad_and_igaudium_et_spesi.aspx#. UmSfQ40o6zl

34. *GS*, 43.

35. Pope Francis Interview: "A Big Heart Open to God," *America Magazine,* http://www. americamagazine.org/pope-interview/

36. *GS*, 36.

37. *GS*, 22.

38. C.S. Lewis, "On the Reading of Old Books."

39. John O'Malley, S.J. "Misdirections," *America Magazine* Online, http://americamagazine.org /issue/ article/misdirections

40. *Ibid.*

41. Pope Francis, Public Letter to Eugenio Scalfari, originally in Italian at *La Republica*, translation

by Rorate Coeli: http://rorate-caeli.blogspot.com/2013/09/full-text-of-popes-letter-to-atheist.html

42. Pope John XXIII, *Gaudet mater ecclesia*, The opening address of the Second Vatican Council. http://conciliaria.com/tag/gaudet-mater-ecclesia/

43. *Ibid.*

44. *GS*, 91: "Undeniably this conciliar program is but a general one in several of its parts; and deliberately so, given the immense variety of situations and forms of human culture in the world. Indeed while it presents teaching already accepted in the Church, the program will have to be followed up and amplified since it sometimes deals with matters in a constant state of development. Still, we have relied on the word of God and the spirit of the Gospel. Hence we entertain the hope that many of our proposals will prove to be of substantial benefit to everyone, especially after they have been adapted to individual nations and mentalities by the faithful, under the guidance of their pastors."

45. www.ninedaysthatchangedtheworld.com

46. The Newman Reader online: http://www.newmanreader.org/works/apologia65/chapter5.html

47. Pope Benedict XVI, address to the Clergy of the Diocese of Rome on 2-14-2013; Vatican Radio transcript: http://en.radiovaticana.va/storico/2013/02/14/pope_benedicts_last_great_master_class: _vatican_ii,_as_i_saw_i/en1-665030

Catholic Education: Providing What Is Missing

By Michael Kenney

Though St. Thomas More lived nearly 500 years before Vatican II, his letter to his children's tutor reads as if he had an advance copy of the *Declaration on Christian Education (Gravissimum educationis)*. In this letter, More urges the tutor to:

> ...put virtue in the first place, learning in the second; and in their studies to esteem most whatever may teach them piety towards God, charity to all, and modesty and Christian humility in themselves.[1]

Vatican II's *Declaration on Christian Education* seems to build on More's directive:

> For a true education aims at the formation of the human person in the pursuit of his ultimate end and of the good of the societies of which, as man, he is a member, and in whose obligations, as an adult, he will share.[2]

And the *Declaration's* opening lines emphasize education's vital and enduring role:

> The Sacred Ecumenical Council has considered with care how extremely important education is in the life of man and how its influence ever grows in the social progress of this age.
> Indeed, the circumstances of our time have made it easier and at once more urgent to educate young people and, what is more, to continue the education of adults.[3]

Over fifty years have passed since the opening of Vatican II. Has Catholic education met Vatican II's goals? If not, why not? And what can be done?

The State of Catholic Education

Vatican II describes Catholic education as a gift from the Church intended to help people throughout their lives to be "imbued with the spirit of Christ."[4]

The Church is bound as a mother to give to these children of hers an education by which their whole life can be imbued with the spirit of Christ and at the same time do all she can to promote for all peoples the complete perfection of the human person, the good of earthly society and the building of a world that is more human.[5]

The *Declaration* presents "fundamental principles"[6] under twelve sweeping headings such as: "The Meaning of the Universal Right to an Education"; "Moral and Religious Education in all Schools"; and "Coordination to be Fostered in Scholastic Matters." The *Declaration* explains that the details will need to be developed and applied to "varying local circumstances."[7]

A comprehensive analysis of the *Declaration* and the past 50 years of Catholic education is beyond the scope of this article; however, two stories offer a basis for consideration, *Jesus Shock* and *On Staying Catholic.*

Dr. Peter Kreeft's book, *Jesus Shock,* asks a provocative question: "Why is Jesus the most controversial and the most embarrassing name in the world?"[8]

No one is embarrassed if you talk about Buddha, or Muhammad, or Moses. Neither Buddhists nor non-Buddhists are embarrassed to talk about Buddha. Why are almost all educated, non-fundamentalist Christians embarrassed to talk about Jesus to non-Christians, and why are almost all non-Christians embarrassed to hear such talk?[9]

Dr. Kreeft probes further:

If you're not sure my assumption is true, test it, in any secular company, or mixed company, especially educated company. The name will fall with a thud, and produce sudden silence and embarrassment. You not only hear the embarrassment, you can feel it. The temperature drops. Or rises. It never stays the same.[10]

Jesus Shock cogently presents the difference Jesus makes for all people, for all time. Jesus is the ultimate educational opportunity. Regrettably, the past 50 years paint a sad picture. Kreeft writes:

Fifty years ago, 75 percent went to Sunday Mass; now it's 25 percent....The numbers for Confession are even worse. The last generation's theological knowledge has been almost abolished: college graduates know less theology today than fifth graders knew fifty years ago. Literally...not one in fifty Catholic college students has ever even heard that Christ is one person with two natures.... Worst of all, when asked why they expect God to accept them into Heaven when they die, only one in twenty even mention Jesus Christ....Can there be any possible educational scandal worse than that?[11]

The second story appeared in Notre Dame's campus newspaper in May of 2013. Entitled "On Staying Catholic," the article opens as follows:

I almost gave up Catholicism twice while at Notre Dame. For two weeks during freshman year, a class I was taking had convinced me that the existence of God was incompatible with rational belief. During the middle of my college career, a traumatic personal experience left me angry, lonely and wanting to give up any faith. Reflecting on those experiences, I am sometimes surprised I am still here, will be graduating in a few weeks and am still Catholic.[12]

Catholic education does not impose, but should continuously propose the Way, the Truth, and the Life, "imbued with the spirit of Christ." In the above illustration, we have the opposite – a professor continuously proposing atheism. We must pray for those who teach at Catholic universities. We also must pray for those who administer Catholic universities that they may have the wisdom to foster truth and the courage to promote authentic academic freedom.

Near the end of *On Staying Catholic*, the student makes this observation:

I recently showed a prospective student around Notre Dame's campus. She asked me what it was like to be Catholic here, the kind of Catholic who believes in and cares about the Church's teachings, who tries to cultivate a life of prayer, who seeks to root every act in the sacramental life. I told her it was difficult.[13]

Difficult? Why? And what can be done? *Jesus Shock* puts it this way:

There is no gimmick. We just (1) believe everything God has told us through Church and Scripture, and (2) respond with adoration. And then everything else that is necessary will follow – as it did for Mary, for whom there was "only one thing needful," and as it did for all the saints, and as it does for Mother Teresa's Missionaries of Charity, who are simply the holiest and happiest people in this entire world.

Adoration means especially Eucharistic adoration. In that silence there is a power greater than a thousand nuclear bombs, greater than the sun, greater than the Big Bang. It is the power of God, released when the atom of the Trinity was split on the Cross and the explosion of redeeming blood came out. In Eucharistic adoration we touch this power, which is the root of everything, for it is Christ the *Pantocrator* (i.e., ruler of the universe, creator, and savior). We touch the candle of our souls to the fire of His passion, His passion for souls, and we catch that flame.[14]

A Way Forward

In 2012, the U.S. bishops proposed a working group to enhance the implementation of *Ex corde ecclesiae* (*From the Heart of the Church*, promulgated by Pope John Paul II in August of 1990). The working group would consist of bishops and presidents of Catholic colleges and universities. The working group's charge was to seek best practices, develop resources, and make suggestions concerning hiring for mission and the formation of trustees, faculty, and staff regarding Catholic identity.

Catholic campuses should be safe harbors where the faculty equips students to cogently and charitably engage an all too often hostile culture. Through God's grace, prayer, study, and the sacraments – particularly the frequent reception of Holy Eucharist and Reconciliation – we are made anew. We grow through *integral human development.*

As described in Benedict XVI's *Caritas in veritate (Charity in Truth)*,[15] integral human development seeks the development of the whole person – intellectually, spiritually, and personally. Catholic colleges and universities have a solemn duty to enhance integral human development rooted in charity and truth, and achieved through service and intellectual formation.

Christian Charity in Two Dimensions: Material and Intellectual

Catholic colleges and universities generally provide multiple opportunities for students to participate in community service. This is good, and yet, the Catholic response must be more. What is this *more*? Mother Teresa put it this way:

We are not social workers, but contemplatives in the heart of the world. For we are touching the body of Christ twenty-four hours a day.[16]

God has not called me to be successful; He has called me to be faithful.[17]

Pope Emeritus Benedict XVI sheds light on this *something more* dimension of Catholic education when he uses the phrase "intellectual charity."[18] Intellectual charity results from faith and reason.[19] As with Catholic identity, intellectual charity is primarily a matter of the will – a decision to pursue, ponder, and embrace Church teachings.

When addressing presidents of Catholic colleges and universities in Washington, D.C. in 2008, Pope Emeritus Benedict put it this way:

> A university or school's Catholic identity is not simply a question of the number of Catholic students. It is a question of conviction – do we really believe that only in the mystery of the Word made flesh does the mystery of man truly become clear? (cf. *Gaudium et spes*, n. 22) Are we ready to commit our entire self – intellect and will, mind and heart – to God? Do we accept the truth Christ reveals? Is the faith tangible in our universities and schools?

By cultivating truth, Catholic colleges prepare students to embrace St. Paul's words to "work out your salvation with fear and trembling."[20] Fr. George Rutler put it this way:

> Everyone has moments of courage, which is a natural virtue, but steady courage all through life, in the daily trials of suffering and discouragement, is a supernatural virtue. Aquinas links that kind of courage with the virtues of munificence and magnificence, which are forms of generosity. It takes courage to give God all we are, when only He notices....To flee from Christ, even if it seems a way of preserving one's life, is to lose the way, truth, and life itself.[21]

Through prayer and with God's grace, we grow in our understanding of God's will and in our capacity to do as St. Peter implored:

> Always be prepared to make a defense to anyone who calls you to account for the hope that is in you, yet do it with gentleness and reverence.[22]

Charity is the love for another, materially and intellectually.[23] Unfortunately, Catholic colleges and universities generally fall short on intellectual charity. This must be corrected. The systematic presentation of truth is essential to an education "imbued with the spirit of Christ" just as faith and reason are essential to Vatican II's universal call to holiness.[24]

A Spirit of Obedience and Faith

Mary is *our life, our sweetness, and our hope*. She models how to say "yes" to God. We proceed with holy purpose when we follow Mary's spirit of love, trust, obedience, and faith. And, we honor God. Life becomes a continuous prayer. As St. Paul writes:

> For God is the one who, for His good purpose, works in you both to desire and to work.
>
> Do everything without grumbling or questioning, that you may be blameless and innocent, children of God without blemish in the midst of a crooked and perverse generation, among whom you shine like lights in the world, as you hold on to the word of life, so that my boast for the day of Christ may be that I did not run in vain or labor in vain.[25]

In his first encyclical, a work of "four hands" acknowledging Pope Emeritus Benedict, Pope Francis presents the light of faith ("from the luminous life of Jesus") as an animating reality:

> Nor is the light of faith, joined to the truth of love, extraneous to the material world, for love is always lived out in body and spirit; the light of faith is an incarnate light radiating from the luminous life of Jesus. It also illumines the material world, trusts its inherent order and knows that it calls us to an ever widening path of harmony and understanding. The gaze of science thus benefits from faith: faith encourages the scientist to remain constantly open to reality in all its inexhaustible richness. Faith awakens the critical sense by preventing research from being satisfied with its own formulae and helps it to realize that nature is always greater. By stimulating wonder before the profound mystery of creation, faith broadens the horizons of reason to shed greater light on the world which discloses itself to scientific investigation.[26]

When we advance integral human development, we advance integrity and promote justice, charity, and peace. With these earthly and eternal implications, all who work in Catholic education should seek to be faithful servants; to do justice and "walk humbly with your God."[27]

Something More – A Template

Pope Emeritus Benedict XVI beautifully expresses the journey of all human beings in his encyclical *Spe salvi* (*Saved by Hope*):

> Human life is a journey. Towards what destination? How do we find the way? Life is like a voyage on the sea of history, often dark and stormy, a voyage in which we watch for the stars that indicate the route. The true stars of our life are the people who have lived good lives. They are lights of hope. Certainly, Jesus Christ is the true light, the sun that has risen above all the shadows of history. But to reach him we also need lights close by – people who shine with His light and so guide us along our way.[28]

Jesus is the Way, the Truth, and the Life, and He summed up our obligation as follows:

> You shall love the Lord your God with all your heart, and with all your soul, and with all your mind.[29]

As Fr. John Hardon notes in *With Us Today*:

> We need to have the Word of God not only sown in our hearts, but also sown in our minds.[30]
>
> The more clearly the human mind understands what the mind believes, the more generously the human will can use what the mind knows is truth.[31]

How can we assure that all students who attend a Catholic college or university will receive the *Word sown in their hearts and minds*? What can be done to ensure a seamless and continuous integration? How can we provide this continuous presentation while also respecting religious freedom?

What if all Catholic colleges and universities were obligated to provide a one credit hour course per semester to advance intellectual charity as a condition of retaining their designation as Catholic? This may seem anathema in the current climate of diversity and pluralism. But isn't this a mere matter of truth in advertising? Certainly canon law would permit this condition.

A positive, professional, compelling marketing and branding effort could be created similar to the impactful marketing effort, *Catholics Come Home*.[32] The campaign would make the case that equipping students at

Catholic colleges and universities with the knowledge "to account for the hope that is in you" is consistent with the message of St. Peter and his successors.

A pronouncement from the United States Catholic Bishops requiring a Catholic curriculum integrated throughout the four years of the undergraduate experience would be a timely response to the New Evangelization. The initiative, rooted in faith, could be called The Mustard Seed.

From the Heart of the Church

A one credit hour course per semester, over eight semesters would provide all students with a foundational education "imbued with the spirit of Christ." This integrated process would equip students to engage the world with integrity for life, *Something More*, as in the words of St. Thomas More:

> These I consider the genuine fruits of learning, and, though I admit that all literary men do not possess them, I would maintain that those who give themselves to study with such views, will easily attain their end and become perfect.[33]

Indeed, a mustard seed that offers a practical, virtuous way to fulfill the promise of Vatican II's *Declaration on Christian Education*.

The Mustard Seed – On Truth and Charity

Recognizing that many students at Catholic colleges and universities are not Catholic, the one credit hour course would need to be presented with charity and clarity. Opposition will come in many forms, some rooted in contrarian agendas. Leaders at Catholic colleges and universities will need to be highly resolved to make the case. Catholic schools have a duty to present Catholic teaching. In the end, as Pope Emeritus Benedict XVI expressed to the presidents of Catholic colleges and universities, "It is a question of conviction."

Here's how The Mustard Seed integrated Catholic curriculum could work:

Year 1 Fall Semester
- *Lumen gentium (Dogmatic Constitution on the Church)*
- *Gaudium et spes (On the Church in the Modern World)*

- *Compendium of the Social Doctrine of the Church* (specific issues across a wide range)
  - *Catechism of the Catholic Church* (specific issues across a wide range)
  - *50 Questions on the Natural Law – What it is and Why We Need It* (Q. 1-25)

Spring Semester
- *Fides et ratio (Faith and Reason)*
- *Veritatis splendor (The Splendor of Truth)*
- *Compendium of the Social Doctrine of the Church* (specific issues across a wide range)
  - *Catechism of the Catholic Church* (specific issues across a wide range)
  - *50 Questions on the Natural Law – What it is and Why We Need It* (Q. 26-50)

Year 2 Fall Semester
- *Deus caritas est (God Is Love)*
- *Spe salve (Saved by Hope)*
- *Compendium of the Social Doctrine of the Church* (specific issues across a wide range)
  - *Catechism of the Catholic Church* (specific issues across a wide range)
  - *Jesus of Nazareth* – From the Baptism in the Jordan to the Transfiguration (ch. 1-5)

Spring Semester
- *Caritas in veritate (Charity in Truth)*
- *Centesimus annus (The 100th Anniversary of Rerum novarum)*
- *Compendium of the Social Doctrine of the Church* (specific issues across a wide range)
  - *Catechism of the Catholic Church* (specific issues across a wide range)
  - *Jesus of Nazareth* – From the Baptism in the Jordan to the Transfiguration (ch. 6-10)

Year 3 Fall Semester
- *Rerum novarum (On Capital and Labor)*
- *Laborem exercens (On Human Work)*
- *Compendium of the Social Doctrine of the Church* (specific issues across a wide range)
  - *Catechism of the Catholic Church* (specific issues across a wide range)

Spring Semester
• *Casti connubii* (*On Christian Marriage*)
• *Humanae vitae* (*On Human Life*)
• *Evangelium vitae* (*The Gospel of Life*)
• *Compendium of the Social Doctrine of the Church* (specific issues across a wide range)
• *Catechism of the Catholic Church* (specific issues across a wide range)

Year 4 Fall Semester
• *Letter to Families*
• *Familiaris consortio* (*On the Role of the Christian Family in the Modern World*)
• *Compendium of the Social Doctrine of the Church* (specific issues across a wide range)
• *Catechism of the Catholic Church* (specific issues across a wide range)
• *With Us Today: On the Real Presence of Jesus Christ in the Eucharist* (ch 1-13)

Spring Semester
• *Lumen fidei* (*The Light of Faith*)
• *Ecclesia in America* (*The Church in America*)
• *Compendium of the Social Doctrine of the Church* (specific issues across a wide range)
• *Catechism of the Catholic Church* (specific issues across a wide range)
• *With Us Today: On the Real Presence of Jesus Christ in the Eucharist* (ch 14-26)

ENDNOTES

1. T. E. Bridgett, *Life and Writings of Sir Thomas More,* (London: Burns & Oates, 1891) at 127-131.
2. *Gravissimum educationis* (*Declaration on Christian Education*), section 1, Oct. 28, 1965.
3. *Ibid.* at opening paragraphs.
4. *Ibid.* at section 3.
5. *Ibid.*
6. *Ibid.* opening paragraphs.
7. *Ibid.*
8. Peter Kreeft, Ph.D., *Jesus Shock,* (Boston, MA: Beacon Publishing, 2008) at 1.
9. *Ibid.* at 1.
10. *Ibid.* at 2.
11. *Ibid.* at 151.
12. "On Staying Catholic," *The Observer,* (April 16, 2013).
13. *Ibid.*
14. *Jesus Shock* at 155-156.

15. http://www.vatican.va/holy_father/benedict_xvi/encyclicals/documents/ hf_ben-xvi_enc_20090629_caritas-in- veritate_en.html

16. http://www.gratefulness.org/giftpeople/teresa_calcutta.htm

17. http://www.osv.com OSV4MeNav/BlessedMotherTeresa/WeAreCalledToBeFaithful/tabid/3143/ Default.aspx

18. http://www.vatican.va/holy_father/benedict_xvi/speeches/2008/april/documents/ hf_ben-xvi_spe_20080417_cath-univ-washington_en.html

19. http://www.zenit.org/en/articles/benedict-xvi-s-call-to-intellectual-charity

20. *Phil* 2:12

21. "Praying with Saint Matthew's Gospel," *Magnificat*, Edited by Fr. Peter John Cameron, O.P., at 328 (2012).

22. *1 Peter* 3: 21

23. http://www.vatican.va/archive/ccc_css/archive/catechism/p1s1c3a1.htm

24. *Lumen gentium* (Light of Nations), chapter 5, para 40-41, November 21, 1964.

25. *Phil* 2:12-16.

26. Pope Francis, *Lumen fidei* (*Light of Faith*), para 34, (June 29, 2013)

27. *Micah* 6:8 http://www.usccb.org/bible/micah/6

28. Pope Emeritus Benedict XVI, *Spe salvi*, , (November 30, 2007).

29. *Matt.* 22:37; cf. *Luke* 10:27; *Catechism of the Catholic Church (CCC)* n. 2083.

30. Fr. John Hardon, S.J., *With Us Today: On the Real Presence of Jesus Christ in the Eucharist*, (Ave Maria, FL. Sapientia Press, 2001) at 1.

31. *Ibid.* at 17.

32. http://www.catholicscomehome.org/

33. T. E. Bridgett, *Life and Writings of Sir Thomas More*, at 127-131 (1891).

MICHAEL KENNEY earned his undergraduate degree and a J.D. from the University of Notre Dame and an LL.M. from George Washington University. He practiced trial and appellate law for 13 years before transitioning to Catholic higher education where he has served in a variety of leadership positions for the past 18 years at University of Detroit Mercy School of Law, Ave Maria School of Law, Notre Dame University, Madonna University and Father Gabriel Richard High School in Ann Arbor, Michigan, one of the oldest Catholic high schools in the U.S. He also serves on the boards of Real Life 101 and Living Faith-Fine Arts Apostolate in metropolitan Detroit. Michael and his wife Mary Claire have seven children.

Vatican II and the Lay Mission: What Is To Be Done?

By James Bemis

The importance of the Second Vatican Council can scarcely be overestimated. The first of the Council's four sessions convened on October 11, 1962 and the last ended on December 8, 1965. Coming within its purview was a breathtaking scope of deliberations, including considerations of the Catholic Church's relationship with the modern world, the liturgy and other sacraments, the entire gamut of the Church's social teaching, education and the role of the clergy, religious and laity.

To grasp what occurred at the Council, one must understand the world undercurrents happening at the time the Council convened. The early 1960s were times of great tumult and change. Two world wars had claimed the lives of tens of millions; a Cold War standoff between the superpowers of the United States and the Soviet Union riveted international attention. The dark specter of Communism seemed everywhere on the march: Europe, Africa, Asia, and North and South America.

Yet, despite the obvious barbarity of the first half of the twentieth century, many – particularly the opinion leaders – had an incongruous ebullience and optimism about "the freedom of the new age." The hubris of the Modern Age led men to the heresy of Modernism, first defined by Pope Saint Pius X in 1907 in his encyclical, *Pascendi dominici gregis*. According to the Pope, Modernism is "the synthesis of all heresies," the belief, fed by intellectual pride, that no eternal truth exists, that everything is relative to the times in which we live. In Modernist philosophy, then, it follows that there is no need for God or the Church. Thus, Modernism was not only a Church issue but a philosophical one that infected the intelligentsia of the day.

Pius X also promulgated *Lamentabili sane*, a second Syllabus of Errors, in 1907, a listing of 65 propositions that were condemned and proscribed.

Among the propositions condemned in *Lamentabili* was the Modernists' credo, "Truth is no more immutable than man himself, since it evolved with him, in him and through him."

Despite the Church's condemnations, by the 1960s the Modernist heresy infected nearly every aspect of contemporary life and as a result the bedrock foundations of civilization – namely, family, religion and property – seemed everywhere under attack. With this as a backdrop, Pope John XXIII opened the Second Vatican Council in October 1962, and the world was never again the same.

Contradictory evidence exists regarding what the Pope hoped the Council would accomplish. Liberals cite John XXIII's comment that the Second Vatican Council would "throw open the windows of the Church and let the fresh air of the spirit blow through." Those of a more conservative bent cite the Pope's Apostolic Constitution, *Veterum sapientia* (On the Promotion of the Study of Latin), published at the same time the convening of the Second Vatican was announced. (*Veterum sapientia* stated in very traditional tones that Latin was the universal language of the Church and its use should be promoted and esteemed - hardly a new spirit of change.)

Further, in the Pope's opening address to the Council, he said, "The greatest concern of the Ecumenical Council is this, that the sacred deposit of Christian doctrine should be guarded and taught more efficaciously." The Church, the Holy Father said, must never depart "from the sacred patrimony of truth received from the Fathers."

Regardless of the Pope's intentions, the Second Vatican Council did result in sweeping changes in the Church, many of which appear in retrospect to be dreadful misinterpretations or mistakes. While changes to the liturgy have received the most attention and controversy, a vast array of other changes were brought in, not the least of which was the mission of the laity, who were called by the Council to more active roles in both the Church and society.

The Lay Mission

In order to properly understand what the Second Vatican Council said about the lay apostolate, it is essential to review the texts themselves and not rely on others' interpretations about the "spirit" of the documents. The two primary texts dealing with the lay mission are *Gaudium et spes* and the *Decree on the Apostolate of the Laity*.

Gaudium et Spes

Gaudium et spes, the *Pastoral Constitution on the Church in the Modern World*, was promulgated by Pope Paul VI on December 7, 1965. The document's Preface states that "the Church has but a solitary goal: to carry forward the work of Christ under the lead of the befriending Spirit."

In an introductory statement entitled "The Situation of Men in the Modern World," it is observed that the modern age is filled with change and contradiction. Nevertheless, the Church "maintains that beneath all changes there are many realities which do not change and which have their ultimate foundation in Christ, who is the same yesterday, today and forever."

The document is split into two parts. Part I relates the Church and man's calling, which seeks to answer three questions: What does the Church think of man? What needs to be recommended for the improvement of contemporary society? What is the ultimate significance of human activity throughout the world? Part II deals with problematic areas with some specificity.

In Part I, it is shown that human dignity lies in man's call to communion with the divine, as mankind was created in the image and likeness of God. Christ himself reveals what it is to be human, as "to the sons of Adam He restores the divine likeness which had been disfigured from the first sin onward."

Chapter IV deals with the Church's role in the modern world, with "an eschatological purpose which can be fully attained only in the future world." But she is already present in this world with a call to form the family of God's children. Thus, while the Church "acknowledges that human progress can serve man's true happiness," the spirit of vanity and malice can transform human activity into an instrument of sin.

Thus, all human activity must be "purified and perfected by the power of Christ's cross and resurrection." The Church, then, "serves as a leaven and as a kind of soul for human society as it is to be renewed in Christ and transformed into God's family.

Part II of the document addresses certain "Problems of Special Urgency," such as marriage, culture, socio-economic life and international peace. The well-being of the individual person and human society is limited to the "community of love" produced by marriage and the family. Nevertheless, "the excellence of this institution is not everywhere reflected with equal brilliance, since polygamy, the plague of divorce, so-called free love and other disfigurements have an obscuring effect."

The primary purpose of marriage is made clear: "Marriage and conjugal love are by their nature ordained toward the begetting and educating of children." Christians should actively promote the values of marriage and the family, both by example and in conjunction with others of good will.

Chapter III examines economic and social life, stating that human dignity and the welfare of society are to be respected and promoted. Catholic Social Teaching reminds us that the goal of economic production is not mere profit but to be at the service of man and his material, intellectual, moral, spiritual, and religious life. Further, the civil community is necessary to promote the common good.

The Church, "by reason of her role and competence, is not identified in any way with the political community nor bound to any political system." Accordingly, the Church maintains "true freedom to preach the faith, to teach her social doctrine, to exercise her role freely among men, and also to pass moral judgment in those matters which regard public order when the fundamental rights of a person or the salvation of souls require it."

Gaudium et spes is grand in sweep and scope, tackling big issues in a big way. However, it also succumbs to the naïve optimism of the sixties, with its presumptuous declaration of standing before "a new age" of limitless potential. For instance, it myopically focuses on the nuclear arms race as the great evil of the day, failing to foresee the destructive consequences embedded in the modernist philosophy.

Decree on the Apostolate of the Laity

Shortly before the release of *Gaudium et spes*, and certainly as a complement to its teaching, Pope Paul VI promulgated the *Decree on the Apostolate of the laity* on November 18, 1965. The decree is divided into six chapters, with topics ranging from the vocation of the laity to the details on the role and form of the apostolate.

Perhaps the decree's most important chapter is entitled "The Vocation of the Laity to the Apostolate," which states that "the Christian vocation by its nature is also a vocation to the apostolate. No part of the structure of a living body is merely passive but has a shape in the functions as well as life of the body." In a commanding statement, the decree notes that "the member who fails to make his proper contribution to the development of the Church must be said to be useful neither to the Church nor to himself." The laity shares in the "priestly, prophetic and royal office of Christ" and therefore in the Church's entire mission.

Living in union with Christ requires Christians to exercise faith, hope and charity, and "free from enslavement to wealth,...aspire to those riches which remain forever." Christians dedicate themselves to the advancement of God's kingdom and reform and improvement of the temporal order.

Chapter II deals with the objectives of the Lay Apostolate. While Christ's redemptive work is primarily concerned with salvation, it also includes renewal of the temporal order. Thus, the Church's mission is not only to bring Christ's grace to mankind but also to penetrate the temporal order with the spirit of the Gospel.

In modern times, new problems and serious errors are circulating which undermine the foundations of religion, the moral order and human society. Thus, laymen are exhorted to be more diligent in doing what they can to explain, defend, and properly apply Christian principles to current problems with the mind of the Church. "The whole Church must work vigorously in order that men may become capable of rectifying the distortion of the temporal order and directing it to God through Christ... the laity must take up the renewal of the temporal order as their own special obligation."

Chapter IV deals with external relationships and the need for cooperation among elements of the apostolate, directed by the Church hierarchy. In the past, the laity in many nations dedicated themselves to the apostolate in societies and associations entitled "Catholic Action," which were promoted by Popes and many bishops and dedicated to bringing the Christian witness to the world. While various projects of the apostolate can take different forms, no project "may claim the name 'Catholic'" unless it has obtained the consent of the lawful Church authority. As an example, St. Gianna Beretta Molla (canonized in 2004) belonged to *Azione Cattolica* and was dedicated to the works of mercy all of her life; in her medical practice, she particularly served the needs of women and children and the poor.

The sixth and final chapter discusses the formation for the apostolate. The synod notes that the apostolate can only attain its maximum effectiveness through a thorough formation. The laity involved need both a spiritual formation and solid instruction in theology ethics, and philosophy. With such a formation, the lay person "as a living member and witness of the Church, he renders the Church present and active in the midst of temporal affairs."

Fifty years after the Second Vatican Council, it is hard to imagine how revolutionary was the call for the laity to play a greater role in Church affairs, not as an optional matter but as a part of the lay vocation. While lay involvement has increased in numerous fruitful ways since the Second Vatican Council adjourned in 1965, many – if not most – of the faithful do not heed the Council's admonition that "the member who fails to make his proper contribution to the development of the Church must be said to be useful neither to the Church nor to himself."

What Is To Be Done?

It is not difficult to see that the promises of Modernity have gone horribly wrong. The greatest horrors of the last century – the bloodiest ever - resulted from Modern Man's monstrous use of science, freed from the restraints imposed by divine revelation. Hitler, Stalin, Mao Tse-Tung and other modern leaders quickly realized technology's usefulness for increasing their power over others. For the millions they ruled, "Progress" came at an unbearably high price.

What does this have to do with the Church and contemporary culture? Everything, for it proves that we need not be intimidated into marching lockstep with the progressive agenda, afraid of being accused of "turning back the clock." We don't have to accept that everything that is "new and improved" is better. We need not accept "enlightened" opinion as gospel, without having another vision of what is right. We can look to our ancient and eternal standards as guideposts to tell us when something is terribly wrong. And the most reliable source of these standards has always been - and remains - the *Magisterium* of the Roman Catholic Church.

But it's not enough to simply debunk the progressive myth. We must stand ready to offer our fellows that more truthful and attractive alternative vision – the Catholic vision.

This leads us to see the valuable – or rather, the essential – role Christians must play in a secular culture like our own, holding up a different image of mankind's place in the universe. First and most importantly, we must be able to view things in their proper perspective by turning our telescopes around from the direction in which modern

Catholics usually have them pointed. That is, we should not endeavor to be 21st century Americans looking at the Church, but rather strive to be well-catechized Catholics critically examining 21st century America.

From this perspective, we can see much more clearly what is before us; we can speak in a more honest and truthful voice about what is happening around us; and we can describe more courageously the epic battle between what Pope John Paul II called the culture of life and the culture of death, the culture of truth versus the culture of lies, between a culture of people and a culture of things, between the culture of richness that can be and the culture of emptiness that is. With these new lenses, it also becomes much easier to make our case.

Thus, the contrasts between the two competing cultural visions couldn't be clearer. If Catholics cannot make the case that the culture of life produces a better, healthier society than does the culture of death, then - to quote Shakespeare - the fault, dear friends, lies not in the stars, but in ourselves.

But we needn't go all the way back to medieval times to establish our case. More recently, during the 1930s, '40s and '50s in this country, the Church spoke with a clear, brave voice that was unmistakably Catholic. Let's look at the positive benefits of the strong Catholic subculture that existed in this country fifty years ago:

- There was an army of effectively catechized Catholics;
- Through family and schools, the Church was an instrument of upward social and economic mobility;
- Laity was loyal to Church leaders;
- Parishes were important local communities, critical to the social life of Catholics;
- There was an emergence of Catholic elite in intellectual, artistic, political circles and Catholic writers and scholars had real prestige.

What resulted was a culture markedly different from today's:

- In movies and television, with the Hayes Decency Code in place, Hollywood was in its Golden Age and Bishop Sheen was a popular TV star.
- In literature, bishops established a National Office for Decent Literature. Was literature impoverished? On the contrary, it

was a great age of Catholic letters with authors such as Evelyn Waugh, Graham Greene, Flannery O'Connor, Walker Percy, Allen Tate, J. R. R. Tolkien, Christopher Dawson, Malcolm Muggeridge, and - dare I say it - C. S. Lewis, a Catholic in heart at least. Image Books was a best-selling line for Doubleday.

- In music, stars were artists like Bing Crosby, Frank Sinatra, Ella Fitzgerald, and Nat King Cole.
- In architecture, churches were, for the most part, still beautiful.
- Family structure was strong.
- Crime and poverty a fraction of what it is today.
- Pornography was out of public view and abortion and sodomy were unmentionable, if you can imagine that.

How did the Church Militant lose her moral influence? In large part, it's the failure of leadership by American bishops, a breakdown that manifested itself in the clerical sexual abuse scandals. Some are, sad to say, just plain apostates who hate historical Catholicism. Others, falling for fads and fashions, use a highly distorted and selective interpretation of Vatican II. This inauthentic implementation of Vatican II has resulted in the weakening of Catholic institutions that would otherwise have been the means of communicating authentic Catholicism to the nation.

But the laity also must share some of the blame. Growing up as a nominal Episcopalian, I could sense my Catholic neighbors were different. Their families were stronger, more vibrant, happier. They exuded a confidence and serenity that was palpable, and I wanted that for myself. I have to believe that others saw that and wanted it for themselves too – hence, the great age of conversions to the Church. No one is ever converted by those with a timid or lukewarm faith. More Catholics then seemed willing to live their faith, willing to stand against modernity's rising tide.

Put another way, Catholic America – both clerical and laity – has increasingly *conformed to* much more than converted the basic secular nature of current American culture. What makes this loss of influence particularly distressing is that given the precipitous decline in American moral and cultural life, with the Protestant Christian influence all but entirely gone, this country needs a strong Catholic influence now more than ever.

An Uphill Struggle

The task seems so daunting. So do we give up and retreat or is there a roadmap back to a sane world? In fact, there is a way and it lies in Catholics bearing witness to the Faith and in doing so helping the Church regain her moral and cultural influence.

How can this be accomplished? We can start by putting our own house in order. One of the most important ways to do this is through the revival of Catholic intermediary institutions, such as religious orders, schools and colleges, orphanages, hospitals, charitable institutions, lay associations like the Knights of Columbus, and newspapers, magazines and other forms of communication. It is these institutions that provide tangible reference points for Catholics to look to in putting their faith into action and help shape the nature and meaning of their work. These institutions signify that the message being transmitted is real and of primary importance.

In America, these Catholic institutions took shape after World War I, hit their full stride in 1940s and '50s, and were severely weakened by both internal and external forces post-Vatican II. The energy and vigor of these organizations go a long way in both the proper formation of Catholics and in helping evangelize the outside culture.

How do we reinvigorate and regain control of our intermediary institutions? It seems to me a counter-revolution must be approached on three levels. As discussed in the *Decree on the Apostolate of the Laity,* the first step is at the personal level. Individuals and families must have a conversion of the heart and avail themselves of frequent reception of the Sacraments, without which all our efforts will be in vain.

Catholic education and evangelization must be geared again toward saving souls. Like medieval parents and grandparents of long ago, instead of raising our kids to be doctors, lawyers or engineer chiefs, we should go back to trying to bring up our children and grandchildren to be saints. We should become models ourselves. If young people see you living your faith, they'll be more likely to live theirs too.

Having said this, what can we as individuals do? How do we start? How can we separate ourselves sufficiently from the culture in which we find ourselves to see it clearly? There is only one way: by immersing ourselves in the Catholic Church's teachings, rich history and great culture, we may set out in search of ancient truths and eternal standards.

These eternal truths and standards are very accessible to us if only we have eyes to see them. They survive because the truth applies to all people in all times - no one outgrows them, no one moves beyond them, no one can ignore them, except at their own risk. In a world where seemingly important current events arc across the media sky like shooting stars, ephemeral illuminations that quickly vanish from view, these great truths of the Faith are the nearest we can get to permanent things.

From there, structural changes can be made. Thus, the second step is that the Church's infrastructure network of organizations and complementary associations must be rebuilt by orthodox Catholics becoming active in parish and other Catholic activities. It is not a case of merely being in the parish church (but not of it). It is a case of becoming a presence, joining with others of like mind to take part in parish events and in the school and even the diocese and be in tune with the mind of the Church in every situation. It's been done before, it can be done again. It is absolutely essential in restoring an authentic Catholicism to the Church's intermediary institutions.

Third and finally, the culture at large can be changed by armies of well-catechized Catholics reinfiltrating key idea-generating sectors of American society such as the government, corporations, mass media, education, entertainment, and others. Further, with their newly regained "credibility," Catholic institutional structures – which have provided the proper formation of these legions of Catholic individuals and groups – can then perform their tasks of enculturation, evangelization, and character formation in civil life.

Key to all this is that the reassertion of authentic Catholicism must always be guided by the Magisterial authority and each of the three parts of the counter-revolution must work cooperatively with each other. By a fundamental restructuring of a decaying American civilization along lines derived from Catholic social doctrine and the natural law, not only will the Church regain her influence but our society will again bloom and prosper.

Now this, it seems to me, is an orthodox call to action – I know a liberal group has hijacked that name but there's no reason traditionalists can't use it too. There is nothing more rewarding or worthy of our time than trying to help the Church recover her lost moral and cultural influence. As I've tried to show, this recovery is vital to our Church, our country, our culture and our civilization. Further, participating in it is something that lies within the talents of every lay person by simply bearing witness to the faith through leading truly Catholic lives each and every day.

JAMES BEMIS has been a frequent contributor to *The Latin Mass Magazine* for over a decade and was a speaker at the 2004 Latin Mass West Coast Conference. In addition, he was the guest speaker at the 2008 and the 2011 General Meeting of the Vancouver Traditional Mass Society in Canada. He has also addressed the National Wanderer Forum and the Denver Regional Wanderer Forum. Formerly associated with the *Los Angeles Daily News* and a columnist for *California Political Review* and *Catholic Exchange*, Bemis currently serves as film critic for *StAR* magazine, a journal of Catholic culture edited by Joseph Pearce, the internationally acclaimed biographer. Bemis' five-part series, *"Through the Eyes of the Church,"* on the Vatican's list of the 45 "Most Important Films in the Century of Cinema," was published in *The Wanderer*. His essays on various Shakespearean plays and their film counterparts have appeared in Ignatius Press Critical Editions. Bemis is a member of the Society of Catholic Social Scientists. He is working on one book on Christianity, culture and the cinema and another on the cost of Europe's apostasy from the Catholic Church.

Am I A Vatican II Catholic

By Cindy Paslawski

"I'm in the peace movement," the woman said to the person in line with her at the bookstore. She was talking about the three or four people with signs on the corner of the highway and Main Street. The two of them chatted as they moved forward in line. Then, "Don't you think Pope Francis is just wonderful? I think he's the one who will bring back the spirit of Vatican II."

Is that spirit stuff still around, I thought as I left the store. But I knew the idea was still alive these many years since the close of the Council. It would be around as long as ideas live and are passed on. Did she mean the anything-goes mentality that characterized the decades after the Council or the spirit of the Catholic Faith as found in the actual Council documents? One does not read those documents without coming away with an idea of the radical commitment to Christ and His truth that is expected of those who sign themselves with His cross.

If, in fact, the Holy Spirit of the Triune God was guiding the Second Vatican Council, then, as Isaiah said:

> For My thoughts are not your thoughts, nor are your ways My ways, says the Lord....As high as the heavens are above the earth, so high are My ways above your ways and My thoughts above your thoughts.
>
> (*Is.* 55:8-9)

The Spirit of God spoke through the Council documents for those who follow Christ, not through the "experts" and theologians who passed off their personal ideas, interpretations, hang-ups as the Gospel of Vatican II. What I read in those pages spoke of reverence at worship, the sanctity and obligations of holy marriage, the need to be a representative of Christ in all venues, to speak the truth before all, to be faithful to commitments of consecration, to evangelize via the newest media methods and to demonstrate by word and action the saving grace of Jesus Christ. We are to *be* the Prayer of St. Francis, doing for others without seeking for ourselves. The documents are a clear call to fidelity and holiness.

I don't get that sense of fidelity from the ever-so-popular "spirit"of Vatican II, perhaps because it came forth not from the Council but from man himself. The Council changed no doctrine or dogma or tradition, thus, we are still bound by the Church, the teachings of Christ, and living *caritas*. Yet after the Council and ever onward, every expert under the sun wrote or spoke of new things, challenged many tenets of the Faith such as the Virgin Birth and infallibility. *Humanae vitae* in 1968 lit a wildfire of open dissent fed by the ultimate expert advice of all: "Follow your own conscience. " Priests left their ministries, Sisters their vows to go off and be something else. The introduction in the secular world of equal rights gave birth to the demand for women priests and parishes became divided between those who energetically embraced all change and those who wanted to keep the Faith. Even those entrusted with sacred tasks such as implementing approved liturgical change would come up with exception after exception put forth by dioceses at the behest of local "experts" to the very simple requirements of the *Constitution on the Liturgy*. Suddenly kneeling was out, the tabernacle hidden, the translation to English watered down and Mass attendance and confession declined.

The spirit was moving all right, but which spirit was it which drew souls away from the teachings of the Church which Christ founded: one, holy (having the sacraments as means of grace), catholic (universal), and apostolic, handed on by the Twelve.

That the tumultuous spirit of dissent is still with us is evident when an unauthorized Canon of the Mass – nowhere to be found in the Roman Missal – is used or an oblique reference is made to general absolution. It is evident in people who sigh for the Vatican II days when all things were questioned, even by priests, or who resented the more conservative decrees of Pope John Paul II and Benedict XVI. It is evident in a catechist's website last year on which she supported abortion and argued angrily with those who dared to point out her wrong reasoning.

Let Isaiah again speak as the Lord told him:

So shall My word be that goes forth from My mouth; It shall not return to Me void, but shall do My will, achieving the end for which I sent it. (*Is.*55:11)

How do we answer the voice of God reaching out to us from so many centuries ago to do His will? His word was sent through Jesus Christ 2000-plus years ago, His word was sent out over fifty years ago by the Council Fathers.

In the introduction to this volume, Bishop Thomas Paprocki wrote of the reform of the reform, meaning some elements of the implementation of the Council needed reformation. The rush of change whipped up soon after the Council needed adjustments shortly after the Council's closing. In Appendix II, Father Timothy Sauppé has listed the Synods of Bishops since Vatican II, their topics, and the titles of the post-synodal apostolic exhortations by which, beginning with Paul VI, the pontiffs have tried to rein in the galloping horses of reform. The very first, in 1967, was on "Preserving and Strengthening the Catholic Faith," as the heretical *Dutch Catechism* gained popularity.

Nothing happens overnight. Like the Israelites following Moses, the time in the desert after Vatican II was lengthy for those who chose not to follow every experiment that appeared in the parish church. Prayer, holy hours – even if discouraged by the parish priest – and being the sign of contradiction to the servants of change in unending meetings became a way of life for many.

Some cities were blessed with one or two churches which followed the *Constitution on the Liturgy* exactly, only in what it required. People drove miles to attend Mass at these places. Parents, gravely dissatisfied with doctrine-less texts, began to homeschool their children in the Faith so that they would learn to know, love, and serve God, not subjectivity and situational ethics.

Then, like islands of fidelity, new religious orders arose, committed to serving, not confusing, the befuddled People of God. New orders of priests replaced those which had died out and missionaries from other countries spread out, even to the United States, to bring the words of Christ and save souls. New orders of Sisters came forth to take up the abandoned classrooms and nursing positions and social ministries. Diocesan seminaries began to change course as well.

Reform of the reform. Popes John Paul and Benedict XVI held fast to the Council in their teachings and insistence on keeping the Faith as it was handed on, keeping the Church in the world but not of it. Liturgical efforts, particularly in the translation of the Mass and calls for reverence, have brought back a bit of the majesty that should characterize the presence of God. The emphasis on mercy inspired many to seek sacramental graces. Teen rallies, conferences with speakers true to the Faith, and Eucharistic processions are much more prevalent to give meaning to the word "witness."

How can we ourselves insure that the word from the mouth of God does not return void?

It isn't just a thing for the Church to do, it is a personal thing for each of us as the body of Christ, the members of His Church. Prayer first and always. Then, as Frank Morriss wrote in this volume, to be heralds of Christ in the marketplace, to act as the Holy Spirit of God inspires charity and merciful acts and courage to be Catholic in all venues of life.

Education must play a part in keeping the reform of the reform alive. Sufficient time has passed so that parish education classes on that mysterious Council fifty years ago should be relevant, this time letting the documents speak for themselves. High schools could incorporate a Vatican study class, and in this volume, Michael Kenney has outlined a semester by semester college curriculum on the teachings of the Church.

Am I a Vatican II Catholic?

In fact, we all are. Our lives have been touched by what the Council said and what people wanted it to say. At this point, whether seen as a curious footnote as Bishop Paprocki wrote, or distant historical event, the Second Vatican Council has permeated our lives through the Mass, our places of worship, our dealings with one another, our fidelity or lack thereof in marriage. The bottom line is how well we have used the Council to help others know Christ, to return this word of God from the Council back to Him, achieving the end for which it was sent.

CINDY PASLAWSKI holds a B.A. in Journalism from the University of Minnesota. She has been active with the Wanderer Forum Foundation almost since its inception, while working as a reporter for *The Wanderer* newspaper. She has also worked on the front lines as a church secretary and most recently as a freelance book editor. As the Wanderer Forum Foundation/Bellarmine Forum's executive secretary and publication editor since 1995, she has overseen production of the *Forum Focus* and the *Bellarmine Forum* magazines, and publication of both *Saving Christian Marriage* (2007) and *Slaying the "Spirit" of Vatican II With the Light of Truth* (2017). From 2001-2004, she coordinated all regional and national forums and Focus on Faith retreats. She and her husband have six grown children.

Benedict XVI: Joy of the Council

*Following are extracts from Pope Benedict's friendly chat
with the clergy of Rome on February 14, 2013.*

"We went to the Council not just with joy, but enthusiastically. There was an incredible expectation. We hoped that everything would be renewed, that a new Pentecost, a new era in the Church, had truly arrived,...rediscovering the bond between the Church and the world's best elements, to open humanity's future, to begin real progress. We began to get to know one another... and it was an experience of the Church's universality and of the Church's concrete reality, which wasn't limited to receiving orders from on high but of growing and advancing together, under the direction of the Successor of Peter naturally." The questions put to the Council Fathers dealt with "the reform of the liturgy,...ecclesiology,... the Word of God, Revelation,...and, finally, ecumenism."

"In retrospect, I think that it was very good to begin with the liturgy, showing God's primacy, the primacy of adoration....The Council spoke of God and this was its first act: speaking of God and opening everything to the people, opening the adoration of God to the entire holy people, in the common celebration of the liturgy of the Body and Blood of Christ."

"The second theme: the Church....We wanted to say and to understand that the Church is not an organization, not just some structural, legal, or institutional thing – which it also is – but an organism, a living reality that enters into my soul and that I myself, with my very soul, as a believer, am a constitutive element of the Church as such....The Church isn't a structure. We ourselves, Christians together, we are the living Body of the Church."

"The first idea was to present the ecclesiology in a theological format, but continuing structurally, that is to say, alongside the succession of Peter, in its unique role, to better define the role of bishops and the episcopal body. In order to do this we found that the word 'collegiality' was very intensely debated, somewhat exaggeratedly I would say. But it was the word...to express that the bishops, together, are the continuation of the Twelve, of the group of Apostles. We said: only one bishop, the bishop of Rome, is the successor of the particular apostle, Peter...Thus the group of Bishops, the College, is the continuation of the Twelve and has its needs, its role, its rights, and its duties."

"Another question in the ecclesiastical sphere was the definition of the concept of the 'People of God,' which implies the continuity of the Testaments, the continuity of the history of God with the world, with humanity, and also implies the 'Christological element.' Only through Christology are we converted into the People of God and thus two concepts are united. The Council decided to create a Trinitarian structure to the ecclesiology: the People of God the Father, the Body of Christ, and the Temple of the Holy Spirit....The link between the People of God and the Body of Christ is, effectively, communion with Christ in the Eucharistic union. Thus we become the Body of Christ, that is, the relationship between the People of God and the Body of Christ creates a new reality: communion."

"On the question regarding Revelation, the fulcrum was the relationship between Scripture and Tradition....Certainly, what is important is that the Scriptures are the Word of God and the Church is subject to the Scriptures, obeys the Word of God, and is not above Scripture. Nevertheless, the Scriptures are only such because there is a living Church, its living subject. Without the living subject of the Church, Scripture is only a book open to different interpretations and gives no definitive clarity." In this sense, "Pope Paul VI's intervention was decisive," with his proposal of the formula "*nos omnis certitudo de veritatibus fidei potest sumi ex Sacra Scriptura,*" that is, "the Church's certainty on the faith is not only born of an isolated book, but needs the enlightened subject of the Church, which brings the Holy Spirit. Only thus can Scripture speak and from this springs all its authority."

"And, finally, ecumenism. I don't want to go into these problems now, but it was obvious that – especially after the 'passion' of Christians during the age of Nazism – that Christians could find unity, or could at least look for it, but it was also clear that only God can give unity. And we are still continuing along this path."

"The second part of the Council was much broader. The theme, arising with great urgency, was today's world, the modern age and the Church, and with it issues of the responsibility of the construction of this world, of society, responsibility for the future of this world and eschatological hope; Christian ethical responsibility...as well as religious freedom, progress, and relations with other religions. At that time, the entire Council, not just the United States, whose people are very concerned with religious freedom, really joined in the discussion... Latin America also joined in strongly, knowing the misery of the people of a Catholic continent and the responsibility of the faith for the situation of these persons. And thus Africa, Asia likewise saw the need for interreligious dialogue....

"The basis for dialogue is in difference, in diversity, in the faith of the uniqueness of Christ who is one, and it is not possible for a believer to think that religions are variations on the same theme. No. There is a reality of the living God who has spoken and who is one God, an incarnate God, therefore one word of God who is truly the Word of God."

"I would now like to add yet a third point: there was the Council of the Fathers - the true Council - but there was also the Council of the media. It was almost a Council in and of itself, and the world perceived the Council through them, through the media. So the Council that got through to the people immediately, efficiently, was that of the media, not that of the Fathers. And while the Council of the Fathers evolved within the faith, it was a Council of the faith that sought the *intellectus*, that sought to understand and try to understand the signs of God at that moment, that tried to meet the challenge of God in this time to find the words for today and tomorrow. So while the whole Council - as I said - moved within the faith, as *fides quaerens intellectum*, the Council of journalists did not, naturally, take place within the world of faith but within the categories of the media of today, that is outside of the faith, with different hermeneutics. It was a hermeneutic of politics. The media saw the Council as a political struggle, a struggle for power between different currents within the Church. It was obvious that the media would take the side of whatever faction best suited their world. There were those who sought a decentralization of the Church, power for the bishops and then, through the Word for the 'people of God,' the power of the people, the laity. There was this triple issue: the power of the Pope, then transferred to the power of the bishops and then the power of all... popular sovereignty. Naturally they saw this as the part to be approved, to promulgate, to help. This was the case for the liturgy: there was no interest in the liturgy as an act of faith, but as a something to be made understandable, similar to a community activity, something profane...

"Sacredness ended up as profanity even in worship: worship is not worship but an act that brings people together, communal participation and thus participation as activity. And these translations, trivializing the idea of the Council, were virulent in the practice of implementing the liturgical reform, born in a vision of the Council outside of its own key vision of faith.

"And it was so, also in the matter of Scripture: Scripture is a book, historical, to treat historically and nothing else, and so on.

"And we know that this Council of the media was accessible to all. So, dominant, more efficient, this Council created many calamities, so many problems, so much misery, in reality: seminaries closed, convents closed, liturgy trivialized...and the true Council has struggled to materialize, to be realized: the Virtual Council was stronger than the real Council. But the real strength of the Council was present and slowly it has emerged and is becoming the real power which is also true reform, true renewal of the Church. It seems to me that 50 years after the Council, we see how this Virtual Council is breaking down, getting lost and the true Council is emerging with all its spiritual strength.

"And it is our task, in this Year of Faith, starting from this Year of Faith [2013], to work so that the true Council with the power of the Holy Spirit is realized and Church is really renewed. We hope that the Lord will help us. I, retired in prayer, will always be with you, and together we will move ahead with the Lord in certainty. The Lord is victorious."

(This report was compiled from text from the websites of Vatican Radio and Vatican Information Service: http://www.news.va/en/news/benedict-xvi-joy-of-the-council#sthash.Bdv2PCJt.dpuf)

Appendix I
Fast Facts about Vatican II
By Michael Adkins

- The 21st Ecumenical Council of the Church

- Notable Previous Councils: the Council of Trent (1545-1563) and the First Vatican Council (1869-79)

- Convoked by Pope St. John XXIII (1958-1963): he announced the intent to host a Council on January 25, 1959 and he opened the Council on October 11, 1962 with the address, *Gaudet mater ecclesia* (*Mother Church Rejoices*)

- Presided over by Pope St. John XXIII, who died in the Council's first year, and Pope Paul VI (1963-1978)

- Attendance: over 2,300 bishops and prelates from around the world participated (only 737 attended Vatican I) and groups of representatives from Protestant communities and Orthodox Churches viewed the proceedings.

- Unlike the other 20 Councils of the past, Vatican II did not aim to clarify Church doctrine against specific heresies and errors, and likewise the Council Fathers did not provide authoritative keys for the Council's interpretation by issuing a creed, canons or dogmas as in previous councils.

4 Constitutions

Constitution on the Sacred Liturgy, Sacrosanctum concilium
December 4, 1963
This document discusses the nature of the liturgy while proposing principles toward the reform of the Roman Rite's *Missal*, rites of all sacraments, sacramentals, the Divine Office (Liturgy of the Hours), the liturgical calendar, sacred music and sacred art; it also considers the unique application of those principles in the context of mission territories.

The Dogmatic Constitution on the Church, Lumen gentium
November 21, 1964
The *Dogmatic Constitution on the Church* discusses the nature of the Church and her connection to all of humanity, the hierarchical structure of the Church and the importance and role of the laity; in addition, the document emphatically calls all Catholics, lay and clergy alike, to a life committed to holiness.

The Dogmatic Constitution on Divine Revelation, Dei verbum
November 18, 1965
This *Dogmatic Constitution* addresses new concerns about natural and divine revelation with special focus on the Sacred Scriptures, clarifying the authority of Scripture, its divine authorship, inspiration, human character and proper hermeneutics; it also describes the interrelated harmony between Scripture, sacred tradition and authority in the Church for interpreting revelation.

The Pastoral Constitution on the Church in the Modern World,
Gaudium et spes
December 7, 1965
In this *Pastoral Constitution*, the Council Fathers, having discussed globalization and the rapid developments in science and technology as both beneficial and dangerous to man, propose Christ as the answer to man's deeper longings. Considering these new circumstances, the Council proposes practical solutions and approaches to several topics of concern: marriage and the family, human progress, life in its economic, social and political dimensions, the bonds between the family of nations, and peace.

9 Decrees

Decree on the Missionary Activity of the Church, Ad gentes
December 7, 1965
With this decree, the Council Fathers insist that missionary work is not simply an activity of the Church, but part of her essential nature and mandate from Christ; missionary work also includes pastoral work among the faithful and work toward Christian unity.

Decree on the Apostolate of the Laity, Apostolicam actuositatem
November 18, 1965)

Apostolicam actuositatem affirms that lay persons can make Christ active and present to the secular world through their witness, contributing to conversion of the temporal order to Christ through their work and prayer; the decree also offers practical ideas for the success of the lay apostolate.

Decree on the Pastoral Office of Bishops in the Church, Christus Dominus
October 28, 1965
This decree examines the role of bishops in the local and universal Church as well as their collegial work in synods, councils and local bishops conferences, a new development of the council.

Decree on Social Communications, Inter mirifica
December 4, 1963
Inter Mirifica provides guidance to the faithful on the consumption and use of mass communication media as a tool for evangelization.

Decree on Priestly Training, Optatam totius
October 28, 1965
Recognizing that priests are at the very heart of Catholic life, the document, "animated by the spirit of Christ," outlines universal reforms of priestly formation for the good and the renewal of the whole Church.

Decree on the Catholic Eastern-Rite Churches, Orientalium ecclesiarum
November 21, 1964
This decree recognizes and affirms the legitimate rights that Eastern Rite Catholic Churches have with respect to their own ancient liturgical traditions and local governance structures, countering suspicions that Eastern Churches will be "Latinized" if they enter into communion with Rome.

Decree on the Adaptation and Renewal of Religious Life, Perfectae caritatis
October 28, 1965
The purpose of this decree is to renew religious life in two ways: renew the interior spirit of religious life and adapt religious life to contemporary conditions in order to strengthen its witness.

Decree on the Ministry and Life of Priests, Presbyterorum ordinis
December 7, 1965
The ministry of the priest is very important and spiritually demanding; this decree outlines practices and duties of priests to cultivate their own

spiritual life in order to fulfill their great mission of bringing Christ to others.

On Ecumenism, Unitatis redintegratio
November 21, 1964
The decree summarizes Catholic principles of ecumenism, the practice of ecumenism, and the relationship of the Catholic Church first to the separated Churches (e.g. Orthodox Churches and the Anglican Church), and then to Protestant ecclesial communities. Expressing a hope and commitment to unity, the Council Fathers recognize the difficulties as well as the serious ecclesiological and doctrinal differences between the Catholic Church and Protestant ecclesial communities, while recognizing a deeper fraternity with separated Churches. The document distinguishes between *spiritual ecumenism*, the cooperation between "separated brethren" through works of charity and prayer, and *practical ecumenism*, which is the work between church authorities to dialogue officially and work toward full and visible unity.

3 Declarations

Declaration on Religious Freedom, Dignitatis humanae
December 7, 1965
Dignitatis humanae is an important and controversial document that affirms religious liberty. Facing the persecution of atheistic Communist regimes, the Council Fathers aimed to protect the rights of all men against oppressive regimes. Likewise, the document aimed to dispel the concern of non-Catholics that if Catholics had power they would establish Catholicism as a state religion. The document states: "the doctrine of the Church that no one is to be coerced into faith has always stood firm" (*DH*, 12). The council distinguishes between religious freedom grounded in natural reason and that grounded in revelation. Traditionalist Catholics (e.g. SSPX) cite the document as a primary reason for rejecting the Council on the grounds that it violates the maxim *error has no rights* and it explicitly proclaims "to develop the doctrine of recent popes on the inviolable rights of the human person and the constitutional order of society" (*DH*, 1). In response, the Council Fathers argue that while error has no rights, errors are attached to persons, and persons do have rights.

Declaration on Christian Education, Gravissimum educationis
October 28, 1965
The document focuses on the rights of Christians to provide a Christian education to their children, the primary rights and duties of parents to educate their children, the role of various Catholic educational institutions and the dangers of a state monopoly in education.

Declaration on the Relation of the Church to Non-Christian Religions, Nostra aetate
October 28, 1965
The declaration is addressed to Christians and urges them to promote fellowship and cooperation with people who do not profess the Christian faith. Among those groups specifically cited in the declaration are Jews, Muslims, Buddhists and Hindus. According to the Council Fathers, Catholics should "through dialogue and collaboration with the followers of other religions, carried out with prudence and love and in witness to the Christian faith and life, recognize, preserve and promote the good things, spiritual and moral, as well as the socio-cultural values found among these men" (*NA*, 2).

It should be noted that on December 7, 1965, the same day the final documents of the Council were promulgated, Pope Paul VI and Athenagoras I, the Orthodox Patriarch of Constantinople, issued a joint declaration of the Catholic and Orthodox Churches whereby the age-old excommunications issued by their predecessors were lifted, opening up a new chapter of Catholic-Orthodox dialogue.

MICHAEL ADKINS is Academic Dean and faculty member of St. Agnes School (K-12) in St. Paul, Minnesota. He has taught various areas of the Humanities in Junior and Senior High School for over a decade, and he currently works on curriculum development and institutional advancement as well as serving as an educational consultant to other schools. A member of the Classical Association of Minnesota and the American Numismatic Association, Adkins holds a Bachelor's Degree in Honors Classics and a Master's Degree in Catholic Studies; he composed his Master's essay on Pope John XXIII's Apostolic Constitution, *Veterum sapientia*, and the importance of the Latin language. He and his wife, Cynthia, have six children and attend the Church of St. Agnes in St. Paul, Minnesota.

Appendix II

Compiled by Fr. Timothy Sauppé

These are the dates of the Synods of Bishops since Vatican II, their topics, and the Pope's post-Synodal Apostolic Exhortation, where applicable:*

- First Ordinary Synod (September 29-October 29, 1967) on Preserving and Strengthening the Catholic Faith.

- Extraordinary Synod (October 11-28,1969) on The Cooperation between the Holy See and the Episcopal Conferences.

- 2nd Ordinary Synod (September 30-November 6, 1971) on "The Ministerial Priesthood and Justice in the World"; *Ultimis temporibus (Vatican Council II, vol. 2, More Post Conciliar Documents*, by Austin Flannery, O.P., (Daughters of St. Paul, 1982).

- 3rd Ordinary Synod (September 17-October 26, 1974) on "Evangelization in the Modern World"; *Evangelii nuntiandi* December 18, 1975.

- 4th Ordinary Synod (September 30-October 29, 1977) on "Catechesis in our Time"; *Catechesi tradendae*, October 16, 1979.

- A Particular Synod for the Netherlands (January 14 - 31, 1980).

- 5th Ordinary Synod (September 26-October 25, 1980) on "The Christian Family"; *Familiaris consortio*, November 22, 1981.

- 6th Ordinary Synod (September 29-October 29, 1983) on "Penance and Reconciliation in the Mission of the Church"; *Reconciliatio et paenitentia*, December 2, 1984.

- Extraordinary Synod (November 25-December 8, 1985) on "The Twentieth Anniversary of the Conclusion of the Second Vatican Council"; "Message to the People of God," and "The Final Report."

- 7th Ordinary Synod (October 1-30, 1987) on "The Vocation and Mission of the Lay Faithful in the Church and in the World"; *Christifideles laici*, December 30, 1988.

- 8th Ordinary Synod (September 30-October 28, 1990) on "The Formation of Priests in Circumstances of the Present Day"; *Pastores dabo vobis*, March 25, 1992.

- Special Synod on Europe (November 28-December 14, 1991).

- Special Synod on Africa (April 10-May 8, 1994) on "The Church in Africa and Her Evangelizing Mission Toward the Year 2000"; *Ecclesia in Africa*, September 14, 1995.

- 9th Ordinary Synod (October 2-9, 1994) on "The Consecrated Life and Its Role in the Church and in the World"; *Vita consecrata*, March 25, 1996.

- Special Synod For Lebanon (November 26-December 14, 1995) on "Christ is Our Hope: Renewed by His Spirit, in Solidarity We Bear Witness to His Love"; "A New Hope for Lebanon", May 10, 1997.

- Special Synod For America (November 12-December 12, 1997) on "Encountering with the Living Jesus Christ: The Way to Conversion, Communion and Solidarity in America"; *Ecclesia in America*, January 22, 1999.

- Special Synod For Asia (April 19-May 14, 1998) on "Jesus Christ the Saviour and His Mission of Love and Service in Asia"; *Ecclesia in Asia*, November 6, 1999.

- Special Synod For Oceania (November 22-December 12, 1998) on "Jesus Christ and the Peoples of Oceania"; *Ecclesia in Oceania*, November 22, 2001.

- 2nd Special Synod for Europe (October 1-23, 1999) on "Jesus Christ, Alive in His Church, Source of Hope for Europe"; *Ecclesia in Europe*, June 28, 2003.

- 10th Ordinary Synod (September 30-October 27, 2001) on "The Bishop: Servant of the Gospel of Jesus Christ for the Hope of the World"; *Pastores gregis*, October 16, 2003.

- 11th Ordinary Synod (October 2-23, 2005) on "The Eucharist: Source and Summit of the Life and Mission of the Church"; *Sacramentum caritatis*, February 22, 2007.

- 12th Ordinary Synod (October 5-26, 2008) on "The Word of God in the Life and Mission of the Church"; *Verbum Domini*, September 30, 2010.

- 2nd Special Synod For Africa (October 4-25, 2009) on "The Church in Africa at the Service of Reconciliation, Justice, and Peace."

- Special Synod For The Middle East (October 10-24, 2010) on "The Catholic Church in the Middle East: Communion and Witness."

- 13th Ordinary Synod (October 7-28, 2012) on "The New Evangelization for the Transmission of the Christian Faith."

- Third Extraordinary Synod for Family & Evangelization (October 5-19, 2014).

- 14th Ordinary Synod (October 4-25, 2015) on "Family and Evangelization"; *Amoris laetitia*, April 8, 2016.

- 15th Ordinary Synod (2018) on "Young People, the Faith, and Vocational Discernment."

Unless otherwise shown, from Synod of Bishops, by Holy See Press Office, www.vatican.va, accessed on October 10, 2013, http://www.vatican.va/news_services/press/documentazione/documents/sinodo_indice_en.html#1%20-%201%20 ASSEMBLEA%20GENERALE %20 ORDINARIA %20(29%20SETTEMBRE-29%20 oTTOBRE%2019Type equation here.67)

FR. TIMOTHY SAUPPÉ entered religious life in 1982 and left before solemn vows in 1989. He holds a License in Sacred Theology (S.T.L.) from the Pope John Paul II Institute for Studies on Marriage and Family Life, 1991 and was ordained in 1992 for the Diocese of Peoria, Illinois. He serves as pastor of St. Mary's in Westville and St. Isaac Jogues in Georgetown, Illinois. He has written several articles for the Bellarmine Forum website and is a doctoral candidate with the International Marian Research Institute, IMRI, Dayton Ohio.